# REVELATION AND KNOWLEDGE

I am under the direction of Messengers from Heaven Daily & Nightly but the nature of such things is not as some suppose. without trouble or care. Temptations are on the right hand & left behind the sea of time & space roars & follows swiftly he who keeps not right onward is lost & if our foot-steps slide in clay how can we do otherwise than fear & tremble.

– William Blake, to Thomas Butts

If we shadows have offended,
Think but this, and all is mended,
That you have but slumber'd here
While these visions did appear.
And this weak and idle theme,
No more yielding but a dream,
Gentles, do not reprehend:
If you pardon, we will mend:

– William Shakespeare, *A Midsummer Night's Dream*

ROSS WOODMAN
WITH JOEL FAFLAK

# Revelation and Knowledge

## Romanticism and Religious Faith

UNIVERSITY OF TORONTO PRESS
Toronto Buffalo London

© University of Toronto Press 2011
Toronto Buffalo London
www.utppublishing.com
Printed in Canada

ISBN 978-0-8020-9213-7 (cloth)

**Library and Archives Canada Cataloguing in Publication**

Woodman, Ross Greig
Revelation and knowledge : Romanticism and religious faith /
Ross Woodman, with Joel Faflak.

Includes bibliographical references and index.
ISBN 978-0-8020-9213-7

1. English poetry – 19th century – History and criticism.  2. Religion and
literature – England – History – 19th century.  3. Religion in literature.
4. Romanticism – England.  I. Faflak, Joel, 1959–  II. Title.

PR585.R4W66 2011      821′.709382      C2011-903072-1

This book has been published with the help of a grant from the Canadian
Federation for the Humanities and Social Sciences, through the Aid to
Scholarly Publications Program, using funds provided by the Social Sciences
and Humanities Research Council of Canada.

University of Toronto Press acknowledges the financial assistance to its
publishing program of the Canada Council for the Arts and the Ontario
Arts Council.

 Canada Council
for the Arts
Conseil des Arts
du Canada
 ONTARIO ARTS COUNCIL
CONSEIL DES ARTS DE L'ONTARIO

University of Toronto Press acknowledges the financial support of the
Government of Canada through the Canada Book Fund for its publishing
activities.

'[…] before me fled / The night; behind me rose the day; the Deep / Was at my feet, and heaven above my head.' To remain unwillingly suspended in such a position, knowing neither the Deep at your feet nor the Heaven above your head, night fleeing in front of you and day rising behind you, is an acrobatic feat of some considerable distinction. This book is dedicated to those who, sometimes perforce, have attempted it as a matter of poetic faith, anything more substantial being too fixed or possibly too fearful to consider.

# Contents

# Acknowledgments

To Marion, who outwatched with me many an envious night;

To Joel Faflak, who wrote and re-wrote this with me in order to maintain a willing suspension between compelling opposites;

To Gerald Filson, who brought a Canadian prairie perspective to a lost and recovered horizon;

To Douglas Martin, whose dedication to world unity exceeded the all-too-human measurement of it;

To Tony Wolfson, who has been here, seen it all, and decided to remain;

To all those whom I taught and who taught me that the dangerous life of the imagination is essential to the human economy;

To Richard Ratzlaff, whose unflagging loyalty and fierce commitment to this project sustained its authors through moments of lesser faith;

To the Aid to Scholarly Publishing Program of the Canadian Federation for the Humanities and Social Sciences, whose financial assistance ensured that this book's knowledge might be revealed;

To the Social Sciences and Humanities Research Council of Canada, which remains committed to the idea that the worlds of faith and speculation are still not without their charms.

To Brad Bannon, who performed the unenviable task of compiling the index with speed, accuracy, and no fuss.

# Sources and Abbreviations

References to the Bible are from the Revised Standard Edition. References to Blake's poetry and prose are to *The Complete Poetry and Prose of William Blake*, revised edition, ed. David V. Erdman (New York: Doubleday, 1988); cited by title, line, and/or page number. References to Byron's poetry are from *Lord Byron: Major Works*, ed. Jerome J. McGann (New York: Oxford UP, 2000); cited by title, canto, and line number. References to Coleridge's poetry are from *Coleridge's Poetry and Prose*, ed. Nicholas Halmi, Paul Magnuson, and Raimondo Modiano (New York: Norton, 2004); cited by title and line number. References to Keats's poetry are from *Poems of John Keats*, ed. Jack Stillinger (Cambridge, MA: The Belknap P of Harvard UP, 1978); cited by title, book, canto, and/or line number. References to Milton's poetry are from *Complete Poems and Major Prose*, ed. Merritt Y. Hughes (New York: Macmillan, 1957); cited by title, book, and/or line number. References to Wordsworth poetry and prose, except where noted, are from *William Wordsworth: The Oxford Authors*, ed. Stephen Gill (Oxford: Oxford UP, 1984); cited by title and line number for poetry and page number for prose.

For the most frequently cited sources, the following abbreviations will be used:

| | |
|---|---|
| *A* | Percy Bysshe Shelley. *Adonais. Shelley's Poetry and Prose.* 2nd ed. Ed. Donald H. Reiman and Neil Fraistat. New York: Norton, 2002. Cited by line number. |
| *BL* | Samuel Taylor Coleridge. *Biographia Literaria.* Ed. James Engell and W. Jackson Bate. Princeton, NJ: Princeton UP, 1983. Cited by volume and page number. |
| *CPP* | William Blake. *The Complete Poetry and Prose of William Blake.* |

Rev. ed. Ed. David V. Erdman. New York: Doubleday. 1988. Cited by page number either as *CPP* or by title, plate number, and/or line number.

DP      Percy Bysshe Shelley. *A Defence of Poetry. Shelley's Poetry and Prose.* Cited by page number.

J       William Blake. *Jerusalem. The Complete Poetry and Prose of William Blake.* Cited by plate and line number.

KL      John Keats. *Letters of John Keats.* Ed. Robert Gittings. Oxford: Oxford UP, 1977. Cited by page number.

M       William Blake. *Milton. The Complete Poetry and Prose of William Blake.* Cited by plate and line number.

MDR     Carl Gustav Jung. *Memories, Dreams, Reflections.* Rev. ed. Ed. Aniela Jaffé. Trans. Richard and Clara Winston. New York: Vintage Books, 1965. Cited by page number.

MHH     William Blake. *The Marriage of Heaven and Hell. The Complete Poetry and Prose of William Blake.* Cited by plate number.

P       William Wordsworth. *The Prelude. The Prelude: 1799, 1805, 1850.* Ed. Jonathan Wordsworth, M.H. Abrams, and Stephen Gill. New York: Norton, 1979. Cited by book and line number from the 1850 version, unless otherwise noted.

PL      John Milton. *Paradise Lost. Complete Poems and Major Prose.* Ed. Merritt Y. Hughes. New York: Macmillan, 1957. Cited by book and line number.

PU      Percy Bysshe Shelley. *Prometheus Unbound. Shelley's Poetry and Prose.* Cited by act, scene, and line number.

SPP     Percy Bysshe Shelley. *Shelley's Poetry and Prose.* Cited by page number for prose, and title and line number for poetry.

TL      Percy Bysshe Shelley. *The Triumph of Life. Shelley's Poetry and Prose.* Cited by line number.

# Beyond Belief / Having Faith

JOEL FAFLAK (*University of Western Ontario*)

> The truth I heard often in sleep from the lips of the Dark Interpreter. Who is he? He is a shadow, reader, but a shadow with whom you must suffer me to make you acquainted. You need not be afraid of him, for when I explain his nature and origin you will see that he is essentially inoffensive; or if sometimes he menaces with his countenance, that is but seldom, and then, as his features in those moods shift as rapidly as clouds in a gale of wind, you may always look for the terrific aspects to vanish as fast as they have gathered. As to his origin, what it is, I know exactly, but cannot without a little circuit of preparation make *you* understand [...] The fact is, in point of awe a fiend would be a poor, trivial bagatelle compared to the shadowy projections [...] which the unsearchable depths of man's nature is capable [...] of throwing off [...] There are creative agencies in every part of human nature, of which the thousandth part could never be revealed in one life.
>
> – Thomas De Quincey, 'The Dark Interpreter'

> Protect me from what I want.
> – Jenny Holzer

> *I Want to Believe*
> – Title of *X-Files* film

## I

This introduction begins with a question: who will read this book? In 1979 I attended my first undergraduate lecture with Ross Woodman at the University of Western Ontario. He walked to the lectern, opened his anthology, and dispensing with preliminaries, began reciting Blake's 'Introduction' to *Songs of Innocence*:

Piping down the valleys wild
Piping songs of pleasant glee
On a cloud I saw a child.
And he laughing said to me.

Pipe a song about a lamb;
So I piped with merry chear,
Piper pipe that song again –
So I piped, he wept to hear.                    (*CPP* 1–8)

Poets take their direction from children who appear on clouds in broad daylight? This was my first introduction to Blake and Romanticism and I was sceptical. Yet this figment of imagination responds as if it were real: it cries as it listens to the poet's voice. Like Blake, Woodman seemed to have no problem with this reality. What seemed to me delusional for Woodman bore the ring of truth. For the first time I glimpsed how delusion might be an acceptable, even fundamental, facet of one's relationship to the world. I felt an immediate sense of revelation, though at the time I had no knowledge to confirm this sense. Instead, I immediately became a stranger to myself. The world of Blake illuminated by Woodman did not cause me to believe; rather, it was a world in which I could have faith. Only sometime later in the course, when Woodman introduced us to Coleridge's notion of a willing suspension of disbelief that constitutes poetic faith, a notion central to this book's argument, did I begin to wonder: is there any other way to know the world?

Of course, one's faith in enlightenment comes at a cost, as Blake goes on to say:

Piper sit thee down and *write*
*In a book that all may read*
So he vanish'd from my sight
And I *pluck'd* a hollow reed.

And I *made* a rural pen,
And I *stain'd* the water clear,
And I *wrote* my happy songs
Every child may joy to hear.          (*CPP* 13–20; emphasis added)

It is not enough to have visions, to possess vision: one often has to pursue one's revelations to the ends of one's human consciousness, even if –

often especially if – they are delusions. Or to use an idea crucial to Woodman's understanding of Romanticism: on the path to enlightenment, one avoids one's unconscious life at one's peril. As you will see, this book begins with a dream: 'The Báb is in Winnipeg ...' The apparently usual, automatic, or regular work of understanding often betrays a dangerous and seductive irregularity that makes us see the authority of enlightenment for what it often is: illusion.

This is what makes the human experience of staining the water clear with thought and writing so laborious. Is one writing on the *tabula rasa* to inaugurate the human, to mark its inevitable stain, or is one staining with clarity, clarifying what is otherwise incomprehensible or unknown, which in any event is also a staining, the risk of a further misapprehension? The ambivalence is crucial, unavoidable, painful. Blake insists upon the arduous psychological attention of what in *Milton* he calls 'ceaseless mental fight,' an attention that demands from the reader all or nothing, life or death. Or as I vividly recall Woodman saying in the next term, Keats holding his pen to write 'Ode to a Nightingale' was like blood dropping on to the white page, the kind of blood Shelley spills to write *Adonais* or *The Triumph of Life* or Keats spilled to write *The Fall of Hyperion* or Blake to engrave any of his epics. To *write* as well as *think* was like life's blood. In *Milton* 'round [Blake's] limbs / The Clouds of Ololon folded as a Garment dipped in blood' (42[49].11–12). To think and create makes the world count for something; without it the world would count for nothing. This is not to make thought useful and thus to invoke the proto-Victorian utilitarianism against which Blake himself railed. Rather, thought signals our inability to settle for the world's given terms. It seemed to me that, for Woodman, thought was more than intellectual practice but rather the intensely lived experience *of* thought. Knowledge is thought's *agon*, the suffering of not knowing, in which with each struggle toward consciousness one risks everything one already knows. In Woodman's account of Romanticism this risk produced an uncanniness felt by many of us who heard him speak. Some thought it was overdramatic. At times I shared their sentiment. I now know better.

As I suggested above, psychoanalysis was one way that Woodman contextualized Romanticism's supernatural naturalism. He focused especially on Jung's break from Freud. Freud saw in Jung's analytical psychology a return to the 'mud and black tide of occultism' (*MDR* 152). Jung detected in Freud's theory of sexuality a blind desire to turn psychoanalysis into a religion, a 'bulwark' against impending chaos (152). Both men held to their positions with some conviction, however much they submitted this fervour to critique in their later writings. Freud was in thrall to the myth of psychoanalysis in the same way that Jung was in thrall to this myth's archetypal dimension. For a time this seduction induced in Jung psychosis, a full break from reality that for the neurotic Freud confirmed his decision to pass over his chosen successor. As much as Woodman negotiated between this religiosity and its psychoanalysis, he was still fervently committed to Romanticism itself, a numinosity that exceeded one's expected critical relationship to the material. Woodman seemed in thrall to Romantic poetry, as if we should weave a circle around him thrice for having fed on honeydew and drunk the milk of paradise. Each time out, Woodman dared us to break the taboo and enter into poetry's often inscrutable *temenos*, which the poetry itself seemed to demand from its listeners. Woodman's lectures seemed intended for converts, and I attended them accordingly and willingly, despite scepticism among my classmates. Woodman's classroom was cabalistic because that *was* the poetry's ultimate power. One was just not always sure if the numinosity of Woodman's Romanticism was in the service of the psychological processing of it or vice versa. The line between them, as this book teaches us, was, and indeed is, fine.

But this seduction was only half of what Woodman wanted his students to understand. Again, it was essential that revelation should produce knowledge. Woodman's lectures also showed that the *gnosis* required psychologically to decipher what was cryptic emerged from inside the poetry, which is why one had to allow oneself at first to be seduced by its prophetic power. *There* lay knowledge, as opposed to answers, a vitally metaphorical rather than rationally scientific understanding of things. Romantic prophecy was not about clarifying the finite horizon of our existence. Rather, it was about our desire for a future insight that, to paraphrase Percy Shelley in *A Defence of Poetry*, might project its dark shadows onto our present, an immanent faith in an imminent vision of things as they are to be things as they might be.

## II

This book represents the first time Woodman has broached in literary criticism the issue of his dream of the Báb and subsequent encounter with the Bahá'í faith. The Bahá'í revelation, like most, first appeared as dreams or visions then documented either first-hand by the prophets themselves or second-hand by those who recorded their revelations. In the case of Bahá'í the documentation has been particularly thorough, though much of these texts remain, as Woodman notes, largely undeciphered or untranslated. This situation poses an especially paradoxical tension between the 'religious' fever for archiving that has possessed our information age since the rise of early nineteenth-century biblical hermeneutics and the (for many dubious) visionary situation it documents. One side of this tension expresses the very human desire to understand how vision underpins all human imagination and accomplishment. The other side expresses a scientific positivism that would rationalize and thus demystify such experiences. The resistance to such rationalization goes to the very core of revelation. Like most religions, Bahá'í does not, like Freud or Jung for instance, think of belief in psychological or archetypal terms. That is, it does not see religion as a matter of poetic faith, the way Freud analysed religion as the discontents of civilization or the future of an illusion, or Jung explored the analytical psychology of this illusion's mythopoeic energy.

Yet the dream-visions that produced 'Kubla Khan,' *The Rime of the Ancient Mariner*, or Wordsworth's encounter with the crazed Bedouin in book 5 of *The Prelude*, not to mention those of Shelley and especially of Blake, had made it perfectly apparent to Woodman that people have revelations every day. Even if his dream was a delusion, others had been similarly deluded. At the very least Romanticism showed Woodman that he was not alone, and not in bad company. It is thus significant that in this book his first impulse is not to analyse the content of his dream of the Báb. As post-Enlightenment creatures, such analysis is our birthright, the easiest path of resistance against the stranger, superstitious, and more occult aspects of our human nature, like our unconscious lives. Instead, Woodman has chosen to ask the more difficult question: how do we risk remaining seduced by the potency of our visions, *especially* in our zealously rational effort to analyse them (away)? For Woodman also realized that his dream, however much he might have disclaimed responsibility for it, also produced in him an immediate sense of a reality, psychological or otherwise, that he could deny, but at his own peril. For, in short, one cannot ultimately disclaim the contents of one's mind, however much others would like to disclaim them (often by relegating them to, and thus condemning, the other who claims them) on our behalf.

There are, of course, various 'strategic' reasons that Woodman left his encounter with Bahá'í largely unspoken in his literary criticism. The academic world is uncomfortable with topics incompatible with its sceptical demands. Like De Quincey's anxiety about confessing his opium

addiction, to 'confess' would be to invoke spiritual or psychological matters dramatically out of sync with a secular age deeply mistrustful of the
kinds of religious affiliations that have informed any number of criti-
cisms, at least since Coleridge and Arnold. Indeed, to raise the spectre
of *any* religious affiliation is to court having others dismiss even raising
the issue to begin with, let alone submit it to analysis. Woodman's situation was especially fraught: what if people saw his association with Bahá'í
as a dangerous slippage in reason? Better to leave things in the closet,
especially in an age anxious to classify and diagnose pathologies that do
not fit its normative order. Woodman's association with Bahá'í, when I
first learned of it, certainly gave me pause. I was raised in a small town.
Christianity I could compass; I had barely met Jews, Muslims not at all.
But this?! The Bahá'í faith was so utterly alien to me at first that it seemed
to entail some kind of cult-like and occult undertaking. This discomfort
relates, among other things, to a particularly Canadian politeness: we
learn to accept things beyond our comprehension by silently agreeing
amongst ourselves that such things *do* exist so long as we proceed as if
they do not. We secretly know that we have made this pact; we publicly
deny that we have.

Something about this politeness speaks to the critical enterprise itself, to the fascinating conviction with which it holds to its views despite
scepticism – the way it holds to this scepticism itself. Perhaps this is some
internalized shame at work here. Slavoj Žižek writes: 'We are ashamed of
[our] shit because, in it, we expose/externalize our innermost intimacy'
(*On Belief* 59). He continues: 'giving way to our innermost self is experienced by the subject as being colonized by some parasitic foreign in-
truder which takes possession of him against his will' (62). And yet such
secreting is fundamentally constitutive of our being, as Julia Kristeva
reminds us about the abject. Once one speaks *this* secret – that subjec-
tivity coheres precisely around what is abject within it that we maintain
*as* abject – one exposes the fundamental rift within an otherwise careful
facade. One confronts, that is, the reality of one's unconscious, which
Jung calls the transcendent, as Woodman argues in chapter 2 of this
book. Jacques Lacan links reality to what he calls the Real, which stands
for our virtual inability to take in, except as illusion, the all-too-real realness of our experience of reality. As Žižek argues, the Real stands for
'a certain *grimace* of reality, a certain imperceptible, unfathomable, ultimately illusory feature that accounts for the absolute difference within
identity' (*How to Read* 80). Put simply: so long as we leave the illusion
intact, we can proceed with reality as usual.

But as Žižek is careful to note, this acceptance entails a further dilemma: the '*Real of the illusion itself*' (81), which hides 'the remainder of [our] *authenticity* whose traces we can discern in an imperfect mechanical reproduction' (81, 45). Or as Žižek summarizes, 'the subject is something that "will have been" in its imperfect representation' (45). The illusion has to exist *as* illusion in order to hide the brute reality of who we are, of things as they are, producing instead at once the spectre and possibility of a subject who 'will have been.' This is the logic of Lacan's point that any confrontation with the unconscious is necessarily a missed encounter. Were we able to see directly, instead of darkly, any notion of the unconscious would be a moot point. Confronting the impact of the Bahá'í faith, Woodman seems to be facing the remainders of his authenticity in the imperfect representation of who he 'will have been.' It is one of the great mysteries of the human psyche that we cannot confront the reality of our 'shit' directly. We need the mediation of some third element. For Woodman, this was Romantic literature, whose suspension of disbelief in what one does not immediately know about oneself seemed the perfect way to process his confrontation with Bahá'í. As if knowing, yet without knowing, Woodman fell upon the Romantics as a way of processing what would to others be a literalist acceptance of religious faith, a poetic faith in his dream, which he had every right to discount but little right or will to disbelieve. In doing so, Woodman's lectures left room for what Wordsworth called, as we shall see in this book, the 'Uncreated' (*P*2.413), that place in creation that Satan cannot find – which is to say, that even God is not aware of. At the very least his encounter with Bahá'í made sense of his lectures' numinosity.

But this is only half the story, for what is more telling about Woodman's revelation is how it implicates us in its telling. Disclosure makes us somehow responsible for its content. Our first, perfectly normal response is to use scepticism to steel ourselves against conversion. Put another way, our discomfort with the challenge of conversion indicates both the fear of and fascination with our susceptibility to it. To confront delusion in another is to name a manic possibility within ourselves. There is a kind of profound silence that greets Woodman's sense of revelation in this book, like the 'mute music' that locked itself away in a 'rugged cell' in *Alastor* when it hears a voice of which it is 'too enamoured' (65). This does not mean the silence is inert. Žižek's name for the strange logic by which we maintain the illusion of our autonomy and so short-circuit our authenticity is 'interpassivity.' This is the phenomenon of videotaping television shows in which the act of recording does the watching for us;

or hiring professional weepers to mourn for our loved ones at funerals while we get on with the business of living; or watching pornography, which fornicates for us. It is also the work of prayer wheels, which perform the labour of belief for us; or of predestination, in which the 'very fact that things are decided in advance – that our attitude to Fate is that of a passive victim – prompts us to engage in incessant frenetic activity' (*On Belief* 27).

I wonder if dismissing another person's dreams and visions is not a way of getting him to do our necessary believing for us. In Lacanian psychoanalysis, the patient automatically presumes that the analyst '*knows* his secret (which only means that the patient *is* a priori 'guilty' of hiding a secret, that there *is* a secret meaning to be drawn from his acts)' so that the analyst is not an 'empiricist, probing the patient with different hypotheses, searching for proofs' but rather 'embodies the absolute certainty [...] of the patient's unconscious desire' (*On Belief* 28). The subject supposed to know, then, is merely a secondary function of the more fundamental '*subject supposed to believe*, which is the constitutive feature of the symbolic order' (29). (We can remind ourselves at this point that the noun form of fundamental, 'fundament,' is a euphemism for 'shit.') The point is not the content of the secret itself, but rather the way in which the symbolic order orchestrates itself and thus our subjectivities around the secret's structuring possibility. The secret becomes the excuse for the subject's being rather than the other way around. Maintaining the secret *as* secret means that its impossible knowledge allows us to get on with the business of living normal lives.

This book breaks with this logic, which otherwise anaesthetises our intellectual senses by suspending us in the warp and woof of enlightenment. If the terrain of what lies encrypted within us marks us, by virtue of its encryption, as 'criminal,' of having been invaded against our will by some foreign force, and thus able somehow never to take ultimate responsibility for the psychic experience it enfolds within itself, this terrain simultaneously confronts us with having permitted the invasion in the first place. This is the troublesome and traumatic logic of sexual abuse, in which the identification between perpetrator and victim becomes very fine indeed. Woodman's sense of revelation, in short, confronts us within the miraculous unfolding of psychic activity a suspended disbelief in which we accept each day we perceive the world around us – so long as we do not have to accept responsibility for the labour of belief itself. That is to say, Woodman confronts us with the remainders of our own authenticity, our capacity to be deluded about our existence. As one of those willing 'converts' to the fact of Woodman's revelation, I have struggled to bring this fact to a suspended state of disbelief for some time, although not nearly as long as it has taken Woodman to confront his own willing conversion to what, as protection, is dismissed as a delusion. Shelley's Apollo is held in heaven by wonder because in his lyrical drama *Prometheus Unbound* the sun will not rise until noon. As Jung writes at the end of *Memories, Dreams, Reflections*, 'it seems to me as if that alienation which so long separated me from the world has become transferred into my own inner world, and has revealed to me an unexpected unfamiliarity with myself' (359). The difficult, uncanny, and numinous evidence of this life-long process, which required no less than the Romantic poets to make whatever sense of it that we can by the end of our lives, is in the present book.

Woodman's first Bahá'í meeting; his dream of the Báb following shortly after; his subsequent involvement with Bahá'í; the impact of this involvement on his understanding of Romanticism, which has passed itself along to hundreds if not thousands of students of Romantic literature over the past fifty years – it all speaks profoundly to me about what is at once enlightening and dangerous about revelation. I am not keen to demystify the experience or the numinosity it clearly *does* have, for that would be to deny the compulsively repetitive way in which we are necessarily deluded by things every day of our lives. Indeed, this is the way faith sustains belief, without which enthralment we could not exist in the world. Confronting the alien experience of the other inevitably breeds in us discomfort, anxiety, even dissociation, as the other's experience *of* the other inevitably does for him in the first place, from which we demand immunity. Such a response is the basic mechanism that underpins any number of phobic reactions: religious, racial, sexual, political, ethnic, cultural. I do not mean, then, either to embrace or impugn the silence that might greet revelation. Rather I want to ask where the silence comes from. Suffice it to say that, like Jacques Derrida silenced by Michel Foucault's account of madness in the age of reason, Woodman had to break the silence in order to release the madness into its transformative potential. That process, begun in *Sanity, Madness, Transformation*, now reaches its beautifully unsettling, unfinished apotheosis in the present work.

# III

The Báb is like the Dark Interpreter of De Quincey's unconscious. Woodman can 'suffer' to make his reader 'acquainted' with the Báb, but he knows that 'there are creative agencies in every part of human nature, of which the thousandth part could never be revealed in one life.' The Báb 'recall[s] [him] to [his] own lurking thoughts, hidden for the moment or imperfectly developed,' confronting him with what 'would or might have occurred to [his] own meditative heart, had only time been allowed for its motions' (De Quincey, *Works* 15:184). Our identities have various points of gestation – biological, familial, sexual, historical – but our fundamental origin remains inscrutable. How we reveal ourselves to ourselves, then, is a process of dark enlightenment, what Woodman, after Jung, calls the '*ignotum per ignotius*' (*MDR* 354), the unknown known by the more unknown, what Shelley calls the 'dark abyss of how little we know' (*SPP* 478). The Báb just happened to be (or what the converted would declare was destined to be) the darkly interpretive way in which Woodman's unconscious chose to speak to him. Yet even if our unconscious recoils back upon our senses in utterly arbitrary ways, we are nonetheless left making sense of this arbitrariness. That is to say, humans possess a desire for revelation and knowledge as mysterious yet inevitable in our natures as the existence of the Dark Interpreter himself, *whatever* form he happens to take for us. To this deceptively simple issue this book addresses itself.

Shelley's statement speaks to the moment of perception as the entire ground of revelation. When the world apprehends our senses it automatically demands our *sense-making* response. At this point where psyche and matter 'touch and do not touch' (Jung, 'On the Nature' 215) the world can be found or lost. Such is the power of the psyche, as Jung knew when he contemplated Nietzsche's Zarathustra, or as Wolfgang Pauli knew when he saw the outcome of quantum physics in the Manhattan project, that it could transform the world into ash. In a post-9/11 world, as we dig deeper for oil, peer farther into the cosmos, and try to adapt to the aftershocks of a radically shifting global economic and geopolitical terrain, we still seem to be at the mercy of such a perception *of* perception. Confronted with such matters, what could one man's dream encounter with an Eastern visionary figure possibly matter? The Báb's significance in the history of Islam is at once revolutionary and threatening: at some level Islam has utterly refused to take stock of the progressive revelation, traceable to the vision of Muhammad, that resulted in the Bahá'í faith, whose spiritual home is on the side of Mount Carmel in Haifa, Israel, but whose global vision is of a peace-loving and just community of one faith eliminating all religious differences. At a much earlier point in his life, shortly after his dream, Woodman, like Northrop Frye riding on horseback from town to town as a Methodist preacher, participated with some fervour in helping to manifest this vision in Canada. As Woodman makes abundantly clear throughout, however, *that* historical and spiritual evolution is not the subject of this book. Rather, he asks the more profound and fundamental (though never fundamentalist) question: what does it mean for a human being to have visions, more particularly to have *vision*? Would it be possible for a country, a community, an individual to exist without it?

The occurrence in Woodman's life was strange enough. That it occurred in 1941 in the prairie city of Winnipeg, Manitoba, in Canada makes it that much more of an alien occurrence. That said, this book, like Guy Madden's film *My Winnipeg*, should also remind us how truly and necessarily estranging the supposedly local and everyday can be. It is this sense of the alien that makes the Canadian strain of Romantic studies itself so singular and estranging. Woodman reminds us that whole worlds of understanding rest upon how we confront (our own) otherness, as in our dreams, the terrain of which is anything but regional. How one *chooses* to interpret one's psychic life determines how one witnesses the world, for in the difference between seeing things either one way or another, whole worlds are made and others lost, no matter what the context or locale. To risk *knowing* something – how Woodman has imagined that he *knows* the Báb – is to risk claiming a rather satanic authority for our sense-making abilities. Woodman began exploring this madness of reason in *Sanity, Madness, Transformation*, which the current study continues by examining Romantic thought's enquiry into the psychological rather than the religious dynamics of revelation.

Woodman takes very seriously the poetic faith that Coleridge defines by way of describing his supernatural contribution to *Lyrical Ballads*. Indeed, Coleridge's famous statement from chapter 13 of *Biographia Literaria* shapes this book's movement by way of distinguishing faith from belief, and at the same time marking their uncanny relationship. Belief is a form of knowing – 'I know that something exists' or 'I know that such a thing will happen.' Having faith goes like this: 'I believe such a thing exists or might happen whether I know it will or not, even if I know it might not.' Put another way, the agency of belief – an *un*willing disbelief – depends upon the uncertainty of faith as much as the authority of faith – blindly accepting the apparent irrefutability of fact – sustains belief. Belief, which is a fundamental element of human being and knowing, fundamentally depends upon faith, which marks the rub of religion's survival. We forget such ironies at our peril.

Negotiating the fine line between belief and faith explains why Woodman has written *Revelation and Knowledge* at least four times. The struggle came with his attempt to impose a preconceived shape on the material; the release came when he set the book free to announce its own particular form to its author and reader. The result is a rather startling critical psychoanalysis whose path is certain but whose trajectory is anything but linear. On one hand, the book's recurrence to various themes, texts, and ideas is compulsively repetitive and death-driven, like the fetish that unwittingly attaches itself to the lost object of its desire. On the other hand, the book moves forward by incremental repetition, refining its critical vision by going back to its own future, finding with each return a new beginning that at the same time moves closer to the inscrutable core of Woodman's particular vision of Romantic revelation. Insofar as such things can be, Woodman's choice to produce the book in its current form was a conscious one, urged by the question, 'What does it mean to believe in something, and thus in ourselves?' To find the answer, however, is to trace the path of our unknown selves as they move toward the unknown. To borrow a distinction central to this book's methodology: compulsive repetition is the work of *religious faith*, the unconscious, automatic, unthinking return to what we think we know to be true; incremental repetition is the movement of *poetic faith*, the eternal recurrence to what we do not know as the numinous core or matrix of what we believe or *imagine* to be true.

Imagination is key here, as it was for the Romantics and as it is for Shia Islam. Imagination mediates the moment at which our senses touch the world beyond them, which both is and is not the world of sense, a world both at and beyond our touch. This reaching beyond ourselves means coming up against the enigmatic substance of otherness that is always beyond our comprehension. This confrontation is especially crucial in the present instance because for Shia muslims understanding the imagination is an organ of truth rather than suspended disbelief, the psychological luxury of which is a celebration of the unknown godhead. The current book suspends itself between these Western and Eastern perspectives, like Woodman's turning a somersault in the air in his dream of the Báb. This revolution is how the unconscious stages a deeper, more impenetrable moment of perception, less than the pulsation of an artery, to borrow Blake's phrase. This flash of insight is the psyche's movement toward consciousness, which is also a fall: in the dream Woodman floats like a feather to the feet of the Báb, the point at which suspended disbelief and truth reach a momentary truce as the true friendship of their opposition. This book is an attempt to reach this state of suspension between truth and disbelief. The result is not without its madness, for in madness lies the restlessness of thought, which in turn marks the vitality upon which our lived and shared experience as human beings depends.

# IV

In *Sanity, Madness, Transformation* Woodman explored an idea of Romantic madness not unlike Slavoj Žižek's idea of the mind's psychotic withdrawal from the world, which in Hegel's idealism founds the subject 'man.' Consciousness mediates between Nature and its symbolic reconstitution by working through the psychosis that constitutes the originating difference between them. The current book pursues this issue further to ask: by what faith do we know that the world that has vanished from our sight in order for us to reconstitute it as human (symbolic, virtual) still exists as the negative touchstone of our perception, without which we would be truly psychotic? In *The World as Will and Representation* (1818) Schopenhauer argues that man reverts to his senses only 'to convince [himself] that [his] abstract thinking has not strayed far from the safe ground of perception, [...] [as] when walking in the dark, we stretch out our hand every now and then to the wall that guides us' (1:449). This is one of the paradoxes by which reason itself functions: relying on our senses to see nature, we must then set them aside in order to understand what we've just seen. To make sense, we must move past the making *of* sense, as distinct, say, from the making of babies. This dilemma is what troubled Mary Shelley about her husband's Promethean vision. But it also reveals how the poetic faith of Romantic idealism casts the shadows of an earlier religious faith onto our own futures. If the Romantics were left to ask what it means to believe in a world beyond belief, then we need to ask further why we're still looking for the answer.

Addressing the 'clash of religions' remapping the global terrain, Kristeva argues that the 'problem we're facing at the beginning of this new millennium is not one of religious wars but rather the rift that separates those who want to know God is unconscious and those who prefer not to, so as to be pleasured by the show that announces he exists.' We are, she argues, confronted 'with prepolitical and transpolitical experiences that render obsolete any appeal for a normative conscience or the reason-revelation duo, for these notions head us toward a reconstruction of humanism derived from *Aufklärung* without any recourse to the irrational.'

'It is precisely at this key point of modernity,' Kristeva concludes, 'that the Freudian discovery of the unconscious and the literary experience – an experience inseparable from theoretical thought – are positioned' (15–16).

For Woodman, the struggle with such irrational returns comes slightly earlier in Romanticism's confrontation with its own madness. Put another way, the more Romanticism wrestles the angels to the ground, the more it confronts their numinosity. To paraphrase Kristeva: if we want to dream like God, we also have to confront His unconscious. Or to paraphrase David Clark paraphrasing Schelling: what was God thinking before He created the world? In *Answer to Job* Jung explores this issue by psychoanalysing *why* God withdrew from the world he made. Like God, humans possess an endless productivity, but their dreams confront them with the return of what God repressed, the Chaos that did not fit the system of the world's making. This is perhaps why Woodman, implicitly confronting the world order taking shape in the revelation of Bahá'u'lláh, avoids its dogmatism by confining himself instead to an exploration of this vision's unconscious dreaming life. Like Woodman's dream of the Báb, we are faced with our essentially *unheimlich* existence, our inability to find a place in the very world we make by perceiving it.

For Žižek this estrangement produces the illusions of humanism or gnosticism, which presupposed a 'home, a "natural" place for man: either this world of the "noosphere" from which we fell into this world and for which our souls long, or Earth itself.' Instead Žižek turns to 'Heidegger's notion of *Geworfenheit*, of "being-thrown" into a concrete historical situation': 'Heidegger points the way out of this predicament: what if we effectively are "thrown" into this world, never fully at home in it, always dislocated, "out of joint," and what if this dislocation is our constitutive, primordial condition, the very horizon of our being? What if there is no previous "home" out of which we were thrown into this world, what if this very dislocation grounds man's ex-static opening to the world?' (*On Belief* 8–9). But once again, this dislocation merely recasts Nietzsche's death of God, which demolishes the shibboleths of doctrinal belief, in terms of the far more laborious work of faith itself. When Toto pulls aside the curtain in *The Wizard of Oz*, we see an ordinary man frantically attempting to keep the mechanical reproduction of divinity working, which puts man back in the position of God contemplating the abyss in the first place, wondering what to make of its chaos.

Put another way: worse than God abandoning the world is the terror of God's aura falling upon man's face. Žižek argues that divinity is a 'kind

of obstacle, [...] that unfathomable X, on account of which man cannot ever fully become MAN, self-identical. The point is not that, due to
the limitation of his mortal sinful nature, man cannot ever become fully
divine, but that, *due to the divine spark in him, man cannot ever fully become
MAN*' (90–1). This dilemma speaks to the current book's exploration of
the Blakean or Jungian desire of man for the fourfold transformation
of his human situation. The very thing that mobilizes our faith, beyond
which belief abandons us, is precisely the obstacle to our becoming human. Divinity isn't the solution; it's the problem. Žižek argues that the
'intermediate status of man IS his greatness, since the human being IS
in its very essence a "passage," the finite openness into an abyss' (36). Or
as Jung asks, partly in response to his and Pauli's confrontation with the
terrifyingly unconscious dimension of the subatomic world, 'Why open
all the gates?' (*MDR* 171). Christ must have wondered this when he cried
out for having been forsaken on the cross. Moses must have understood
this when he saw the burning bush. No wonder Charlton Heston went up
the mountain looking like a buff if beleaguered seeker, and came down
looking as old as Methuselah. Cruising for God at the borders of one's
finitude tends to add a few years to one's psychic life. Cruising through
the ruins of Romanticism for the ultimate Man Who Got Away is what
gives this book its profound valence.

    This troubled idealism makes Woodman's suspended disbelief in the
core prophetic texts of Romanticism rather startling in the present state
of Romantic studies, which seems to have moved far beyond the critical
moment of his earlier *The Apocalyptic Vision in the Poetry of Shelley* (1964).
We are now aware that Romanticism was aware of what Clifford Siskin
calls the construction of its own 'self-made mind, full of newly constructed depths' (*Historicity* 13), a Romanticism responsive to the dangers of
its own myth-making capacities. Yet such an approach, powerfully diffuse
in its attention to Romantic blindness and insight, seems unwilling itself
to remain deluded about Romanticism's own willing delusions, its knowledge that the delusions of revelation were unavoidable. For to establish
a critical relationship to any particular aspect of history is to entertain
one's delusions about that history, to tarry with a faith that is always more
than critical. Perhaps this is why Bloom is careful to distinguish Romantic
mythopoeia from the reductive distinction between myth and a 'Scientific, critical, rational *Greek* thought [...] completely emancipated from,
and eventually hostile to, myth' (*Shelley's Mythmaking* 4). 'With Plato,'
Bloom continues, '[myth] re-entered philosophy and has never quite
since departed.' Myth's tenacious aftermaths, Bloom argues, point to

Romantic myth-making's darker psychology, which remains at the core of how the Romantic mind might have fallen victim to its own ideological constructions. Following in this exploration of Romantic psychology, yet radicalizing its claims, the current book explores the psychodynamics of a revelatory poetic imagination for which criticism has yet to account. One might call this the poetic experience of religious revelation that is the uncanny or unconscious nature of all our critical faiths, however sceptically enlightened. Romanticism confronts at the intersection between religion and poetry the unconscious dimension of both.

*Caveat lector*, then. Woodman takes Romantic prophecy and its revelatory power very seriously. He knows that believing in ideals is a painful and bewildering process. As Harper, the valium-addicted Mormon wife of the closeted Joe in Tony Kushner's *Angels in America*, says,

> I feel like shit but I've never felt more alive. I've finally found the secret of all that Mormon energy. Devastation. That's what makes people migrate, build things. Heartbroken people do it, people who have lost love. Because I don't think God loves His people any better than Joe loved me. The string was cut, and off they went. (119)

We can trace such a theme back to Woodman's exploration of Zoroastrianism in *The Apocalyptic Vision in the Poetry of Shelley*, which anticipates the present text's treatment of revelation. Here Woodman confesses a critical faith that Romantic prophecy speaks the voice of delusion itself, which, like Ruth listening 'amid the alien corn' (67) in Keats's 'Ode to a Nightingale,' necessarily forces us into the wilderness. We *resist* doing so, Woodman suggests, at our peril. We may miss what lies 'hidden' within it.

# V

Whereas Coleridge treats revelation with some suspicion, Wordsworth treats it as a flash that reveals the invisible world of nature. For Wordsworth, that is, revelation produces faith, an immediate knowledge or *gnosis* of things as they are. Yet the poets' struggle between the natural and the supernatural points to the larger way in which revelation and ordinary perception share an uncanny bond. Perception depends upon a mostly unconscious and unmediated faith in its own continuity and legitimacy, upon the unwavering movement of revelation within it. Mere sight is revelation sustained at the level of the everyday. Conversely, revelation is merely ordinary perception. Moses merely saw a burning bush; Blake merely dined with the prophets Elijah and Ezekiel. Coleridge had some sense of this fact when he defined the primary imagination as the 'living Power and prime Agent of all human Perception, [...] a repetition in the finite mind of the eternal act of creation in the infinite I AM' (*BL* 1:304). This repetition is further repeated through the activity of the secondary imagination, which works with the 'conscious will' to dissolve, diffuse, and dissipate the primary imagination's autonomous and unconscious labour in order to recreate it in more conscious terms.

That the secondary imagination is a repetition of a repetition, however, suggests both a refinement of vision and a blink in its perceptual apparatus. Put another way, the secondary imagination traumatically encrypts within its own operation the repetition of a primary act that is itself already a repetition or coming after. Coleridge's brief theory of imagination doesn't put it this way, nor does one sense, particularly in and as this theory's unfinished form, that Coleridge wants it this way. But one recalls how Coleridge, relying on Kant's theory of imagination, runs into Kant's dilemma of how to represent the thing-in-itself, a perceptual gap that gives Coleridge's poetic vision its *unheimlich* valence, the way in which for Coleridge the world is a sight to dream of but not to tell. Cathy Caruth argues that trauma is traumatic because of its forgetfulness, its inability to take itself in at one go: 'the event is not assimilated or experienced fully at the time, but only belatedly, in its repeated *possession* of the one who experiences it' ('Introduction' 4). Trauma produces the gap in our knowledge that comes with our inability to take in the world empirically at the moment of perception, a bewilderment that necessitates perpetually making sense, perpetually telling more. That is to say, trauma demands recall (for Coleridge, opium), yet only through the (im)possible detours and returns of the unconscious. For Caruth this is why 'trauma and its uncanny repetition' are at the heart of psychoanalysis 'as it listens to a voice that it cannot fully know but to which it nonetheless bears witness' ('Introduction' 9). Woodman's attempt to absorb in his dream the unknown that cannot be psychologically absorbed centres on this traumatic demand for total knowledge.

Bearing witness to this voice of the other within ourselves, however, is further complicated by our negotiations with others about such voices. Faith cannot be a matter of merely individual belief without it also being one of social negotiation. We want our vision(s) to be seen or not seen, confirmed or denied by the other. We want others to agree with us about the terms of our lived existence, our faith that the world exists the way we imagine it to exist. Such agreement becomes a rather tricky prospect, however, when faith turns upon what we *cannot* see but believe to be true. This assent becomes especially crucial in Romanticism, in which matters of faith previously mediated by the church get renegotiated through other means, as in philosophy or science. As Elinor Shaffer notes,

> The critiques of the Enlightenment went to the roots of religion's claims to supernatural authority, rational validity, divine inspiration of the sacred books, and historical evidence [...] Against these devastating critiques there was a counter-movement [...] The argument from the 'need' for religion (regardless of its capacity for rational justification) gained ground, sometimes by reassertion of the traditional 'original sin,' or in Kantian terms of 'radical evil,' or, increasingly, human 'psychological needs.' (138–9)

An uncanny bond exists between the demystification of revelation and the argument from 'psychological needs.' For the latter, by turning God's creational authority over to what Shelley in 'Mont Blanc' calls 'the human mind's imaginings' (143), makes the question of a now purely human perception of the world a question of faith in the world's existence, which is in turn to make this perception a matter of the psychological need to have the world *seen* in a particular way. The flashpoint here is the empirical status of religious revelation itself: 'The historical religions, whose claim rested on supposed miraculous interventions by a deity in the order of nature (Christianity, Islam), were suspect by virtue of such claims; and the Scriptures themselves, once subjected to the same tests as secular documents, were unsound bases for such claims' (142). The movement from the sanctuary and confessional to the laboratory – from a religious faith in revelation to a forensic faith in facts – did not, that is, alleviate the burden of proof.

One figure who focused this dilemma rather sharply was David Hume. In the Abstract to *A Treatise of Human Nature* (1740), Hume 'promises to draw no conclusions but where he is *authorized* by experience,' which will have to do because 'we can never arrive at the ultimate principles' (xvi, 646) of reality. Making experience his touchstone, Hume goes on in *An Enquiry Concerning Human Understanding* (1748) to argue that 'we may observe, that there is no species of reasoning more common, more useful, and even necessary to human life, than that which is derived from the testimony of men, and the reports of eye-witnesses and spectators' (74). Such histories are not credible because of 'any *connexion*, which we perceive *a priori*, between testimony and reality, but because we are accustomed to find a conformity between them' (75) based upon the habit of experience. The customary recurrence of experience is what creates belief, which is 'some sentiment or feeling [...] excited by nature' and 'is nothing but a more vivid, lively, forcible, firm, steady conception of an object than what the imagination alone is ever able to attain' (32). Belief is the natural feeling that binds thought and imagination, especially because, on its own, the latter can deviate in its cognition of reality. Hence belief is 'that act of the mind, which renders realities, or what is taken for such, more present to us than fictions, causes them to weigh more in the thought, and gives them a superior influence on the passions and imagination' (32).

Yet in that phrase, 'what is taken for such,' one realizes how belief still sustains perception, especially at the limits of experience. Hume addresses this issue in 'On Miracles' (1752), which Shaffer cites. Miracles evoke the 'passion of *surprise* and *wonder*' and 'give a sensible tendency towards the belief of those events' (78). But they are ultimately a 'violation of the laws of nature; and as a firm and unalterable experience has established these laws, the proof against a miracle, from the very nature of the fact, is as entire as any argument from experience can possibly be imagined' (76). Moreover, miracles are most susceptible to the forgeries of human testimony. Like prophecy, miracles work by '*Faith*, [...] which subverts all the principles of [...] understanding, and gives [...] a determination to believe what is most contrary to custom and experience' (90). The communication of experiences 'contrary to custom and experience' is the unconscious of perception that haunts eighteenth-century empiricism as what Jung calls the '*opus contra naturam*.' Paraphrasing Caruth on the excessive rationality of Locke's writings, we might call this the 'trauma of empiricism.' Empiricism's desire to read in the association of ideas the soul's formation, Caruth argues, disguises a traumatic lack of self, 'displaced in the neurosis of empiricism': the fact that 'associative substitutions are displaced versions of the attempt to establish a unified self-consciousness' (*Empirical Truths* 34, 37). Belief, that is, covers up the unknowable origin of self and existence. It turns the cognitive productiveness of Locke's *tabula rasa* into a site of traumatic blankness, understanding's irrecoverable primal scene of cognition. Armed with this kind of awareness, Woodman confronts an extension of the Semitic tradition of revelation that reaches beyond it by boldly breaking the seal set by Muhammad.

One way Romanticism deals with Hume's sceptical legacy is via the aesthetic. Shaffer argues that in Romanticism the 'imaginative functions would serve as apologetic grounds for religious experience, shifting from dogmatic and institutional authority to aesthetic validation of the reflective ideas essential to religion' (141). For instance, Kant argues for the imagination's ability to shape and thus free itself from the contingency of experience. Kant sidesteps the fact that one can never definitively trust one's perception of the world by sublating the mind's empiricism as part of the broader idealism of a *sensus communis* that agrees on the tenets of this empiricism. The post-Enlightenment aesthetic refashioning of the world reveals the political unconscious of a concern to manage both individual and collective psychologies, to make individual psychologies cohere within and thus conform to the body politic's larger consciousness. One of the paradigmatic examples of this management of personal vision is Coleridge's later prose writings. Since the 1790s, Coleridge writes, 'the hand of providence has disciplined *all* Europe into sobriety' and all 'youthful enthusiasts, [...] [have] been taught to prize and honour the spirit of nationality as the best safeguard of national independence' (*BL* 1:189–90). Eventually philosophy and religion conflate to form a political theology that became one of the powerful currents of nineteenth-century British imperial identity. For Coleridge, imagination, informed by philosophy, is the '*nisus formativus* of the body politic, the shaping and informing spirit, which *educing, i.e.* eliciting, the latent *man* in all the natives of the soil, *trains them up* to citizens of the country, free subjects of the realm' (1:286). Imagination orchestrates coherence, stability, and progress and governs how good citizens learn to *internalize* the ideas of Church and State as part of a larger, permanent national culture, knowledge, and education. In *On the Constitution of Church and State* Coleridge names a 'permanent class or order' of individuals, a 'National CLERISY' who oversee the nation's 'continuing and progressive civilization' and who 'remain at the fountain heads of the humanities, in cultivating and enlarging the knowledge already possessed' (42, 46, 43). That is to say, 'it is the privilege of the few to possess an idea: of the generality of men, it might be more truly affirmed, that they are possessed by it' (12–13). Indeed, the line between a sober reflection upon and a zealous faith in the nation's idealist State is fine indeed. As Anthony Harding notes, Coleridge's political vision is a type of revealed religion that preserves 'an "inner sense," a spiritual meaning in scripture, understood by select interpreters' (7). This political vision, it would appear, is radically opposed to Woodman's dream of the Báb.

By overseeing an exchange of knowledge that is at once esoteric and confidential, therefore, the Clerisy symbolize the religious enthusiasm of political theology itself, one that encrypts the preternatural experience of revelation and its supernatural comprehensions of faith. Speaking of the visual as the pre-eminent sense in his 1832 *Letters on Natural Magic*, David Brewster states: 'This wonderful organ [the eye] may be considered as the sentinel which guards the pass between the worlds of matter and spirit. [...] The eye is consequently the principal seat of the supernatural' (10). Brewster cites the Spectre of the Brocken, an atmospheric phenomenon by which our shadows, cast upon mist, both magnify and distort the human form. The Spectre reflects the spectral nature of vision itself, the way in which reality passes into consciousness via a logic beyond comprehension. In 'Constancy to an Ideal Object,' Coleridge uses the apparition to explore how only 'yearning Thought' can station a world of things that 'veer and vanish' (4, 2). The woodman in the poem's final apostrophe sees an 'image with a glory round its head' advancing toward him in the 'viewless snow-mist [that] weaves a glist'ning haze.' Yet although the 'enamoured rustic worships its fair hues,' he does not know that 'he makes the shadow [...] he pursues' (28–32). Moreover, this self-projection also marks his self-alienation, the *unconstancy* of thought's 'yearning.'

In his 1845 *Suspiria de Profundis*, Thomas De Quincey figures the Spectre as a 'solitary apparition' that is 'not always solitary in his personal manifestations' (15:183). This multiple personality, which De Quincey aligns with the Dark Interpreter, signifies how the unconscious challenges the senses by spectrally disembodying the self at the limits of empiricism. By associating this dislocation with the 'gloomy realities of Paganism' (15:183n), De Quincey also invokes the dangers of a religious enthusiasm that by the first quarter of the nineteenth century and beyond had acquired a distinctly political valence. Perhaps he is recalling *The Private Memoirs and Confessions of a Justified Sinner* (1823), in which James Hogg uses the Spectre to trope the psychotic nature of human identity, ethical action, and the fanatical religiosity of social cohesion – the way in which the political use of perception, testimony, and common sense turns violently manipulative and coercive. The prostitute Bell Calvert sums up this crisis rather succinctly when she asks, '"We have nothing on earth but our senses to depend upon: if these deceive us, what are we to do?"' (80). Calvert speaks to the novel's parody of the uncanny relationship between the delirium of reason, which in *Biographia Literaria* Coleridge associates with the mechanical logic of eighteenth-century associationism, and the enthralments of faith. Calvinism is the novel's metonymy for a communal revelation gone awry, a ludicrous forensics that produces in its adherents a virulently psychosomatic struggle with the unthought, unseen or unconscious of faith. Calvinism offers an improbable but self-justifying metapsychology, a delirious rationality that in the novel's words 'seems [...] like enchantment,' so that each character 'can hardly believe [his or her] senses' (72).

By yoking the zeal of Calvinist revelation and its vertiginous moral universe with the fervent rationality of the nineteenth century's scientific imagination, Hogg's novel points to the survival of a troubling enthusiasm anchored in the trauma of cognition as a supernatural process beyond rational comprehension. Hogg's novel stages the poetic faith of Romantic supernaturalism in Coleridge, Brewster, or De Quincey as the hysteria of belief. It thus returns to the spectral scene of the intersubjective communication of revelation that troubles Hume's concern with the miraculous. One's faith in the perception of things, depending upon the compulsive repetition of custom and experience, turns symptomatic of a terror that the world we imagine we see and know might not be there at all, or what perhaps is worse, might be there after all. Relying upon the recurrence of pattern and habit for our perceptions, custom and experience are thus driven by largely automatic and unconscious processes. Such unconsciousness evokes in turn how the customary observation of events, requiring consensus and confirmation, is simultaneously open to conjecture, hypothesis, dispute. Observation means that all experience is up for grabs. Part of Shelley's anxiety about convincing himself that 'Mont Blanc appears,' 'Remote, serene, and inaccessible' (61, 97), is the solitary and potentially psychotic break that haunts that text's revelatory and prophetic pursuit of the otherwise communal experience of perception. Shelley proclaims,

> Thou hast a voice, great Mountain, to repeal
> Large codes of fraud and woe; not understood
> By all, but which the wise, and great, and good
> Interpret, or make felt, or deeply feel,         (80–3)

invoking a 'faith so mild' (77) that reconciles men to nature as 'a mysterious tongue / Which teaches awful doubt' (76–7). Shelley needs the intersubjective dimension of vision, for the option is the 'vacancy' of 'Silence and solitude' (144) or the autonomous authority of a voice.

## VI

In his notebooks Coleridge speaks in a voice frequently more sceptical than the political theology of his later writings. In an 1805 entry, he explores Romantic revelation in terms of psychology rather than philosophy or religion:

> Among the numerous examples of confusion of Heathen & Christian Mythology in the Poets of the 15th Century (pleasing inasmuch as they prove how intimately the works of Homer & Virgil &c were *worked* in & *scripturalized* in their *minds* – I. was taught this hour, the other the next – or both together & by the same man with the same countenance, with the same seriousness and zeal, at the same early age – & in a time when Authority was all in all – and what was publickly *taught* of Aristotle, was individually & perhaps more generally, *felt* of *Homer* in the various broken reflections of him throughout the Latin Poets & all men of Education & in the original & the echoing series of the other Greek Poets to the Politians, & c &c, – indeed, it requires a strong imagination as well as an accurate psycho-analytical understanding in order to be able to conceive the *possibility*, & to picture out the reality, of the *passion* of those Times for Jupiter, Apollo &c & the nature of the *Faith* (for a Faith it was – it vanished indeed at the Cock-crowing of a deliberate Question, in *most* men; but in the ordinary unchecked stream of Thought it moved on, as naturally as Contraband & Legal Goods in the same Vessel, when no Revenue Officers are on the Track.) (*Notebooks* 2:2670)

This passage marks the first appearance of the word 'psycho-analytical' in the English language. It constellates two issues: faith and our ability to read the past. Coleridge alludes to how Renaissance poets, 'con-fusing' the 'Heathen & Christian' as part of the same 'mythology,' '*worked* in & *scripturalized*' Homer or Virgil. For the Renaissance ancient poetry was a form of belief rather than doctrine because it fundamentally expressed how 'Jupiter, Apollo & c' were daily merely present to the ancient imagination. Faith was not a question of the gods' being, but of a passion *for* the gods. Or rather, there was no question of faith itself; it simply *was*. The difference between belief and faith, that is, disappeared or perhaps had not yet appeared. Only with the dawn ('cock-Crowing') of Enlightenment in the Renaissance was the 'deliberate Question' itself posed. At this point, faith 'vanished' and poetry stepped in to speak for the reality of the gods that the ancients took for granted as surely as Christianity spoke for the existence of God. At this point philosophy and science on one hand and literature on the other found themselves in separate camps, divided between 'what was publickly *taught* of Aristotle,' who spoke for the mind of science, and what 'was individually [...] *felt* of *Homer*,' who spoke through the more intuitive paths of feeling.

Yet faith never really vanished. It moved on 'in the ordinary unchecked stream of Thought,' 'as naturally as Contraband & Legal Goods in the same Vessel [of thought that contains philosophy and science], when no Revenue Officers are on the Track.' Thus, when in *Biographia Literaria* Coleridge aligns poetry with myth and belief in order to speak of the 'poetic faith' that comes from a 'willing suspension of disbelief,' he treats the psychology of faith as desire and illusion as well as hope and certainty. Coleridge is not talking about the delusions of ideology's social mythos, although the 1805 passage suggests that the 'deliberate Question' of rationality stakes its own belief claims on reality. Rather, he addresses the human capacity *to* believe, especially in what we do not necessarily know to exist or to be true – again, what he calls the 'supernatural.' This psychology of faith constitutes an *other* register of cognition that goes underground. This is not the Freudian unconscious per se, the depth or interior of a repressed or buried psychic half-life. Rather, it is a 'Contraband' reality buried within the everyday, in the 'ordinary unchecked stream of Thought,' a shadow economy within reason, the unseen part of its operations. It is thus also 'naturally' or unavoidably part of the 'same Vessel' as reason, consciousness, the visible. Poetry speaks of and from this Hades (in 'Ode to a Nightingale' Keats will say that the work of poetry is always borne 'Lethe-wards' [4]), where the dead, never really dead, continue to wander in a forgetting that, as Freud will remind us, is its own form of remembering. Or as Jung will remind us, this is the land of the dead formed when the gods fall into psychosis, the archetypes of a collective unconscious awaiting formulation in depth psychology, like the dead in *The Seven Sermons to the Dead* returning from Jerusalem because they could no longer find what they were searching for. It could also be Woodman's dream of the Báb.

The resilience of this other form of memory comes from its being *felt* rather than seen, from its resistance to enlightenment's demand for visibility. Its transmission from past to present is thus different from reason's 'public' education, and its knowledge and historical form elude official expression. For one thing, faith is felt 'individually,' invoking in Coleridge's time the post-Revolutionary spectre of a knowledge that might counter the status quo. Faith is truly radical, that is, because of its psychological dimension. It cannot be located in the origins or ends of identity but rather makes itself felt throughout history, another trajectory of feeling that transmits itself as broken reflections and echoes. This body of feeling registers thought's cognition as it is, as Wordsworth will say in 'Tintern Abbey,' felt on the pulses before passing into the purer mind, Blake's 'Pulsation of the Artery' (*M* 29[31].3). Yet, as Coleridge suggests, thought can never overcome or set feeling aside. Rather, feeling is the psychosomatic body of cognition integral to thought. And to apprehend this body, the passage calls upon another way to 'conceive the *possibility*' – as opposed to 'explain the meaning' – of 'the *passion* of those Times.' Again, the point is not to understand reality itself but to comprehend one's passion *for* this reality, knowledge's human dimension. This 'requires a strong imagination as well as an accurate psycho-analytical understanding.' One invokes the Enlightenment precision of reason while the other invokes a Romantic faith in imagination. But the 'psycho-analytical' confuses the psyche with reason, introducing the psychological as a third component between imagination and reason. This third thing between theology and philosophy is like the 'tertium aliquid' of the Coleridgean dialectic in *Biographia Literaria*, 'an inter-penetration of [...] counteracting powers, partaking of both' (1:300). Psychology is the reciprocity of understanding between imagination and the analytical. That is to say, psychology *conceives* or *imagines* how the mind *makes* reality, which in the Jungian terms of the collective unconscious is a feeling confrontation with the archetypes as a constellation of previous modes of how thought *was felt*.

This is the nature of poetic faith. To suspend one's disbelief in a metaphorical reality is also to *be suspended by* this disbelief in feeling, caught in a struggle of faith that by its nature can never be resolved. 'Poetic faith' *is* the struggle that makes itself felt as the possibility *of* faith. At the point that metaphor negotiates reality a different body of faith emerges, what Woodman might call the metaphorical body of faith itself. Coleridge's notebook passage suggests in the profoundly human struggle of faith a turn inward to its unconscious dimension, which calls for a psychoanalytical understanding. Psychoanalysis itself, that is, calls for a certain faith in unconscious phenomena – dreams, symptoms, archetypes – as the register of a world beyond our rational comprehension. That Freud was so anxious to legitimate psychoanalysis as a respectable science indicates the extent to which he was aware that the analysis of the unconscious was the pursuit of a forbidden or occult knowledge. In his turn to alchemy or the paranormal, Jung accepted this pursuit as integral to the psychoanalytic project. Coleridge's awareness of the 'contraband' quality of faith, its supernatural poetic character, becomes itself symptomatic of a certain wariness about that which resists the 'normal' paths of empirical study, which is what makes Coleridge, as Woodman makes him, more Jung's than Freud's precursor. The pursuit of reality's limits has about it the quality of the dangerous and the arcane. It also bears the taint of shame or guilt. Once again: to take prophecy seriously, as Woodman does, is to delude ourselves – necessarily, inevitably – about the reality of things.

# VII

At the launch of *Sanity, Madness, Transformation* at the University of Toronto Press in 2006, I said something that, in hindsight, startled me as much as hearing Woodman speak for the first time startled me. I suggested that, even if I were deluded, I, like Coleridge's Wedding-Guest, would gladly follow Woodman into his madness. Such absolute commitments do not come without their dangers, especially in the present climate of critical and cultural relativism. Negotiating such dangers isn't easy, though *to* negotiate them is also to participate in that same suspicion to which I also remain committed. And yet, to paraphrase Shelley's essay 'On Life,' I am now convinced of what I was earlier convicted: that something fundamental happened to me in Woodman's undergraduate class, some shift in my perception of things that altered irrevocably how I see the world. Remembering that class's transformative power, I am often bewildered that literature and literary studies have become sites of such bitter contestation on one hand and near irrelevance on the other. I've spent much of the past thirty years pondering these issues, equally wondering if one's investment in them isn't just a way of making one's life count. But then I wonder further: what would it matter if I had been, or am still, deluded? Whence, one needs to ask, comes the imperative to invest one's life with meaning? The making of such meanings is inherently what defines us as humans, defines *the human*, and the study of literature, or of the literary more broadly, still seems to me the most potent way of assessing the situation. The particularly complex motility of our creaturely sense means, as everyone from Locke onward has attempted to understand, that we are in the business of making sense. We are by nature *sensoria*, machines for making sense, of which mechanical reproduction we are simultaneously compelled to make sense – that is, to find the kernel of an authenticity we both imagine and desire. These two productions of sense are unavoidably intertwined, like the Moebius strip that carries the two sides of the consciousness that is the very matrix of our sentience.

But then the next question arrives: how do we come to believe in this process? What makes this production of human being an article of faith, despite all efforts to resist such belief? For we know even in the midst of such radical deconstructions of being that is our legacy from the previous century, that this matrix *is* our being, that we can't dismiss ourselves as human without the very process of our being human, of human being. Keats knew such paradoxes to tease us out of thought when he contemplated a Grecian urn, ancient yet still vital. This is, as Woodman reminds us, how Blake conceives of Eternity. In an earlier version of this book, Woodman wrote: 'Like the mind itself, the present is "wandering through eternity." Eternity is not a place of rest, a state of being. It is something we are wandering through like a whale looking for the ocean.' Put another way, one cannot empty the ocean in which one swims without contemplating utter annihilation. Those saddled with the immense burden of thinking the quantum physics that would help to realize Oppenheimer's dream understood this paradox. Likely the point of faith comes, then, with necessarily swerving aside from such annihilation. This is the vertiginous point of the Real of Freud's death drive, the point of utter nothingness beyond all capacity of human symbolization that, by virtue of its utter irrepresentability to human consciousness anchors the very economy of being human as a vast repression of the very thing that would refute its very being, all the while knowing that such spectral nothingness *is* our being.

In his recent essay 'Church, State, and Resistance,' Jean-Luc Nancy writes:

> Being in common, or being together – or even more simply, and in the barest form, being several – is being in affect: being affected and affecting. It is being touched and touching. 'Contact' – contiguity, brushing together, encountering, and clashing – is the fundamental modality of affect. What touch touches is the limit: the limit of the other – of the other body, because the other is the other body, that is to say, what is impenetrable (penetrable only by a wound, not penetrable in the sexual relation, where 'penetration' is only a touch that pushes the limit to its farthest point). What is at stake above all in being-with is the relation to the limit: How can we touch and be touched there without violating it? And we desire to violate the limit, for the limit exposes finitude. The desire to merge and the desire to murder constitute the double modality of an essential trouble that agitates us in our

finitude. Wanting to swallow or to annihilate others – and yet at the same time wanting to maintain them as others, because we also sense the horror of solitude (which is properly the exit from sense, if sense is essentially exchanged or shared). That being said, humanity regulates or has regulated the relation to the limit in two ways: either by some modality of sacrifice, which consists in crossing the limit and thus establishing a link with totality (more generally still, I would say, a modality of consecration, since bloody sacrifice is not the only one at stake); or by means that lie outside of consecration – and that is the West, that is politics and the law, in other words, and essentially the recourse to an autonomy of finitude. (111)

Negotiating the boundary between a Western 'autonomy of finitude' and an Eastern 'consecration' to a totality always beyond ourselves is at the heart of this book's argument. The former poses at once an apparently respectful distance yet also a firm apprehension of the world, a conquest of finitude in order to render its boundaries transparent and thus to enwrap the subject in the illusion of his self-sufficiency. In this scenario the world can never be too much with us because we are at once its agent and master.

Yet the latter position suggests a parallel delusion in that it equally desires to still, in some cases to annihilate, the *habitus* that is the context of the subject's struggle with finitude. Woodman confronts this annihilation in Shelley's 'one annihilation,' in the Persian prophet Bahá'u'lláh's declaration that the entire creation has passed away, and in Blake's apocalyptic vision of the 'rotten rags' of memory destroyed in order to create a new Fourfold humanity (*Epipsychidion* 587; *M* 41[48].4). Each scenario, that is, betrays a position of some violence, of a desire to rend the limits of finitude that, properly speaking, is an impossibility of the human condition, insofar as we mean to define ourselves, however ambivalently, fragmentarily, or opaquely as human. That is to say, both scenarios sidestep the position of the human from that we sense, speak, think, create, and destroy. Here I invoke Schopenhauer's darkly human sense of existence, which Nancy paraphrases when he goes on to state that the 'city [the *polis*] may want to be regulated according to some cosmic, physical, or organic model, but the very fact of this will and this representation indicates that it is totality, "consecration to the whole," that is felt to be lacking' (111). For Schopenhauer, who influenced Jung, representation is how we understand the *ur*-drive of being that he calls 'will,' the world of the will comprising the totality of being itself. Will is always the goal of our desire's trajectory as representation's bringing of the will to consciousness, the human process that articulates this process for us, the way we constitute ourselves as subjects, the way we bring the will to human understanding and thus constitute the human itself. Yet representation is only ever partial, fragmentary, impermanent, always thrust toward that which is beyond it that will still its endless longing for clarity. For Schopenhauer we free ourselves from the blindness of representation's 'illumination' of the totality of things when we accept the will's drive toward insight not as a transcendentalism but as a kind of blind determinism: 'We are like entrapped elephants, which rage and struggle fearfully for many days, until they see that it is fruitless, and then suddenly offer their necks calmly to the yoke, tamed for ever' (1:306). For Schopenhauer the 'will itself cannot be abolished by anything except *knowledge*' (1:400), but this means that we do not overcome the will through enlightenment, but rather by radically accepting the will in order to remain no longer susceptible to it. We seek an end to the desire *for*, rather than the cure *of*, enlightenment.

At the core of the kind of impossible affect Nancy describes, then, is a more fundamental question that goes back to the empiricist arguments of the eighteenth century, one of the fulcrums of history at which we find matters of faith turned over to matters of reason and these latter issues in turn turned over to the psychology of understanding the 'failure' of both religion and philosophy. The crisis defined by such a momentous shift (with which after-effects we are still dealing today as they define the curvature of a historical movement into the quantum spaces of modernity) is, I have argued elsewhere as Woodman argues in this book, the crisis that gives birth to, and is accepted as the fundamental locus, of psychoanalysis. This is the crisis of the unconscious – of the unknown of infinitude and finitude – which in the sense-bound condition of our humanness constitutes the failure of sense in all valences of that word.

We can thus reform the question 'What does it mean to believe in something?' as 'How is it that we believe in things?' which is also to ask the contrary question, 'What happens when our senses deceive us?', the fundamental question demanded of religious faith and of our belief in the horizon of God beyond our finitude where sense cannot carry us. The urgency of this question is summed up in a recent address by Julia Kristeva to the Modern Language Association entitled 'Thinking in Dark Times,' which I've quoted from above. Kristeva reads the recent rioting in French suburbs by North and West African youths as but one symptom of a 'malady of ideality,' which 'confronts us with a prereligious and prepolitical form of belief; it is a matter of needing an ideal that contributes to the construction of the psychic life but that, because it is an absolute exigency, can easily turn itself into its opposite: disappointment, boredom, depression, or even destructive rage, vandalism, and all the imaginable variants of nihilism that are but appeals to the ideal' (18). If we accept Kristeva's notion of this 'prereligious need to believe' as 'constitutive of the psychic life with and for the other' (20), and if we accept this 'psychic life with and for the other' as a fundamentally sympathetic binding predicated on the trajectory of human desire toward a beyond it can never know definitively to exist, we begin to realize what is at stake in our survival as a species. The attack here is not on religion or on public institutions. The attack is on belief itself. As the world burns, we are left with the most fundamental question: why have faith at all?

# VIII

Some years ago I asked Woodman to give a guest lecture to a fourth-year seminar I was teaching at the University of Western Ontario on the topic of Kushner's *Angels in America*. Woodman began by invoking Bloom's *The American Religion*: 'Bloom describes the Mormon religion as the American religion and America itself [...] as religion-crazed or mad. Calling himself [...] an unorthodox Jewish Gnostic, Bloom explains his position as the archetypal American position. The creation of the world was for the Gnostic a terrible mistake, the work of the Demi-urge who, like Satan, rebelled against the absolute perfection of the patriarchal Father by creating a highly imperfect world committed to "more life"' ('Kushner's *Angels in America*' 1). Needing the entire world to pass away in order for the world to be reborn in, or to return to, its 'absolute perfection' is the crucible of departure and return, destruction and creation, endless wandering across the frontier for the promised land that defines the ceaseless desire of America's Manifest Destiny. This endlessly promised fulfilment, endlessly deferred, is epitomized by Jay Gatsby yearning toward the green light at the end of Daisy's dock across an expanse of water that ceaselessly drowns the past and future in an acutely interminable present where everything that is capable of happening happens while nothing is accomplished. Such a frenetic mobility, Woodman suggests, uncannily resembles the frozen terrain of doctrinal belief. Walter Benjamin, to whom Kushner's vision is crucially indebted, images such immobile possibility as the ashes of history from which ceaseless destruction the angel of historical experience ceaselessly renews itself.

The ceaseless renewal of apocalypse is always around the corner.

The call to 'more life' is Bloom's translation of the Hebrew word for 'blessing.' It is also one of the penultimate lines of Kushner's play, spoken by its central character, Prior Walter, who throughout the play is dying of AIDS. Facing the Myriad Infinite Aggregate Angelic Entities or Continental Principalities in Heaven, who are in Permanent Emergency Council, which in Kushner's imagination looks like San Francisco after the big Quake of 1901 – undying, undead – Walter gives back The Book that they have conferred upon him as the chosen one or Prophet. He prefers a catastrophic, shiftless, suffering, disease-ridden, and imperfect earthly existence to the immobility and stasis of eternity. He wants 'to be alive,' even when being alive is too painful to bear. The Angel of the Continental Principality of America, like Keats's Moneta, admonishes Prior for wanting to 'date on his doom':

> You only think you do.
> Life is a habit with you.
> You have not *seen* what is to come:
> We *have*:
> What will the grim Unfolding of these Latter Days bring?
> That you or any Being should wish to endure them?
> Death more plenteous than all Heaven has tears to mourn it,
> The slow dissolving of the Great Design,
> The spiralling apart of the Work of Eternity,
> The World and its beautiful particle logic
> All collapsed. All dead, forever,
> In starless, moonlorn onyx night.
> We are failing, failing,
> The Earth and the Angels.

The Angel thus asks 'Who demands: More Life?' when Death protects the living from 'More horror than can be borne' and 'bares the Earth clean as bone.' To which Prior replies:

> But still. Still.
> Bless me anyway.
> I want more life. I can't help myself. I do.
> I've lived through such terrible times, and there are people who live through much much worse, but [...] You see them living anyway. When they're more spirit than body, more sores than skin, when they're burned

and in agony, when flies lay eggs in the corners of the eyes of their children, they live. Death usually has to take life away. I don't know if that's just the animal. I don't know if it's not braver to die. But I recognize the habit. The addiction to being alive. We live past hope. If I can find hope anywhere, that's it, that's the best I can do. It's so much not enough, so inadequate but [...] Bless me anyway. I want more life. (131–3)

'But still. Still.' To hope for and believe in more life, to want to keep the machinery of our senses going, insofar as they deign to operate on our behalf: perhaps that is our greatest delusion. In a remarkable juxtaposition Woodman reads this passage as one of the shadows that futurity casts upon the present of Romanticism. Prior wanting more life is Apollo dying into life at the end of Keats's fragment *Hyperion*, replayed in Keats's equally truncated revision of that poem as *The Fall of Hyperion* when Moneta challenges the Poet either to ascend the steps of Saturn's temple or 'die on that marble where thou art' (1.108). The Poet chooses the latter, and thus the life of poetry (which in Keats's text is the only life worth living), and not a moment too soon: 'One minute before death, my iced foot touch'd / The lowest stair; and as it touch'd, life seem'd / To pour in at the toes' (1.132–4). 'Thou has felt / What 'tis to die and live again before / Thy fated hour,' Moneta explains. 'That thou hadst power to do so / Is thy own safety; thou hast dated on / Thy doom' (1.141–5). To commit oneself to faith in the face of the death drive becomes for Woodman most crucial, not within the vexed epic terrain or dream vision of Keats's Hyperion poems, but in a stanza written just before his death, one of this book's origins:

This living hand, now warm and capable
Of earnest grasping, would, if it were cold
And in the icy silence of the tomb,
So haunt thy days and chill they dreaming nights
That thou would wish thine own heart dry of blood,
So in my veins red life might stream again,
And thou be conscience-calm'd. See, here it is –
I hold it towards you.                                              (1–8)

We are trained not to trust that Keats's hand is reaching out from the page. What, then, is the moment of uncanny affect, the moment of shimmering silence, in which one imagines that it is? For what does it mean to say that in such poetic moments – in the *Liebestode* from *Tristan und Isolde*;

in the final scene of Von Trier's *Dancer in the Dark*; in the final pages of Coetzee's *Waiting for the Barbarians* – we can attain a poetic faith in what we have seen or felt that is otherwise enigmatic to our perception? What is this faith in more life that makes one risk death itself, just to know for certain – that is to say, without knowing at all – that the world exists?

Even in the most profoundly uncommitted scepticism there is a committed, even fervent relation to something, even if nothing, that is nonetheless a relation *to* and that thus implies the commitment and obligation, however willing or unwilling, of a necessary and inescapable transference between the self and that which lies beyond it. Simply to exist, to mark a place in the overwhelming tide of existence means to *hold* a place and thus to occupy a position, even if by virtue of one's complete indifference to the place itself. Merely to breathe, to take in air, is to mark one's place in existence as a momentary contribution to and exhaustion of, and thus occupation of, the *habitus* of existence itself. Indeed, even to commit suicide, as Shelley understood only too well in *Adonais*, is to mark a tear in the world's fabric that nonetheless *leaves* its mark – the negative mark of a haunting that, framed within the fundamentally human work of the psyche, indicates that it may be virtually impossible for the world of humanity ever to pass away simply by virtue of the fact that one is necessarily born *into* and thus in relationship *to* the world.

In *Fear and Trembling* Kierkegaard explores the *agon* of the sheer absurdity of Abraham's decision to sacrifice his only son Isaac based on God's injunction to do so. Abraham's act is not really a decision because it exists beyond the morality of deeds or the rationality of cognition. Faith is a 'prodigious paradox [...] a paradox that is capable of making a murder into a holy act well pleasing to God, a paradox that gives Isaac back again to Abraham, which no thought can lay hold of because faith begins precisely where thinking leaves off' (46). The current conflict between a Western belief in the incarnation of God's power in human form and an Eastern faith that wants no truck with such materialities asks us to think this paradox of faith beyond thought itself. Yet in such apparent differences lie profound similarities. The possibly fatal embrace comes at the point that such beliefs cannot read their own internal, human functioning as a poetic faith that turns upon an endless psychoanalysis of itself. Another remarkable encounter in Kushner's play stages just such a moment of intersubjective dialogue in which the apparent intransigency of Mormonism confronts the apparently liberal resistance to homophobia with the primal scene of the raw human dynamics of faith mobilizing both. Prior, visited by visions that he cannot explain, the 'infallible barometer' for which is his very erect penis, appeals to Hannah Pitt, the apparently very straight, very pious Mormon mother of his ex-lover's lover, to explain such visions and thus allay his fears, through their shared understanding, that he isn't losing his mind:

*Hannah:* ... One hundred and seventy years ago, which is recent, an angel of God appeared to Joseph Smith in upstate New York, not far from here. People have visions.

*Prior:* But that's preposterous, that's ...

*Hannah:* It's not polite to call other people's beliefs preposterous. He had great need of understanding. Our Prophet. His desire made prayer. His prayer made an angel. The angel was real. I believe that.

*Prior:* I don't. And I'm sorry but it's repellent to me. So much of what you believe.

*Hannah:* What do I believe?

*Prior:* I'm a homosexual. With AIDS. I can just imagine what you ...

*Hannah:* No you can't. Imagine. The things in my head. You don't make assumptions about me, mister; I won't make them about you. (102)

It's that simple. Faith is a matter of tolerance, of tolerating the other's possible delusions, of, as Wordsworth says of the crazed Bedouin, going on 'like errand' (*P* 5:161) knowing that 'in the blind and awful lair / Of such a madness, reason did lie couched' (5:161, 151–2).

Yet even more simple is the cure for the disease of belief if it grows intolerant and intolerable. Hannah concludes, 'An angel is just a belief, with wings and arms that can carry you. It's naught to be afraid of. If it lets you down, reject it. Seek for something new' (103). Such simplicities perhaps explain why the Ancient Mariner cruises from kirk to kirk, looking to find someone to share his 'fond anxiety' (*P* 5:160) and to go with him to church, even if to sit in such sanctuaries leaves him with a 'conflict of sensations without name' (10:290). Woodman marks what is at stake in desiring more life, in seeing the march of history as the possible march into its own delusions. Yet in reading Blake's apocalyptic journey through Milton's body, the final judgment of which is the moment of revelation, 'less than a pulsation of an artery' (*M* 28[30].63) in which he arrives, awake, in his own body, he also marks the psychoanalysis of such delusions, the moment at which we awaken into the delusive terrain of belief, there being no place else to reside with such basic and fundamental human desires.

In 'On Truth and Lies in a Non-Moral Sense' Nietzsche argues that

Only by forgetting [the] primitive world of metaphor can one live with any repose, security, and consistency: only by means of the petrifaction and co-agulation of a mass of images which originally streamed from the primal faculty of human imagination like a fiery liquid, only in the invincible faith that *this* sun, *this* window, *this* table is a truth in itself, in short, only by forget-ting that he himself is an *artistically creating* subject, does man live with any repose, security, and consistency. If but for an instant he could escape from the prison walls of this faith, his 'self consciousness' would be immediately destroyed. (86)

The contours of faith that sustain self-consciousness and give us our hu-man form are, in Blake and Shelley as in Nietzsche, entirely up for grabs. When Blake asks who dares to frame the tyger's fearful symmetry, he asks by what supernatural process the tyger comes within our human frame of reference. The framing of the question itself has a capacity to entertain the dangers of delusion that makes sense of why he dines with prophets. Blake and Shelley, that is, are already in Nietzsche's 'primitive world of metaphor.'

## IX

A final question, then: Why now, this book? In response to the problem of the 'place and ... possible power in our troubled world as we enter the third millennium' of the 'intellectual [who] bases her thought in the human sciences,' Kristeva appeals to the dark intelligence of the public intellectual. I quote her at some length on the matter:

In taking over from theology and philosophy, the humanities replaced the 'divine' and the 'human' by new objects of investigation: social bonds, the structures of kinship, rites and myths, the psychic life, and the genesis of languages and written works. We have acquired an unprecedented under-standing of the richness and risks of the human mind, and this understand-ing disturbs and meets with resistance and censure. Still, as promising as they are, the territories thus constituted fragment human experience; heirs to metaphysics, they keep us from identifying new objects of investigation. Transdisciplinarity does not in itself suffice to reconstruct the new human-ism we need. What matters is that from the outset the thinking subject con-nects his thought to his being in the world through affective, political, and ethical transference. My practice as a psychoanalyst, my novel writing, and my work in the social domain are not 'commitments'; rather these activities are an extension of a mode of thinking I look for and conceive as an *energeia* in the Aristotelian sense of thought as act, the actuality of intelligence. (14)

Such an *energeia* 'opens up a new approach to the world of religion':

> The discovery of the unconscious by Freud showed us that far from being illusions, while nevertheless being illusion, different beliefs and forms of spirituality shelter, encourage, or exploit specific psychic movements, which allow the human being to become a speaking subject and either a locus of culture or a centre of destruction [...] We can henceforth not only recognize the complexity of the inner experience that faith cultivates but also bring to light the hate that takes the guise of lovers' discourse as well as the death drive channelled into political vengeance and merciless wars. (14–15)

It is to this complexity that the *energeia* and actualized intelligence of the present volume addresses itself. It answers an urgent call to see the bigger picture:

> It is clear that today the intellectual is confronted with a difficult, historic task commensurate with the crisis of civilization: coaxing this new type of knowledge to emerge progressively. We should not hesitate to use technical terms, but we should be careful not to reduce them to their strict meaning, which is always too narrow. By positioning ourselves at the interface of these diverse disciplines, we give ourselves the chance to clarify, even if only a little, that which remains enigmatic: psychosis, sublimation, belief, nihilism, passion, the gender war, maternal madness, murderous hate. (15)

Since our illusions about the world's stability have been painfully demystified, the need to clarify that which 'remains enigmatic' seems especially urgent. Would that our leaders had visions of children on clouds, without preying on our desire to believe such myths as doctrines of belief. Are these the myths of politics, the myths of religion, or both? Have things always been this way? This book participates in the endless critique of the reason of these myths in order continually to release us into their endless power as myth-making, into a profound ambivalence about their sanity. In *this* world of poetic faith, more than what we have settled for might just be possible. By positioning ourselves with Woodman at the interface of these diverse disciplines, what might just be possible has at least a chance.

My own proclamation of faith in this book comes from some 'remote, serene, and inaccessible' core. I do not take credit but must certainly accept responsibility for my participation in the present volume. That is to say, I cannot but choose to mark my decision to follow in the wake of another's vision. I knew at the moment I heard Woodman speak in that first undergraduate class that I had heard the voice of a madness to which I could all too easily commit myself. Like Woodman standing up at the Bahá'í meeting and declaring everything he heard to be true, without understanding one word of what was being said, I knew that a fundamental truth had been revealed to me, the knowledge of which I would not have, if I am ever to have it, until a time much later. Such truth was not in the nature of either of our individual identities, although for the longest time I attempted to process it at that level. Rather it was in the nature of a perception transmitted to us via the Romantic poets that Woodman taught exclusively in his course, transmitted, that is, through a kind of preternatural transference of insight about the fundamental nature of human perception, about the human faith that the world exists as it does, or as it seems to, rather than as it *ought* to, although it was certainly a crucial part of the Romantic frame of things to wonder about how the world could be imagined, and thus imagined otherwise.

To paraphrase Wordsworth, at such moments of commitment one makes no vows; vows are made *for* us. Such throwing over to the visionary was for me, and still is, essential. I wouldn't say that I am now armed with greater consciousness to defend myself against such seductions, except to say that I possess, insofar as one can possess, a growing awareness of the human desire to be seduced. By 'visionary' I mean not the metaphysical or transcendental fabric of being, such as an earlier line of Romantic critical vision defined the Romantic imagination. Rather I mean the simple expectation that the world will be there *to* perceive. I knew at the moment I heard Woodman speak as another human being (which is to say, without at all knowing) that such listening was a matter of psychic survival, which I have always understood to be the only terms by which we *do* survive, the only terms by which our material, social, political, sexual, economic existences can be broached. Shelley explores this kind of expectation in 'Mont Blanc' when he wonders how the mountain appears at all in the first place. To which speculation I can now say, with some vital degree of 'energetic pessimism': thank God – whomever, whatever – that it does, and did, and might still.

REVELATION AND KNOWLEDGE

# Dream

The Báb is in Winnipeg. He is staying on the fourth floor of the DuBarry Apartments where I once lived with my parents on the top third floor. I am eager to see him. My father offers to take me. My brother joins us. When we arrive my father says he will wait. I try to persuade him to come. My brother and I take a dumb waiter to the fifth floor pulling on the ropes. When we arrive he too says he will wait. I go alone to the apartment. I am let in. On the floor in front of me is a luminous Persian carpet. The intricate pattern is in motion like the surface of a calm sea. It is also murmuring like the sound of a breeze gently tossing waters. I am told to remove my shoes. I see an empty chair at the other end of the room. I hesitate to step on the rug. When I do, the pattern divides, clearing a path. I take the chair at the other end and sit down. I wait. The Báb enters on my left. When he steps on the rug, it gathers around him like an *aba*, or cloak. He turns and looks at me. In an instant he is standing before me. He takes a chair identical to the one I am on. He sits down facing me. Our knees are almost touching. I try to speak, but I cannot. Struggling to make a sound, I rise in the air, turn a somersault, and land like a feather at his feet. Dissolving into air, I awake with a start: a streak of lightning, a distant thunder.

# To the Reader

I give you the end of a golden string,
Only wind it into a ball:
It will lead you in at Heavens gate,
Built in Jerusalems wall.

– Blake, *Jerusalem*

Over a period of some forty-two years (1946–88), the lecture hall became for me a *temenos* in which what Blake calls the 'Corporeal Understanding' was imaginatively transformed by the 'Intellectual powers' into what Keats calls a 'continual allegory,' which he describes as 'a life like the scriptures' (*CPP* 730; *KL* 218). Keats refers to the 'hebrew Bible,' but he has in mind what Blake calls 'poetic tales,' whose mystery most people reduce to 'forms of worship' (*MHH* 11). Keats's task is to restore religion to its original state as 'poetic tales,' which enact a mysterious process he calls 'Soul-making' (*KL* 249). This process is 'a grander scheme of salvation than the chrystain religion' (250) because its efficacy does not depend upon the grandiose claims of the ego to know God, if not *be* God. Instead, it depends upon a '*Negative Capability*' in which the 'Intellectual powers' operate in a willing state of suspended disbelief described by Coleridge as 'poetic faith' (43; *BL* 2:6). Poetic faith, as distinct from religious faith, is the capacity to entertain 'uncertainties, Mysteries, doubts.' It does not, by 'any irritable reaching after fact & reason,' claim to have penetrated to the inmost core of the mystery. It is, rather, content with 'a fine isolated verisimilitude' (*KL* 43). Perhaps having just encountered Coleridge's newly published *Biographia Literaria*, Keats could only regret that Coleridge, 'incapable of remaining content with half knowledge,' ended up sacrificing his poetic genius in order to discover the 'Penetralium of mystery' (43), like a high priest who alone can enter the secret parts of the temple. Equally determined to penetrate the mystery, the atheist Shelley worked at the opposite pole of Coleridge's religious faith, though Keats was equally certain that Shelley possessed negative capability.

The issue of religious vs poetic faith dialectically informs the argument of this book. Romanticism writes this issue large as the struggle to release the soul from its burial in matter. Here, as Shelley argues in 'Ode to the West Wind,' it lies 'like a corpse within its grave,' waiting for the imagination's 'clarion' to awaken it (8, 10). Shelley describes this grave as 'the dreaming earth' (10), which tropes Shelley's complex metaphorical system as the soul's enactment of itself. Blake uses the trope of his 'Vegetable Body' (*M* 42[49].27), which is the corporeal image of the five senses as the soul sleeping in nature's unconscious body dreaming it is awake. Nature, which is the physical body's unconsciousness of its own operations, becomes metaphor, the soul's embodiment of itself in and as the process of its making. One of the arguments made about the Romantic imagination is that a Romantic poem *is* this very process of soul-embodiment, like Adam awaking in *Paradise Lost* to find that his dream is truth. Blake calls this process 'Resurrection & Judgment in the Vegetable Body' (42[49].27). The 'Judgment' is what Coleridge calls the 'Night-mare Life-in-Death' that gets constellated when the soul is reduced to that 'portion of Soul discernd by the five Senses' (*The Ancient Mariner* 193; *MHH* 3). 'Resurrection' is the soul's release from this state.

To say that a Romantic poem is a substitute for religion, however, is not the same as saying that it renews religion. Whereas Keats and Shelley each in his own way substituted poetry for religion by rejecting religion and thus freeing the soul from superstition, Wordsworth and Coleridge saw in the substitution an isolation from religion that left poetry a 'delusion' that was at best 'fond,' at worst terrifying ('Elegiac Stanzas' 29). They thus came to view poetry as the renewal of the Christian faith within themselves, so that ideally poetry and religion, like Wordsworth and Coleridge, belonged together as a kind of secular scripture. When Coleridge argues that 'it had pleased Providence that the divinest truths of religion sho[uld] be revealed to us in the form of Poetry,' he most likely means the effect of first hearing Wordsworth chant his poetry, which sounded to Coleridge as though it had 'sprang forth' as from 'the first creative fiat' (*Lectures* 326; *BL* 1:80).

Blake is unique among the Romantics in that he saw his poetry as nei-

ther a substitute for nor a renewal of religion. For him, poetry is an apocalyptic unveiling of the 'Mystery' of the scriptures, a divine revelation
that constellates the return of Christ as the biblical descent of the New
Jerusalem. Blake describes this process as the 'Starry Eight' descending
into 'the Fires of [his] Intellect' (*M* 42[49].9–10), which is at once his
own resurrected body and the new body of the world. Entering this visionary state 'Within a Moment: a Pulsation of the Artery,' Blake falls initially into his 'Vegetable Body,' whose state of pure unconsciousness he
calls a 'Void Outside of Existence' (29[31].3, 41[48].37). This descent
of the creative imagination personified by Los into 'the Void Outside of
Existence' brings the 'Void' into 'Existence.' As in the opening verse of
Genesis, the 'Void' becomes a 'Womb' (42[49].1), which, as Blake describes it, gradually assumes the shape of that 'portion of Soul discernd
by the five Senses,' which, he argues, are 'the chief inlets of Soul in this
age' (*MHH* 4). As Deism or natural religion, this portion is the 'Vegetable Body' of the world, which Coleridge describes as the 'mechanical
philosophy' (*BL* 1:261), Christ becoming in Milton's Deistic account of
the creation 'a Ratio of the five Senses' (*MHH* 6). Blake's reference is to
Newton's compasses, which Jehovah as 'Destiny' had constructed 'to circumscribe / This Universe, and all created things' (*PL* 7.226–7), leaving
the Holy Ghost as the imagination a 'Vacuum' (*MHH* 6). To release the
soul from this arrested state in which Milton left it ('Milton's Religion is
the cause' [*M* 22[24].39]) and restore it to its original state as the 'human form divine' ('The Divine Image' 11) is, Blake insists, the divine
task of the creative imagination.

Finally dissatisfied with the 'human form divine' as it assumes a limited shape in the act of composition, which he describes as a 'fading
coal' awakened to a 'transitory brightness,' Shelley rejected it as a 'feeble
shadow of the original conception of the poet' (*DP* 535). In its non-place
as the 'void circumference' (*A* 420) or 'intense inane' (*PU* 3.4. 204),
he conceived instead a 'great poem' by the 'one great mind' which can
never be written. He associates this unwritten 'great poem' with the
'sacred few' who, in his final fragment, 'as soon / As they had touched
the world with living flame / Fled back like eagles to their native noon'
(*TL* 128–31).Rejecting the Christian dogma of incarnation, which he
parodies in *Prometheus Unbound* as Jupiter begetting a son who will perpetuate forever his tyrannical role, Shelley in *The Triumph of Life* replaces the
dogma with a 'shape all light' (352). As the 'white radiance of Eternity,'
this 'shape all light' finally extinguishes its refracted form as a 'dome of
many-coloured glass' (*A* 463, 462). 'Eternity,' declares Blake, 'is in love

with the productions of time' (*MHH* 7.10), a love which he further describes as 'Cominglings: from the Head even to the Feet' (*J* 69.43). These 'Cominglings' between eternity and time are, for Blake, the making of the resurrected body of the imagination, a body which Shelley ultimately rejects as a 'feeble shadow.' As the 'light's severe excess' (*TL* 424), it finally extinguishes poetry itself, an extinction that Blake rejects by identifying the operations of the imagination with the biblical descent of the New Jerusalem. This creative process at work in his brain where God first planted His Paradise restores physical sensations as the 'Spectres of the Dead' to their original form as the likeness of God Himself. In his 'Printing house in Hell' (*MHH* 15), Blake's metaphor of his working brain, Blake's engraved text is raised to its resurrected or illuminated form. This elaborate metaphor of the operations of his brain embraces Blake's epic vision of those mythical operations as what in *Paradise Regain'd* Milton describes as

> deeds
> Above Heroic, though in secret done,
> And unrecorded left through many an Age,
> Worthy t' have not remain'd so long unsung.                    (1.14–17)

Having in 1912 written *Symbols of Transformation*, in which he announced his break with Freud, Jung, as he describes it in his memoirs, realized that he now possessed 'a key to mythology' and was 'free to unlock all the gates of the unconscious psyche.' 'But then,' he continues,

> something whispered within me, 'Why open all gates?' And promptly the question arose of what, after all, I had accomplished. I had explained the myths of peoples of the past; I had written a book about the hero, the myth in which man has always lived. But in what myth does man live nowadays? In the Christian myth, the answer might be, 'Do *you* live in it?' I asked myself. To be honest, the answer was no. 'For me, it is not what I live by.' 'Then do we no longer have any myth?' 'No, evidently we no longer have any myth.' 'But then what is your myth – the myth in which you do live?' At this point the dialogue with myself became uncomfortable, and I stopped thinking. I had reached a dead end. (*MDR* 171)

Though Jung had not read Blake, his break with Freud returned him to a realm of the unconscious that the Romantics had explored, Blake to an unprecedented degree. What the Romantics came gradually to recognize was that, as Jung describes it, the hero myth was a myth that had, in exhausting its resources, turned back on itself to unveil its dark side, which Wordsworth describes in his experience of the French Revolution by comparing the summoning of 'a Pope [Pius VII] [...] to crown an Emperor [Napoleon]' to a 'dog / Returning to his vomit' (*P* 11.358–63). Warning against the Romantic association of the hero with Milton's Satan, Coleridge in *The Statesman's Manual* identifies it with the will abstracted from reason and religion to become, as idolatry, a 'state of reprobation,' which, he argues, too often has given 'a dark and savage grandeur to the historic page' (*Coleridge's Poetry* 364). Its 'COMMANDING GENIUS' then assumes the form of 'Hope in which there is no Chearfulness' ('hope, till Hope creates / From its own wreck the thing it contemplates,' writes Shelley [*PU* 4.573–4]), or an 'Interminableness of Object with perfect Indifference of Means' (*Coleridge's Poetry* 364).

Jung's reluctant and fearful decision to 'open all gates' into the unconscious by, among other things, first killing in a dream the Siegfried in himself, led me to an exploration of the Romantic vision to which I have largely devoted my academic life. This exploration, however, had a more personal dimension, which, prior to the writing of this book, *Revelation and Knowledge,* I have never publically analysed. This more personal dimension was a dream of a young Persian prophet named the Báb (which means Gate), about whom, prior to the dream, I knew almost nothing. Descending upon me or rising up in me, the dream, though strangely expected, struck me, a twenty-year-old Canadian prairie-bred, middle-class, Anglo-Saxon boy who had been reared in the midst of a Great Depression that required a Second World War to find release, as if I were experiencing a visitation from another planet which, in the immediacy of it, was transforming my life. Certainly looking ahead, perhaps with less eagerness than most, to joining the Canadian Air Force, my dream of the Báb opened a Gate so alien to the future that was now on all sides 'heroically' open to me as a war against a seemingly invincible enemy. Though totally unprepared, I found myself in a psycho-spiritual place that only much later would I relate to Jung's radical opening of 'all gates.' This dream, as it gradually took up residence in my reluctant soul, changed the direction of my life, a change that, assisted by the archetypal psychology of Jung, my study of the Romantics helped me, if not to affirm, at least to understand. The affirmation, like a divine fiat, came from an uncreated source, which Jung describes as '*ignotum per ignotius,*' the unknown known only through the more unknown, which Jung calls 'the name of God' (*MDR* 354). 'If he possesses a grain of wisdom,' Jung concludes, 'he will lay down his arms and name the unknown by the more unknown. [...] That is a confession of his subjection, his imperfection, and his dependence; but at the same time a testimony to his freedom to choose between truth and error' (354). While this dream will inform the argument of this book, it will not, God willing, take possession of it. There is, as we shall see – and as Jung warns – a madness lurking within it, which consciousness must struggle to absorb. Handed by an angel a little book in what became the final book of the Bible – a gap or void joining it to, while separating it from, its beginning – John of Patmos is told to eat it: 'Take it and eat it up; and it shall make thy belly bitter, but it shall be in thy mouth sweet as honey' (10.9).

Inspiration, the Romantics realized, however 'sweet' in the mouth, is 'bitter' in the belly, sometimes, as Keats knew, 'Turning to poison while the bee-mouth sips' ('Ode to Melancholy' 24). 'But,' Shelley nevertheless insists in his *Defence of Poetry* before abandoning it to write *Adonais,* his elegy on the death of Keats,

> poetry defeats the curse which binds us to be subjected to the accident of surrounding impressions. And whether it spreads its own figured curtain or withdraws life's dark veil from before the scene of things, it equally creates for us a being within our being. It makes us the inhabitants of a world to which the familiar world is a chaos. It reproduces the common universe of which we are portions and percipients, and it purges from our inward sight the film of familiarity which obscures from us the wonder of our being. [...] It creates anew the universe after it has been annihilated in our minds by the recurrence of impressions blunted by reiteration. It justifies the bold and true word of Tasso – *Non merita nome di creatore, se non Iddio ed il Poeta* [None deserves the name of Creator except God and the Poet]. (533)

The recognition of the act of perception as an act of creation is a transformative discovery that I associate with my study of Romanticism as that study, unknown to me at the time, was initiated by my dream of the Báb. Prior to my dream, I had not experienced as a curse 'the recurrence of impressions blunted by reiteration.' I had no conscious sense of a 'film of familiarity' obscuring 'the wonder of [my] being,' an obscuring that had in effect 'annihilated' the universe so that as 'one verse' it had ceased to exist. 'One song they sang,' declares Wordsworth describing what, 'beyond the reach of thought / And human knowledge,' was as a child audible to his senses as they 'looked / Towards the Uncreated'

(*P* 2.415, 403–4, 412–13). 'Most audible, then,' he continues, 'when the fleshly ear, / O'ercome by humblest prelude of that strain, / Forgot her functions, and slept undisturbed' (2.416–18).

Reading as I fell asleep an account, in part first-hand, of the revelatory episode of the Báb, I would now say that my literal grasp of what I was reading – so strange to me it barely made sense – was so 'o'ercome by humblest prelude' of its prophetic import that my senses 'forgot [their] functions and slept undisturbed,' only as dream to awaken, as in Wordsworth, 'beyond the reach of thought / And human knowledge.' Listening to Wordsworth at their first meeting chanting a portion of an unpublished poem ('Guilt and Sorrow'), Coleridge was so overcome by what he was hearing that it struck him as if it 'had then sprang forth at the first creative fiat.' It was, indeed, as if Wordsworth had entered 'the riddle of the world' and was 'help[ing] to unravel it' (*BL* 1:80). Coleridge experienced the action of Wordsworth's mind as an act of creation, which, as the 'living Power and prime Agent of all human Perception' repeats in 'the finite mind [. . .] the eternal act of creation in the infinite I AM' (1:304). He experienced in Wordsworth the act of perception at its 'primary' or unconscious level as an act of creation. So radical was his experience, that Coleridge in himself underwent a veritable derangement of sense that, further explored through a deepening addiction to opium, conducted to a theory of the imagination. Imagination became the act of perception itself without which act nothing humanly exists. The act of perception is the continuous, instant by instant (Blake's 'Pulsation of the Artery') creaturely incarnation of God, which brings to completion the arrested act of divine creation from which, as fallen, the human creature is cut off. Jung later reached much the same conclusion in his argument for continuous 'creaturely incarnation.'

Needless to say Wordsworth, though flattered, was alarmed by the apparent impact on Coleridge of his chanting of part of his unpublished poem. Persuaded that 'all Truth is a species of Revelation,' Coleridge in a series of long letters to Thomas Poole, points out that, 'if it please the Almighty to grant [him] health, hope, and a steady mind, (always the 3 clauses of [his] hourly prayers), Before [his] 30th year [he] will thoroughly understand the whole of Newton's Works.' Working at present on 'his easier work, that on Optics,' he finds '[Newton's] whole Theory [...] so exceedingly superficial as without impropriety to be deemed false.' Newton,' he insists, 'was a mere materialist – *Mind* in his system is always passive – a lazy Looker-one on an external World.' 'If the mind be not *passive*,' he continues, if it be indeed made in God's Image, & that too in the sublimest sense – the Image of the *Creator* – there is ground for suspicion, that any system [such as Hartley's theory of association] built on the passiveness of the mind must be false, as a system. / I need not observe, My dear Friend, how unutterably silly & contemptible these Opinions would be, if written to any but to another Self. I assure you, solemnly assure you, that you & Wordsworth are the only men on Earth to whom I would have uttered a word on this subject – . It is a rule, by which I hope to direct my literary efforts, to let my Opinions & my Proofs go together. It is *insolent* to *differ* from the public *opinion* in *opinion*, if it be only *opinion*. It is sticking up a little *i by itself i* against the whole alphabet. But one *word* with *meaning* in it is worth the whole alphabet together – such is a sound Argument, an incontrovertible Fact. – (*Collected Letters* 2:709)

At the same time, however, he confesses to Poole that '[a]t Wordsworth's advice, or rather fervent intreaty, [he has] intermitted the pursuit [against Newton's *Optics*] – the intensity of thought, & the multitude of minute experiments with Light & Figure, have made me so nervous & feverish, that I cannot sleep as long as I ought & have been used to do: & the Sleep, which I have, is made up of Ideas so connected, & so little different from the operations of Reason, that it does not afford me the due Refreshment' (*Collected Letters* 2:707). The mind as active in perception brings into play the mind as 'the living Power and prime Agent of all human Perception' in which its history 'rise[s] up before you [...] from its birth to its maturity' (*BL* 1:297). Unlike '[e]very other science,' which 'pre-supposes intelligence as already existing and complete,' the '[transcendental] philosopher,' Coleridge argues, 'contemplates it' at its source (1:297). This source, which in itself remains unknown, Jung, following in the unconscious footsteps of Coleridge, calls the 'collective unconscious.' In my dream of the Báb, speechless in His presence as an all-consuming expression of my desire to speak, which Coleridge (quoting Friedrich Schelling) calls 'the sacred power of self-intuition' (1:241), I rise up in the air, turn a somersault, and float down like a feather to His feet. 'In common actions,' Coleridge writes, translating Schelling, 'the *action* itself becomes forgotten due to the object of the action; the philosophic process is also an *action*, yet not an action only, but at the same time a constant *self-intuition* in this action' (1:241n6). My dream, as I came to understand it, contained within it my '*self-intuition*' of the action performed, a '*self-intuition*' for which at a conscious level I was completely unprepared. As a 'primal' act of perception, which Coleridge describes as 'the original intuition, or absolute affirmation' of 'the IMMEDIATE, which dwells in every man' ('but does not in every man rise into consciousness'), my dream confrontation with the Báb conferred upon me an identity which would require the rest of my life to absorb. The process of this absorption constitutes the mythos of this book (1:243).

The danger inherent in my dream of the Báb lay in its powerful numinosity, which, far from addressing itself to what, as true allegory, Blake describes as the 'Intellectual powers,' appeared to address itself to what, as false allegory, Blake describes as the 'Corporeal Understanding.' The numinosity of the dream lay in the sheer physicality of its bodily presence in which, as if in defiance of the body – what Wordsworth describes as the 'gravitation and the filial bond / Of nature that connect [the infant Babe] with the world' (*P*2.243–4) – I rise up and turn a somersault in the air. In this apparent inflationary defiance of gravity, a defiance Wordsworth embraces, though not as a matter of religious belief, in adopting the Platonic doctrine of pre-existence in his 'Intimations of Immortality' ode, I, as Jung argues, risked, as Nietzsche and others risked, the psychotic danger of identifying myself with the archetypal world. By making a dogma of it, as, for Jung, Freud made a dogma of sexuality, I was in danger in my processing of the dream of turning it into a 'metaphysics of presence,' which, as we shall see, Derrida identifies with the madness of the Cartesian 'Cogito.' I had, therefore, to differentiate myself from the physical numinosity of the dream ('Lord! what demonic hyperbole' Plato's Glaucon cries out) by deconstructing it, thereby assigning its numinosity to the realm of a metaphorical rather than literal understanding. As metaphor, the Báb in the dream embodies the 'sacred power of self-intuition,' which, under a particular set of circumstances, conferred upon me, who remains otherwise the prisoner of those circumstances, an identity that releases me from them, while yet remaining the condition essential to this identity. 'There is this difference,' writes Shelley,

> between a story and a poem, that a story is a catalogue of detached facts, which have no other bond of connexion than time, place, circumstance, cause and effect; the other is the creation of actions according to the unchangeable forms of human nature, as existing in the mind of the creator, which is itself the image of all other minds. The one is partial, and applies only to a definite period of time, and a certain combination of events which can never again recur; the other is universal, and contains within itself the

germ of a relation to whatever motives or actions have place in the possible varieties of human nature. Time, which destroys the beauty and the use of the story of particular facts, stript of the poetry which should invest them, augments that of Poetry, and for ever developes new and wonderful applications of the eternal truth which it contains. Hence epitomes have been called the moths of just history; they eat out the poetry of it. The story of particular facts is as a mirror which obscures and distorts that which should be beautiful: Poetry is a mirror which makes beautiful that which is distorted. [...] Poetry redeems from decay the visitations of the divinity in man. (*DP* 515, 532)

In his brief career, Shelley struggled to reconcile the demands of story as narrative with the greater demands of poetry as lyric. In this struggle he developed a metaphysics of presence that became in the end a metaphysics of suicide. The greater demands of the 'divinity in man' overpowered the lesser demands of his mortal nature. As a result he, rejecting human life, gave up both 'story' and 'poetry.' His notion of the 'intense inane' or 'void circumference' constituted madness. Such a madness might have left me somersaulting in the air as my worship of the Báb as a 'sacred power' which, far from conferring an identity upon me, robbed me, however ecstatically, of it. For this reason, Blake and Shelley will provide in this book a central axis of 'Contaries' upon which I will process my dream. Jung's question – 'Why open all gates?' – is a question I shall attempt to answer.

There is an essential transpersonal or impersonal dimension to the answer *Revelation and Knowledge* explores to this question. Without this objective dimension this book, as 'story' or narrative, would be purely subjective; it would enact the myth of Narcissus drowning in his own projected image as the feeble Echo of this myth. (Shelley's drowning here comes to mind.) This danger serves as the shadow side of the Romantic vision. For this reason, while I do not ignore the personal circumstances of the dream (in which I did nearly drown), I explore the dream and its circumstances as part of a broader consideration of a mutation of consciousness that involves the earth as one country and humankind as its citizens. This mutation – humanity's collective coming of age – has thus far confronted us with a catastrophic series of false attempts to achieve this maturity, and this failure contains within it the imminent danger of human extinction as humanly essential to the actual, conscious realization of human oneness.

The 'IMMEDIATE' that confronts us as the 'sacred power of self-intuition,' Coleridge points out, 'becomes intelligible to no man by the ministry of mere words from without' (*BL* 1:243–4). 'The medium, by which spirits understand each other,' he explains, 'is not the surrounding air; but the *freedom* which they possess in common, as the common ethereal element of their being' (1:244). This '*freedom*,' he insists, transcends the narrative of its historical achievement by releasing it at its source from the enactment of it upon which, as source, all enactment depends. Freedom, as Coleridge understands it, is another name for the 'sacred power of self-intuition' best understood as the freedom of the will as the only 'ground' (itself 'groundless') of the 'absolute self.' 'But if we elevate our conception to the absolute self, the great eternal I AM,' Coleridge points out, 'then the principle of being, and of knowledge, of idea, and of reality; the ground of existence, and the ground of the knowledge of existence, are absolutely identical, Sum quia sum; I am, because I affirm myself to be; I affirm myself to be, because I am' (1:275). Bahá'u'lláh, to whom the Báb addressed His revelation less as the recipient of it than as its author ('Sum quia sum'), makes the same point when He too elevates 'self-intuition' to Coleridge's conception of 'the absolute self.' 'Could ye apprehend with what wonders of My munificence and bounty I have willed to entrust your souls,' Bahá'u'lláh declares, 'ye would [...] gain a true knowledge of your own selves – a knowledge which is the same as the comprehension of Mine own Being' (*Gleanings* 326–7).

Bahá'u'lláh, it will be noted, here speaks as the voice of 'the absolute self, the great eternal I AM.' As the voice (' O Most Exalted Pen' [*Gleanings* 27]) of the 'eternal I AM,' Bahá'u'lláh, as I will later explore in terms of progressive revelation, assumes a role that Blake imaginatively affirms as the descent of the New Jerusalem apocalyptically enacted in his epic vision as the birth of a new consciousness. The '*Hysteron-Proteron*' (*BL* 2:131) of this global consciousness is, as the Jungian analyst, Wolfgang Giegerich, describes it in his account of the soul's logical life, a '*real* psychology of the Self,' which, he argues, 'has to *start out* [*proteron*] from the *accomplished* Self, otherwise there can be no Self-development':

> The Self [as Coleridge also describes it in terms of the *Hysteron-Proteron*] has to be there from the outset, i.e., *prior* to the attempt of realizing the Self, if the Self is to be realized at all. This is an obvious contradiction. But this contradiction *is* what the entrance problem ['Why open all gates?'] is about. The transgression across the threshold is nothing else but this *hysteron proteron*, this 'crazy' reversal of the order of time: what is 'later' (*hysteron*) in time (here, the realization or finding of the Self) has to be *proteron*, 'earlier,'

'prior'; it has to be the precondition of a search for the Self. You have to already be there if you want to get there. You have to arrive before you set out on the way that is to take you to where you want to arrive. On this *hysteron proteron* hinges the whole question of realness (actuality) or irreality of psychological work. Without it, you condemn yourself to a position where you can only peep through the door, watching the images [Shelley's 'Figures ever new' (*TL* 248)], teaching the message of what is yonder ['intense inane'], but never getting to the other side of the threshold. (21)

Jung, Giegerich argues, intuitively got to the other side of the threshold without consciously, as the soul's logical life, realizing that he was there. He did not open all gates. He merely peeped through the final one. 'The hypothesis of the threshold and of the unconscious,' Jung argues, 'means that the indispensable raw material of all knowledge – namely psychic reactions – and perhaps even unconscious "thoughts" and "insights" [intuitions] lie close beside, above, or below consciousness, separated from us by the merest "threshold" and yet apparently unattainable. We have no knowledge how this unconscious functions, but since it is *conjectured* to be a psychic system it *may possibly have* everything consciousness has [...] in subliminal form' ('On the Nature' 171–2; italics added).

For Coleridge, peeping – as conjecture, as endless possibility, as a 'willing suspension of disbelief' – is, as the 'transcendent' rather than the 'transcendental' (fancy as distinct from imagination or reason), disallowed because, he argues, it reduces a true revelation of the 'infinite I AM' to a '*something-nothing-every-thing*, which does all of which we know, and knows nothing of all that itself does' (*BL* 1:120). As a result, he insists, 'the whole universe co-operates to produce the minutest stroke of every letter, save only that I myself, and I alone, have nothing to do with it, but [am] merely the causeless and *effectless* beholding of it when it is done' (1:119). 'Yet,' he continues, 'scarcely can it be called a beholding; for it is neither an act nor an effect; but an impossible creation of a *something-nothing* out of its very contrary! [...] The sum total of my moral and intellectual intercourse dissolved into its elements are reduced to *extension, motion, degrees of velocity*, and those diminished *copies* of configurative motion, which form what we call notions, and notions of notions' (1:119).

Coleridge argues that by his day the 'mechanical philosophy' had reduced us to this sorry state of perception as the 'causeless and *effectless*' response to matter in motion ('scarcely can it be called a beholding'). He proceeds to demonstrate these 'mechanical *effects*' by citing an authenticated case of 'absolute *delirium*' not unlike the '*delirium*' informing his *Rime of the Ancient Mariner* (1:110, 111). Addressing this 'absolute *delirium*' to which materialism has reduced us, Baha'u'llah declares: 'Lo, the entire creation hath passed away! Nothing remainteth except My Face, the Ever-Abiding, the Resplendent, the All-Glorious.' To which He then adds: 'We have, then, called into being a new creation, as a token of Our grace unto men. I am, verily, the All-Bountiful, the Ancient of Days' (*Gleanings* 29–30).

Developing his Hegelian notion of the Logos or *Geist* as Jung's '*real* psychology,' Giegerich explains the passing away of the entire creation in terms of the Hegelian term *Aufhebung* (sublation). 'Jung's psychology,' he argues, 'is both *sublated* religion and *sublated* science' (67). '"Sublation,"' he goes on, 'is the translation of the Hegelian term *Aufhebung* in the threefold sense of a) negating and cancelling, b) rescuing and retaining, c) elevating or raising to a new level.' Jung's 'psychology,' Giegerich explains, 'negates the immediate religious interpretation *with which* the contents of the inner experience *come*,' an interpretation that has been extinguished by the new reality arising from the inner experience of this interpretation. At the same time, however, this new reality also 'preserves the religious contents and atmosphere of what has been extinguished as a '"moment"' in the process of extinction as that 'moment' becomes a memorial of it, which is essential to a conscious understanding of the new level that has replaced it. *Aufhebung* therefore 'negates the naïve positivistic reductivism' that would dismiss the memorial as mere superstition. It will not, that is, embrace a view of progress, in which the past is extinguished, leaving us perpetually unenlightened at a new historyless beginning, which, according to Paul de Man, modernism sought to achieve, while yet remaining chained to a past it was forced to drag along. While the soul's logical life leaves 'both science and religion beneath itself,' it nevertheless still 'contains them as sublated moments within itself. It is their *successor* (much as cars, trains, airplanes are the successors of the [sublated!] horses and horse-drawn carriages in the technical sphere. The sublation character comes out quite nicely in our talking of the 'horsepower' of cars)' (67).

The 'crazy' argument of *Revelation and Knowledge* is that the divine revelations of the twin prophets, the Báb and Baha'u'llah, the one present in the announcement of the other, is the 'other side of the threshold' in which, in the larger context of progressive revelation epitomized in the essential oneness of the twin revelations, we are always already immediately there as the very condition of our becoming conscious of it. This immediacy (Coleridge's 'IMMEDIATE, which dwells in every man') I bring to my reading of the Romantics as my way of processing my dream of the Báb, though at a distance from it. To the Romantics I entrusted my sanity, persuaded that it resided in their madness as, for Wordsworth, the sanity of Coleridge lay, as reason, 'couched' in 'the blind and awful [awe filled] lair' of the crazed Bedouin's madness, Wordsworth, sharing 'That maniac's fond anxiety,' by preparing himself, perhaps in the proposed *Recluse,* to go upon 'like errand' (5.151–61). The fact that, though setting out, neither Wordsworth nor Coleridge got there, resides perhaps in the fact that they settled for the institutional finality of a revelation whose impressive inner resources were by their day spent.

The threshold to be crossed may be consciously recognized as the soul's logical life. It is, however, as the act of creation itself, always already crossed. Revelation as I explore it in this book is the crossing that unconsciously repeats itself in every act of perception until, as consciousness, it is hopefully recognized. As progressive this repetition is an evolutionary process that has now, as '*proteron*,' brought us, as '*hysteron*,' to the terrifying recognition that the earth is one country and humankind its citizens.

In *Biographia Literaria* Coleridge, analysing what he considers the chief defects of Wordsworth's poetry, subjects Wordsworth's 'moral' choice of 'low and rustic life' to what Coleridge calls 'a small *Hysteron-Proteron*': '*truth*' usurps '*pleasure*' to become Wordsworth's '*immediate* object.' 'Now,' Coleridge concludes, 'till the blessed time shall come, when truth itself shall be pleasure, and both shall be so united, as to be distinguishable in words only, not in feeling, it will remain the poet's office to proceed upon that state of association, which actually exists as *general*; instead of attempting first to *make* it what it ought to be, and then to let the pleasure follow' (*BL* 2:130–1). In his Preface to *Lyrical Ballads,* however, Wordsworth is deliberately rejecting 'that state of association, which actually exists in *general*,' by dealing with what he calls 'the essential passions of the heart which find [in 'low and rustic life'] a better soil in which they can attain their maturity' (597). Wordsworth, that is, is writing the 'spousal verse' whose epic form is the 'simple produce of the common day' that attends upon the marriage of the human mind 'to this goodly universe / In love and holy passion' (Prospectus to *The Recluse* 53–5). In this '*Hysteron-Proteron*' state, biblically described as the New Jerusalem, truth and pleasure are one. Revelation is the creation of this state as the divine act of creation itself. 'Veiled in My immemorial being and in the ancient eternity of My essence, I knew my love for thee; therefore I created thee, have engraved upon thee Mine image, and revealed to thee My beauty' (*Hidden Words* 4) is the '*Proteron*' which informs the argument ('*Hysteron*') of this book.

# 1 'I hold it towards you'

I hold it towards you.     .

– Keats, 'This Living Hand'

## 1

As a companion to *Sanity, Madness, Transformation: The Psyche in Romanticism*, this second volume offers a series of shifting perspectives on the Romantic *Weltanschauung* or 'spirit of the age' (to borrow Shelley's use of Hazlitt's phrase) within the larger framework of the descent of the New Jerusalem. The Bible ends with John of Patmos's prophesying this descent, thereby completing the act of creation with which the Bible begins. This completion does not repeat the act but rather transforms it into a divinely human perception of the act. Coleridge describes this perception as the 'primary IMAGINATION' and the struggle to bring this perception to consciousness as the 'secondary imagination' (*BL* 1:304). In this book, as in the previous one, I am primarily concerned with this secondary struggle. With this difference: the previous book focuses upon a psychological reading of Romanticism; the subliminal mythos or narrative of the current book is my highly subjective experience that initiated the first book. This experience may well make undue demands on the reader's belief. When the reader further realizes that the experience was initiated by a dream that took me into a territory likely even more unknown to her than it was to me, she may find her willingness to suspend disbelief severely challenged. In short, I begin with a caveat, which I would like now to expand into a more promising invitation.

I shall explore the mythos of the dream in due course. For now, I start with the fact that the dream opened in my life to what Keats describes in 'Ode to Psyche' 'some untrodden region of my mind' (51). This terra incognita led me to engage with the Romantic imagination by a circuitous route not entirely unknown to students of Romanticism. My dream enacted the primary form of this imagination, and my struggle to bring this primary imagination to consciousness continues to enact this imagination's secondary form. Keats's ode was inspired by his coming 'on the sudden, fainting with surprise,' upon the tale of Eros and Psyche as he 'wander'd [...] thoughtlessly' through Apuleius's lascivious novel, *The Golden Asse* (8, 7). In short, he had stumbled upon Psyche, whom the Greeks had not yet fully recognized as a goddess. To rectify this failure, Keats will build a 'fane' or temple for her as her dedicated poet, priest, and prophet, but not by treating her as a goddess in the 'antique' sense of 'Olympus' faded hierarchy' (50, 36, 25). Instead, he will explore her in the radically new sense of the unconscious, the realm of dream to which Keats was committed, though at first more to escape from rather than confront reality. In his ode, however, Keats is now determined to regard the dream with newly 'awaken'd eyes' (6). The true worship of Psyche is the new poetry of the Romantic imagination in what Coleridge calls the 'living Power and prime Agent of all human Perception,' which Shelley describes as the 'mind in creation' (*DP* 531). For Keats, this new poetry enacts the process of soul-making as 'a grander system of salvation than the chrystain religion.'

My dream of the young Persian prophet, the Báb, found its analogue in Keats's discovery of Psyche. I first heard about the Báb only a few hours earlier at a meeting, which I rather thoughtlessly attended because I wanted my way with the young lady who invited me. 'On the sudden, fainting with surprise,' I received, quite beyond the reach of my consciousness, which was focused on other matters, what I nevertheless acknowledged as 'a grander system of salvation than the chrystain religion.' The elaborate 'fane' I have since built for the Báb in a previously 'untrodden region of my mind,' like Wordsworth's ongoing work on *The Recluse* as an unfinished Gothic church, constituted my own process of soul-making. The writing of this book is my struggle to bring this previously unacknowledged narrative to consciousness. Put another way, this book is the creative work of my secondary imagination struggling to repeat at a conscious level 'co-existing with the conscious will' 'the eternal act of creation in the infinite I AM.' Or, I am careful to add, as Coleridge does, 'where this process is rendered impossible, yet still at all events it struggles to ideal-

ize and to unify' (*BL* 1:304). For Shia Islam, as for Coleridge, the imagination unveils the symbol, an act of human perception that constitutes
the immediate reality of the physical world. Without this act, the world's
materiality, the physical sensations that Coleridge aligns with 'the mere
motion of [his] muscles and nerves' (1:118), would remain unperceived.
My reading of the Romantics according to this revelatory act of perception became the imaginal key unlocking the poetic meaning of my dream.
At times I struggled in vain to repress this meaning, eventually knowing
that if I did, the repression would become the soul's grave.

I have already suggested that the Romantics were vexed by the difference between poetic and religious truth, and that Blake, Shelley, Keats,
and Byron opposed Wordsworth's and Coleridge's turn to religion because religion imprisoned poetic power. Because the 'Reformation
produced such immediate and great benefits,' Keats writes, the Protes-
tantism of Milton 'was considered under the immediate eye of heaven.'
As a result, Milton found in 'its own remaining Dogmas and supersti-
tions, then, as it were, regenerated, [...] resting places and seeming sure
points of Reasoning' (*KL* 96). Thinking of Milton's Deistic God, Blake
declares that 'Choosing forms of worship from poetic tales' is the beginning of 'Priesthood' (*MHH* 11). This statement does not mean that
building a 'fane' is the same as creating a form of worship, for the construction depends almost entirely on the materials used and the ways
of using them. I do not experience the writing of this book as a form of
worship, which is now for me, as it is for Keats, 'too late for antique vows'
('Ode to Psyche' 36). Like Keats, I must be 'by my own eyes inspired'
(43). I must, that is, be inspired by the 'awaken'd eyes' of the symbol-
making Psyche, which Coleridge understood as the 'living Power and
prime Agent of all human Perception.'

# 2

Coleridge sees the primary imagination as the act of perception itself,
which at an unconscious level he calls the 'whole soul of man into activity' (*BL* 2:15–16). Coleridge's mariners mobilize this activity when they
hail the albatross 'As if it had been a Christian soul' (65). Shooting the
albatross, on the other hand, enacts the mere motions of muscles and
nerves in which 'God himself / Scarce seemed [...] to be' (599–600).
Coleridge describes this state as 'the Night-mare Life-in-Death [...] /
Who thicks man's blood with cold' (193–4), a state Keats explores

> when suddenly a palsied chill
> Struck from the paved level up [his] limbs,
> And was ascending quick to put cold grasp
> Upon those streams that pulse beside the throat. (*Fall of Hyperion* 1.122–5)

Fighting his addiction to opium, Coleridge felt that the Mariner's betrayal of the imagination only reinforced imagination as a matter of religious belief, for which Coleridge became England's chief intellectual spokesman. '[A]t the more than magic touch of the impulse from without,' the imagination 'create[s] anew the correspondent object.' Without this transformation, perception would only be 'the mere motion of [...] muscles and nerves' and would lose 'all reality and immediateness,' leaving us 'in a dream-world of phantoms and spectres' (*BL* 1:137). All of the major Romantics feared this nightmare. For Blake, it is the 'Phantom of the over heated brain' (*J* 4.24). Shelley describes it as a 'mad trance' in which the 'spirit's knife' strikes 'Invulnerable nothings' (*A* 347–8). Keats describes it as 'the operations of the [imaginal] dawn / Stay'd in their birth' (*Hyperion* 1.294–5). Wordsworth describes it as 'a brain confounded, and a sense, / Death-like, of treacherous desertion, felt / In the last place of refuge – my own soul' (*P* 10.413–15). And, echoing Coleridge, Byron calls it 'ships sailorless [...] rotting on the sea' ('Darkness' 75).

The Romantics are compelled to return to this soulless state of matter as the 'Negation' or 'Spectre' that 'must be destroyd to redeem the Contraries' via the imagination's '*Esemplastic*' operations (*M* 40[47].33–4; *BL* 1:168). For Keats, Shelley, and Byron, this redemption constitutes a 'spell' that unites matter and spirit as symbol or 'poetic tales.' When these become 'forms of worship,' however, they are reduced to the superstition or delusion of the kind of belief system Coleridge saw in David Hartley's 'mechanical system,' which Shelley describes in 'On Life' as a 'seducing system to young and superficial minds' because it 'dispenses them from thinking' (*SPP* 506). Coleridge liberated himself from Hartley's system by binding the imagination's 'finite' operations to the Christian Creator's supreme mind, thus distinguishing imagination from fancy, which he aligns with Hartley's law of association. In an 1801 letter to Thomas Poole, Coleridge writes that he has 'overthrown the doctrine of Association, as taught by Hartley, and with it all the irreligious metaphysics of modern Infidels – especially, the doctrine of Necessity' (*Collected Letters* 2:706).

In a statement that anticipates his later metaphysics of the imagination in *Biographia Literaria,* influenced by German idealism, Coleridge goes on to say that he hopes to 'be able to evolve all the five senses, that is, to deduce them from *one sense,* & to state their growth, & the causes of their difference – & in this evolvement to solve the process of Life & Consciousness' (*Collected Letters* 2:706). The statement seems to stop short of Blake's bold claim that the imagination was the immediate revelation of the Word, though Coleridge believed he had found this revelation in Wordsworth's writing. Hearing Wordsworth chant an unpublished poem ('Guilt and Sorrow') early in their relationship, Coleridge felt that Wordsworth's verse had sprung forth as 'at the first creative fiat.' Wordsworth was alarmed by this effect on Coleridge's mind, especially as the effect became a symptom of Coleridge's contributions to *Lyrical Ballads.* To Coleridge's mind, as he writes in *Biographia,* Wordsworth, who associated Coleridge's poems merely with fancy, had failed to comprehend 'that fancy and imagination were two distinct and widely different faculties' (1:82) and that the entire mythos of his *Rime* was grounded in this distinction. Fancy binds the brain to the motions of matter, reducing the soul to its ghostly form. Imagination in its primary form constitutes 'an instinct of growth, a certain collective, unconscious good sense' (1:82) releasing the mind from matter.

Yet Coleridge's dialectical approach to the imagination as the 'eternal act of creation' was also for him a matter of religious faith, not unlike a belief in the divine imagination, which belief Shia Islam sees as a ceaseless war with Satan to raise the sensible to the supersensible and thus unite them. Shia Islam identifies the legitimate uses of the imagination with the religious embrace of the Qur'an as the revealed Word upon which Muhammad in the name of Allah placed His Seal. Because the Seal is the illumination of the Word as the religious nature of all true art, any breaking or perversion of the Seal is blasphemy. That is to say, Shia Islam sees the creative imagination as an organ of truth rather than fiction, like Coleridge's primary imagination. It is the immediate revelation of God's eternal act, raising the 'living Power' of perception to a recognition of the 'prime Agent' that is its divine source. Like Coleridge, therefore, Shia Islam identifies art with the secondary imagination, in which the human will ideally becomes the Will of God in its affirmation of God's eternal act. One secular Western analogue for this act is Shelley's 'one Spirit's plastic stress' (*A* 380). As progressive revelation, this force unites Shelley in *Adonais* with its source as the 'fire for which all thirst.' Another analogue is Blake, who describes a 'fierce glowing fire' that 'enterd into [his] soul' (*M* 22[24].8, 13) as Los at the same time that 'the Fires of Intellect' descended into Blake's garden as the 'Starry Eight' (35[39].34). In Blake's dialectical process of progressive revelation, the soul is gradually awakened from its sleeping state as the Seven Eyes of God to its fully awakened state as the Eighth Eye.

In Blake I found the fullest embodiment of a Romantic dialectic into which my dream of the Báb initiated my intellect. The Eastern analogue for Blake is the Shia account of progressive revelation, which culminates in the revelation of Muhammad as what Shia Islam calls the Eighth Climate or Eye. Blake identifies this Eighth Eye with the Second Coming of Christ. As Norman O. Brown argues, in this radical sense we will not understand Blake until the West embraces Islam as the continuation of the West's 'Prophetic Tradition' from which it has remained catastrophically cut off in the name of Mammon or materialism. Brown identifies this catastrophe with a 'Westernizing triumphalism' (367) now threatening the future of humankind. This 'triumphalism,' equally catastrophic for Islam, has inwardly propelled me to process my dream in order to engage the global village in which, as aliens, we now confront ourselves as survivors. If, as Brown argues, Blake's vision contains 'Judaism, Christianity and Islam; and heresies in Judaism, Christianity and Islam' (367), this vision also contains a notion of the prophetic oneness of all religions, a ceaselessly unfolding *poetic* tale of imagination that remains perpetually threatened by 'Priesthood.'

For the Muslim, every verse of the Qur'an as the 'Seal' of prophetic revelation contains multiple meanings. Each of these greets the soul of the true believer as the soul's bride. 'Behold how within all things the portals of the Ridván [Paradise] of God are opened, that seekers may attain the cities of understanding and wisdom, and enter the gardens of knowledge and power,' declares Bahá'u'lláh. 'Within every garden they will behold the mystic bride of inner meaning enshrined within the chambers of utterance in the utmost grace and fullest adornment' (*Kitáb-i-Íqán* 140). Announcing His revelation, which 'Priesthood' fears, Bahá'u'lláh declares: 'Let the future disclose the hour when the Brides of inner meaning, will, as decreed by the Will of God, hasten forth, unveiled, out of their mystic mansions, and manifest themselves in the ancient realm of being' (175–6). In Islam God's eternal act is progressively revealed by the living chain of prophets culminating in Muhammad, Who assembles them in the Eighth Heaven into their inherent oneness. The revelation of Muhammad seals or abrogates the Seven Eyes or Heavens of God of which, as in Blake, Jesus is the Seventh. Understood as blindness, this sealing cuts off the disciples of previous dispensations – Judaism and

Christianity – from Muhammad's revelation. As a result their religious insight becomes blind orthodoxy, which is God's judgment upon it.

In Blake's account of Milton bound in judgment to his 'Sixfold Emanation' (*M* 2.19), his three wives and three daughters who figuratively embody his blindness, Milton is brought to 'Resurrection & Judgment' in Blake's 'Vegetable Body.' The sleeping Milton enters this body at the metatarsus of Blake's left foot. Unknown to Milton, 'the Spirits of the Seven Angels of the Presence' enter with him, providing him with the 'still perceptions of his Sleeping Body.' These dream images, Blake explains, 'now arose and walk'd with them in Eden, as an Eighth / Image Divine tho' darken'd; and tho walking as one walks / In sleep; and the Seven comforted and supported him' (*M* 15[17].1–7). In nearly the same way, the spiritual philosophers of Shia Islam describe the orthodoxy of Sunni Islam as seven sleepers. For Shia Islam, the return of the Twelfth or Hidden Imam is the awakening from this sleep. I embraced this return, not as orthodoxy, but in the poetic terms of the final 'Resurrection & Judgment' to which Milton is summoned by Blake. In *Milton*, Blake undertakes the radical re-formation of the Christian revelation that Milton had failed consciously to embrace, though for Blake he unconsciously affirmed it as a true poet. Blake thus released Christianity from the orthodoxy in which it had long remained imprisoned. When Blake writes, 'Terror struck in the Vale,' he indicates the beauty of apocalyptic awakening that, 'as Milton sings, / Hath terror in it,' 'the Eternal Life' that informs the perpetual forgiveness of his 'mild song' (*M* 42[49].24; *P* 14.245–6; *J* 4.2, 5). Ultimately, Blake cannot bring this forgiveness to consciousness in his unfolding epic, beginning with *The Four Zoas*, so great are the human terrors informing the primary act of perception. Hence the union of Milton with his muse, which constitutes the wondrous action of the primary imagination, remains 'unknown / Except remotely' (*M* 40[46].2–3). The divinity of the imagination ultimately lies not in its creative power but in itself as 'the Uncreated.'

In *Milton*, the apocalyptic awakening of Blake's unconscious 'Vegetable' body takes place in 'Bowlahoola,' Blake's 'Furnaces the Stomach for digestion' (*M* 24[26].59) whose violent agitations seek appeasement. These agitations accompany Blake's reading aloud of *Paradise Lost* to his trembling wife, Catherine, in their garden at Felpham. 'Thundering the Hammers beat & the Bellows blow loud / Living self moving mourning lamenting & howling incessantly' (24[26].52–3). The 'Vegetable' action of Blake's epic is constituted by the struggle to digest Milton's epic. As the perverse vision of Urizen or 'Sleep of Ulro,' this struggle is the literal interpretation of the Seventh Eye or Jesus excreted by Blake's bowels. As a dream, the unconscious activity of Blake's 'Vegetable Body' releases this vision from its spacio-temporal state to unveil this body's eternal form as its 'Resurrection & Judgment.' Viewed in this eternal form, Blake's epic takes place 'Within a Moment: a Pulsation of the Artery,' in which he 'fell outstretchd upon the path / A moment' in his garden at Felpham. In this 'moment' his soul is released from the bondage of his senses, the moment itself becoming 'equal in its period & value to Six Thousand Years,' in which 'the Poets Work is Done' (28[30].63, 29[31].1–3). As Los declares,

> Six Thousand Years
> Are finishd. I return! both Time & Space obey my will.
> I in Six Thousand Years walk up and down: for not one Moment
> Of Time is lost, nor one Event of Space unpermanent
> But all remain: every fabric of Six Thousand Years
> Remains permanent: tho' on the Earth where Satan
> Fell, and was cut off all things vanish & are seen no more
> They vanish not from me & mine, we guard them first & last
> The generations of men run on in the tide of Time
> But leave their destind lineaments permanent for ever & ever.
>
> (22[24].16–25)

Here Blake describes what is going on in his own immortal 'Soul' before it 'returnd into its mortal state' (42[49].26). Wordsworth called this the soul's pre-existent state in which the soul dwells with God, entering the body, 'Not in entire forgetfulness, / And not in utter nakedness, / But trailing clouds of glory' ('Intimations of Immortality' 62–4). Blake further describes this 'moment' as Ololon's descent into the 'Starry Eight' or 'Fires of [Blake's] Intellect,' who become the 'One Man Jesus' (*M* 42[49].12). Shia Islam, as we have seen, identifies this instant with the 'Resurrection & Judgment' of the unsealing of the Seven Eyes at the return of Hidden Imam, who will unseal what Muhammad sealed.

## 3

Blake identifies imagination with divine revelation by enacting the prophetic truth of the Hidden Imam's return as a poetic tale. For Blake imagination thus becomes, not a fixed and dead 'Priesthood,' but the inspired repetition of revelation, eternally renewed as its progressive unfoldment. It is in this improbable sense, as I suggested earlier, that I associated Blake's apocalyptic vision with my dream of the Báb, in which I turn a somersault in the air and land like a feather at his feet. One of my first attempts to deal with this dream was in a paper I wrote on Blake's *Milton* for Northrop Frye's graduate course, which at the time almost cost me my sanity. Certainly I thought it would cost me my career. At that time I did not know that years earlier Frye had a not dissimilar experience with Blake's *Milton* in Herbert Davis's graduate course. Had I known, I might have approached him as a fellow-sufferer who agreed to write the paper only to discover that I could not. Only much later did Frye confess that his problems with *Milton* were suddenly resolved in Bowles Lunch on Bloor Street in Toronto, a familiar haunt of my own, a few hours (about 3:30 AM) before he was to deliver a paper on the subject. Blake's Los, it may be argued, stooped down at a critical moment and put his prophetic sandal on Frye's left foot. At the time I experienced no such divine intervention. This much: in Frye's first graduate course on Blake in my first post-graduate year at the University of Toronto (1948–9), I had mentally gone under in an uneven encounter with the sheer dialectical brilliance of Frye's first-class Hegelian mind. What I experienced in myself at the time as a demonic parody of Blake's vision unveiled a psychotic corner. I was forced to descend into this abysm to find there a madness in myself. I was prepared to ascribe this madness to my dream of the Báb until, with the help of Blake and his fellow Romantics, I found my way through madness to its other side or, more precisely perhaps, its other pole.

In his notebooks Frye describes his 'intensely superstitious' nature as

> removing all censors & inhibitions on speculation: it's almost exactly what Coleridge calls fancy. It may eventually be superseded by imagination: but if there's no fancy to start with there won't be any imagination to finish with. Let's call it creative superstition. It works with analogies[,] disregarding all differences & attending only to similarities. Here nothing is coincidence in the sense of unusable design; or, using the word more correctly, everything is potential coincidence – what Jung calls synchronistic. (*The 'Third' Book* 211)

Frye's particular genius, I suggest, was fanciful. It rejected nothing to start with, and then consciously reshaped the fancy's unconscious and mechanical associations to conform with the unifying and idealizing power of the secondary imagination. Spiritually persuaded by his revelatory reading of Blake as the imaginative form of what his Methodist parents superstitiously believed, but which nonetheless shaped his future development, Frye recognized that, at a logocentric level, Christ dwelt within him as the 'living Power and prime Agent' of his acts of perception. Frye saw himself as destined to bring this primary process to consciousness as the 'echo' or 'finite repetition' of the Christian God's 'eternal act of creation.' In this sense, Frye's *Anatomy of Criticism* is like Coleridge's unrealized *Logosophia*, on the 'PRODUCTIVE LOGOS human and divine; with, and as the introduction to, a full commentary on the Gospel of St. John' (*BL* 1:136), which Coleridge worked at most of his life, unable in the end to release it from his 'creative superstition.' That is to say, Coleridge's fancy, as the cursed spell of addiction, received more than his imagination could absorb and transform.

I quickly realized that Frye's great advantage over me in his graduate class was the fact that as an ordained minister in the United Church of Canada he was a devout, if heterodox, Christian. (Frye's word is 'underground.') He had at his creative disposal in the honours English program at the University of Toronto a long tradition of Christian humanism. He brought this tradition persuasively to bear upon Blake in *Fearful Symmetry* in ways I found as temperamentally alien to Blake as it finally proved to be to me, a tradition I would increasingly resist as what Blake calls the 'Opposition' of 'true Friendship' (*MHH* 20). 'It is,' writes Brown,

> no accident that Hegel's meditations on world-spirit, world-history, and world-religion, yield only a caricature of Islam. In the prophetic tradition, properly understood, Islam must be perceived as a legitimate dialectical response to the failure of orthodox Christianity. Protestants should be able to see that the need for a Protestant Reformation was there already in the 7th century C. E., to be perceived by prophetic eyes. Blakeans should be able to see that there is no way to accept 'Again He speaks' in Blake unless we accept that again He speaks in the Koran. (368–9)

'The repetitiveness of the Koran would drive a reader out of his mind if he were reading it as he would read any other book,' Frye writes in his Notebooks (*Notebooks and Lectures* 195). The same thing, I suggest, could be equally said about Blake's poetry, especially *Milton*. I knew if I was ever going to succeed in reading *Milton* – and in Frye's class the time was now short – I had to read it in the same way I had tried to read the Qur'an. For Muslims, the Qur'an was directly dictated to Muhammad over a period of some twenty-three years by the archangel Gabriel, whose embrace was powerful enough to squeeze out Muhammad's natural breath and replace it with *pneuma*, the divine breath of the Holy Spirit. In Blake's poem, imagination speaks in 'the voice of the Devil' (*MHH* 4) to issue as madness from 'the depths of Hell' in 'the unfathomd caverns of [Blake's] Ear' (*J* 3.28-29), the 'Corporeal Understanding' of which becomes, when transformed by the 'Intellectual powers,' 'mysterious Si- nais awful cave' (*J* 3.24), or the cave on Mount Hira where Muhammad received his revelation.

'The history of the Bible is story: the Koran has shape (at least the individual suras have) but it doesn't tell a story,' Frye continues in his Notebooks (*Notebooks and Lectures* 260). He returns to this point in *The Great Code*: 'The emphasis on narrative, and the fact that the entire Bible is enclosed in a narrative framework, distinguishes the Bible from a good many other sacred books. [...] [T]he Koran consists of revelations gathered up after Mohammed's death and arranged in order of length, with no discernible narrative principle in their sequence' (198). As Frye himself makes abundantly clear, however, the biblical apocalypse also enacts the release of the soul from its narrative framework by returning it to a beginning that has no beginning, and is therefore identical to an end that has no end. In this radical sense he returns the Bible to the same formlessness he associates with the Qur'an, a formlessness of God that, with reference to the Bible, he describes as 'all things, yet no thing, and yet not nothing' (*Fearful* 431). Frye struggles to explain how God, who dwells beyond an '*analogia visionis*' like the one Blake constructs, 'is not the orthodox Creator, the Jehovah [...] who must always be involved with either an eternal substance or an eternal nothingness, depending on the taste of the theologian, but an unattached creative Word who is free from both.' In such a statement, Frye confronts the mystic in himself who knows that 'the creaturely aspect of man does not exist at all and yet is [as history] a usually victorious enemy of the soul.' That is to say, Frye confronts, as 'an effort of vision, so called,' the 'One,' though 'neither as a human attempt to reach God nor a divine attempt to reach man, but as the realization in total experience of the identity of God and Man in which both the human creature and the superhuman Creator disappear' (431). Shelley confronts this 'total experience' in the final movement of *Adonais*, where life is figured analogically as a 'dome of many-coloured glass' that is 'trample[d] [...] to fragments' (462, 464). In Frye's gradu- ate class, but well beyond my conscious reach, I similarly confronted 'the identity of God and Man' which, in some terror, I at first rejected.

Read as Blake's epic struggle to release the soul from the Orc-Urizen cycle, the story becomes what Shelley, quoting Bacon, calls 'the moths of just history; they eat out the poetry of it.' Blake describes these 'moths' as the 'rotten rags of Memory' or history that must be 'cast off' and replaced by 'Inspiration' (*M* 41[48].4). Understood as 'divine madness,' the decaying sense of this casting off is precisely what revelation *as* revelation does, what Muhammad does and what Blake does. Contrasting the New Testament as narrative or story with the Qur'an, Frye argues that the New Testament has depended from the beginning on translation. Among other things, this translation guaranteed the New Testament's ready entrance into the world of the popular imagination in different times and places. By way of contrast, he rightly insists that the Qur'an 'is so bound up with the linguistic characteristics of Arabic that in practice the Arabic language has had to go everywhere that the Islamic religion has gone' (*Notebooks and Lectures* 419). This linguistic notion of revelation is, I suggest, equally true of Blake's illuminated works: Blake's texts are so bound up with their illumination that, as Blake conceived and wrote them in his 'Printing House in Hell,' they have to go everywhere that his poetry has gone. Frye tends to ignore the fact that Blake's epics are, first and foremost, revelation in which the narrative or story, the binding of the soul to the fallen world, has to be 'cast off.' I struggled to read Blake as revelation because no other way made any more sense to me than did a narrative reading of my dream of the Báb. As history, this reading brought me close to psychosis, which, Frye insistently argues, is what history essentially is without apocalypse. Blake's Urizen declares, 'Lo! I unfold my darkness,' into which the imagination, as history, falls: 'and on / This rock, place with strong hand, the Book / Of eternal brass, written in my solitude' (*The [First] Book of Urizen* 4.31–3).

For Blake, to write in solitude means to write cut off from divine inspiration. Without divine revelation, which Blake like the Sufis identifies with the creative imagination, the mind becomes enslaved to the senses that, as the 'Vegetable' work of the muscles and nerves in writing, produces 'the Book / Of eternal brass.' By submerging this Book in 'corrosives, which in Hell are salutary and medicinal,' 'apparent surfaces' are melted away, displaying 'the infinite which was hid' (*MHH* 14). Here Blake describes how engraving symbolically enacts the apocalypse present in every 'Pulsation of the Artery' when it is no longer identified with 'mere motion of my muscles and nerves,' which Blake assigns to the 'Void Outside of Existence.' To cast out the 'Vegetable Body' by thus alchemically transforming it in 'the Fires of Intellect' is to cast out narrative or story by bringing this body to 'Judgment.' This apocalyptic action propels the Romantic imagination, compelling the Romantic poet to construct a demonic parody of apocalypse as the custodian of its dissolution. Priesthood, as Blake understands it, is the ritual preservation of this dissolution in ecclesiastical alcohol, which he describes as the religion of the Elect. For Blake, the 'Reasoning Power in Man' (*M* 40[47].34) is doomed endlessly to repeat this ritualization as habit and custom. When Frye argues that 'the heart of the Bible is ritual drama' (*Notebooks and Lectures* 206), he similarly describes how his mind ritually enacts its own operations as a ceaseless repetition of certain motifs, which arrests apocalypse by converting it, not into art, but into an 'anatomy' of apocalypse.

Romanticism largely avoids this conversion by building dissolution into the action of apocalypse. One could argue that this dissolution has the advantage of treating apocalypse as a mystery, a condition of mind that Frye vehemently rejects. 'There is nothing like the colossal explosion of creative power in the ninth Night of *The Four Zoas* anywhere else in English literature,' Frye writes. '*Prometheus Unbound* comes a little way along Blake's path, but Shelley's imagination plunges upward to burst into a shower of lyrical sparks, hiding the stars in an instant with a strange illumination of its own, then fading quickly and leaving us with what Blake calls "the black incessant sky" once more' (*Fearful* 305). Of course, Blake left *The Four Zoas* unengraved and unbound, many of its pages indecipherable and some of its illustrations obscene. The poem endures as its own unbound wreck in something of the same way that Tintern Abbey endures in Wordsworth's text. Such absence indicates a ruin that Wordsworth's unconscious chose not to confront except as his own reflection in Dorothy's 'wild eyes' (149) or in his dream of the crazed Bedouin.

## 4

In *The Fall of Hyperion* the narrator witnesses the sacrifice in Saturn's ruined temple. This scene stages the failing powers or shadowy figures of what Keats in 'When I have fears that I may cease to be' calls the poet's once 'teeming brain' (2). To compensate for this bewilderment, Moneta responds by showing his 'dull mortal eyes' the 'scenes / Still swooning vivid through [her] globed brain / With an electral changing misery' (1.244–7). Because these are to her 'still a curse' (1.243), her gift is the antithesis of Shelley's 'electric life which burns within [the] words' of 'the compositions of the most celebrated writers of the present day' (*DP* 535). Keats's narrator

> ha[s] a terror of her robes,
> And chiefly of the veils, that from her brow
> Hung pale, and curtain'd her in mysteries
> That made [his] heart too small to hold its blood.

Nevertheless, he 'with sacred hand / Parted the veils.' Not satisfied with what he physically sees, a kind of nightmare life-in-death whose half-closed eyes held 'a benignant light' that turned inward and 'saw [him] not,' he 'ached to see what things the hollow brain / Behind enwombed.' It is as if the 'benignant light' was a 'grain of gold upon a mountain's side,' which 'twing'd with avarice strain'd out [his] eyes / To search its sullen entrails rich with ore' (1.251–77). (Keats, playing among many associations with the idea of Moneta as the Roman goddess of money whose temple as Juno later became the mint, figures himself as a poet anxious to pry open the hidden treasures of Moneta's mind for his own intellectual and monetary profit.) Struggling in vain to write an epic that might surpass Milton's, and fearing that he might soon cease to be, Keats, with Shakespeare's *King Lear* partly in mind, turns to tragedy. Once again overcome by what he is struggling to write, 'deathwards progressing / To no death,' once again he gives up (*Fall of Hyperion* 260–1). In what he calls 'the fierce dispute / Betwixt damnation and impassion'd clay,' Keats knows that, though he is on the side of 'impassion'd clay,' 'damnation' has won ('On Sitting down to Read *King Lear* Once Again' 5–6). He no longer has 'new phœnix wings to fly at [his] desire' (14). Moneta's gift is now his curse as well. His poems have murdered him. In *Adonais* Shelley mirrors this dark psychological state in which Keats's imagination is the victim of his 'Vegetable Body.' Though his 'weak hand' can 'scarce uplift / The weight of the superincumbent hour [of his mourning],' Shelley, however 'darkly, fearfully' (*A* 295, 282–3, 492), nevertheless found 'new phoenix wings to fly at his desire,' though by thinking his way much differently to nothingness.

The real or imagined object of poetic faith might be quite distinct from religious faith, but they are informed by the same psychic energy. The Romantic poet who does not have religious faith must act as if he did and willingly suspend his disbelief in the act of composition. That is to say, the desire informing poetic faith must be as absolute as religious faith, for anything less cannot sustain the imagination's apocalyptic flight when propelled by the force of revelation. The 'fire for which all thirst' that descends on Shelley in the final stanzas of *Adonais* to consume 'the last clouds of [his] cold mortality' is the alchemical fire that shapes the poem (486). The fire that makes absolute demands on the poem *is* the poem that is made, and the true measure of a poem's greatness is the absoluteness of the desire that informs it.

More than that: as composition, the absoluteness of this desire is its sacrifice upon the altar of the creative process in which the poem, as distinct from the poet, becomes the object. So long as the poet is the object, the poem cannot emerge to live an independent life. No poet in the act of composition can know whether his works will become fully autonomous or will be stillborn, deformed, or in the end non-existent. As Shelley argues, the 'instinct and intuition of the poetical faculty,' which 'is still more observable in the plastic and pictorial arts, [...] grows under the power of the artist as a child in the mother's womb, and the very mind which directs the hands in formation is incapable of accounting to itself for the origin, the gradations, or the media of the process' (*DP* 532). On the poetic level, desire's absolute nature resides in the immediate life-and-death situation this desire constellates with reference to the creative process in which, as soul-making, the Romantic imagination becomes engaged; on the religious level, this desire is the eternal life-and-death situation that is constellated for the soul in God's revelatory engagement with the soul. The immediacy of the former's poetic faith mirrors the eternity of the latter's religious faith. 'So, till the judgment that yourself arise, / You live in this, and dwell in lover's eyes' (13–14), Shakespeare concludes his sonnet in which he addresses his own 'powerful rhyme' (2), which only the Last Judgment can destroy. Poetry, in this sense, is the temporal as distinct from eternal state of immortality. The eternal state is God, who ultimately judges the soul as redeemed or damned; the temporal is the creative imagination. The danger of the imagination lies in its 'strength / Of usurpation' (*P* 6.599–600), which Wordsworth as a poet confronts, but as a Christian rejects. Foregoing usurpation, he surrenders his 'egotistical sublime' (*KL* 157) to grace, thereby treating his own imagination as what Milton calls deeds 'Above Heroic, though in secret done.'

Blake's position is rather more complex. Assuming the role of Satan in opposition to Milton's Deistic God, Blake transforms Satan's strength of usurpation by using it to restore Milton's fallen God to His original divine form. In this radical way the imagination becomes the fourfold human form of the true God celebrated in the final plates of *Jerusalem*.

But Shelley's case remains even more problematic. The 'one Spirit's plastic stress' of the imagination carries the soul through all the stages of its evolution toward the 'fire for which all thirst' that consumes 'the last clouds of cold mortality,' which is whatever in its 'mortal state' checks the soul's flight. But for this 'plastic stress,' the evolution itself would check the soul's flight 'into the Heaven's light' toward 'the burning fountain whence it came' (*A* 387, 339). Shelley's final vision of the soul's ascent in *Adonais* perhaps best mirrors as purely as verbally possible the highest aspiration of human intelligence. In the *Symposium*, which Shelley translated, Socrates associates this aspiration with Eros as the desire for the One unveiled to Socrates as the goddess Diotima, who is the Greek image of the Hebrew Sophia as the Holy Spirit.

Unless religious faith interpenetrates poetic faith as the finite 'repetition' of 'the eternal act of creation in the infinite I AM,' the finite 'repetition' becomes the demonic parody of this eternal act. Cut off from the 'eternal act of creation,' the primary imagination as human perception becomes 'fixed and dead.' The human creation passes away, leaving as the evidence of its ruins the 'mere motion of my muscles and nerves,' which Shelley calls the 'ghosts of a no more remembered fame' (*PU* 3.4.169). These phantoms are the 'curse' (1.73) Shelley's Prometheus confronts in the Phantasm of Jupiter and that Keats experiences in Moneta. 'Speak the words which I would hear, / Although no thought inform thine empty voice,' declares Prometheus. The Earth replies:

> Listen! and though your echoes must be mute,
> Grey mountains and old woods and haunted springs,
> Prophetic caves and isle-surrounding streams
> Rejoice to hear what yet ye cannot speak.

'A spirit seizes me, and speaks within: / It tears me as fire tears a thundercloud!' (1.73, 248–55), the Phantasm exclaims, describing what the creative process becomes when it is cut off from its source.

It is in this phantasmagoric context that the renewal of divine revelation at its source in God began for me to assume a meaning that it would never otherwise have had, had I not also confronted this renewal's demonic parody. Understood as the absolute denial of revelation except as parody, the demonic is Blake's 'Reasoning Negative' (*M* 5.14) or nonexistence, a negation by which, ironically, revelation is affirmed beyond parody. For Blake, '[h]uman sacrifice – now better understood as genocide – is, as Frye describes it, the most eloquently symbolic act which the dreaming Selfhood is capable of performing. It [...] parodies every aspect of eternal life. In its purest form it is a ritual, taking place at regular intervals and connected with the cyclic order of nature. Its victim represents Luvah or the dying Albion, and repeats in his death the original breaking of Albion's body and the spilling of his blood. (*Fearful* 397)

For Blake, Albion fleeing Blake's 'Saviour,' who stands over Blake every morning at sunrise dictating *Jerusalem* as his 'mild song,' is Christ hanging on the cross upside down, a condition that endures until the epic's final plates. Hence, Frye explains, the breaking of Albion's body as a symbol of the crucifixion is also 'an analogy of the eventual reintegration of that body' (397). This reintegration cannot occur until its demonic parody is finally, in and as its total form, 'snared & caught & taken' (*M* 8.48). For Blake, incising backwards on the copper plate so that it will appear frontwards in its printed form repeats the entire mythos of his apocalyptic vision as a daily tactile contact with this vision.

# 5

Blake's engraving process has its priestly counterpart in the Eucharist, what Frye calls 'an analogy of the last harvest and vintage' (*Fearful* 397). In the final plates of *Milton* Blake assembles many of his 'Giant forms,' which in their 'Litteral expression' condense 'into Nations & Peoples & Tongues' (*M* 42[49].14, *J* 53.8). Most of them are, Blake explains, 'Persons & Machinery intirely new to the Inhabitants of Earth,' a single global body constituting the 'human form divine' (*CPP* 728). This resurrected fourfold body is Blake's epic emerging from his 'Printing house in Hell.' There he transforms the 'Spiritual Acts of [his] three years Slumber on the banks of the Ocean' into his 'long Poem descriptive of those Acts [...] on One Grand Theme Similar to Homers Iliad or Miltons Paradise Lost.' Received as 'immediate Dictation twelve or sometimes twenty or thirty lines at a time without Premeditation & even against my Will,' Blake insists that 'the Time it has taken in writing' is 'renderd Non Existent' (*CPP* 728–29). At the end of *Milton*, 'Los & Enitharmon [rise] over the Hills of Surrey,' 'Oothoon / Pants in the Vales of Lambeth,' "Los listens to the Cry of the Poor Man,'

Rintrah & Palamabron view the Human Harvest beneath

Their Wine-presses & Barns stand open; the Ovens are prepar'd
The Waggons ready: terrific Lions & Tygers sport & play
All Animals upon the Earth, are prepard in all their strength

To go forth to the Great Harvest & Vintage of the Nations.

$\qquad$ (42[49].31–9; 43[50].1)

Blake assembles the energy arising from 'immediate Dictation,' in which 'Time [is] renderd Non Existent,' in 'less than a pulsation of the artery.' In Romanticism, the release of this energy is as close as poetry can come to divine revelation. In Blake's particular case this revelation announces the Second Coming in a manner distinctly different from the tragic fate of Keats's epic, which he was attempting to write while Blake was likely printing and illuminating *Jerusalem.*

When called 'into activity,' Blake's 'whole soul' receives and transforms what Shelley calls the 'ceaseless motion' and 'unresting sound' of 'fast influencings' ('Mont Blanc' 32, 33, 38), which register as sensations in every muscle, nerve, cell and fibre of Blake's 'Vegetable Body.' Transformed by the imagination into creative power, his physical body becomes Los at the forge shaping a spiritual body, Blake's 'Animal Lungs' becoming the 'Bellows,' his 'Animal Heart' the 'Hammers,' and his 'Stomach for digestion' the 'Furnaces.' 'Thousands & thousands labour,' declares Blake,

thousands play on instruments
Stringed or fluted to ameliorate the sorrows of slavery
Loud sport the dancers in the dance of death, rejoicing in carnage
The hard dentant Hammers are lulld by the flutes['] lula lula
The bellowing Furnaces['] blare by the long sounding clarion
The double drum drowns howls & groans, the shrill fife. shrieks & cries:
The crooked horn mellows the hoarse raving serpent, terrible,
but harmonious. $\qquad$ (*M* 24[26].58–66)

The 'sorrows of slavery' reveal the sheer physical agony of creation that nevertheless rejoices in its pain, an image of the sacrificial role of 'Vegetable Body' in the imaginative process of creation, the pain of which Blake refused to ameliorate by medicinal means: 'I know that all Distress inflicted by Heaven is a Mercy. a Fig for all Corporeal' (*CPP* 716).

*The Fall of Hyperion* is Keats's less rejoicing account of the creative process, which becomes a physical struggle to survive what as composition he experiences as his own death, every word dating on his own doom. Shelley describes this process as the 'one Spirit's plastic stress' 'Torturing th' unwilling dross that checks its flight / To its own likeness,' a pain he can scarcely endure (A 384–5). Identifying himself with what he imagined to be Keats's fate, 'the rupture of a blood-vessel in the lungs' followed by 'a rapid consumption,' Shelley weeps his own fate: 'on a cheek / The life can burn in blood, even while the heart may break' (SPP 410; A 287–8). Trapped in the 'Night-mare Life-in-Death' that is the fate of Byron's Cain and the historical fate of the crucified Christ whose name has become 'a curse,' Shelley chooses suicide as martyrdom in the name of all spiritually awakened poets who inhabit an eternal world. Having 'gazed on Nature's naked loveliness, / Actaeon-like,' Shelley is now a 'herd-abandoned deer struck by [his own] hunter's dart' (275–6, 297). The Beauty of Truth that he, like Keats, pursued is, so far as this world is concerned, still forbidden fruit. As Shelley writes in his Defence, 'Veil after veil may be undrawn, and the inmost naked beauty of the meaning never exposed' (528).

For Shelley, Byron is the 'Pythian of the age' (A 250) far better equipped to inflict the 'Vitality' of his time's 'poison' (Childe Harold 3.299) upon which he relied as a poet. Weeping over Keats's corpse, attempting to restore him to life with a kiss, Urania asks:

'Why didst thou leave the trodden paths of men
Too soon, and with weak hands though mighty heart
Dare the unpastured dragon in his den?
Defenseless as thou wert, oh where was then
Wisdom the mirrored shield, or scorn the spear?'          (A 236–40)

Shelley envied Byron, though was not really tempted by poison except as Socrates partook of the hemlock. Shelley nevertheless rather deplores the 'weak hands' that, like Keats's 'hands,' can scarcely inscribe the words of his grief. 'Now more than ever seems it rich to die,' declares Keats wrapped in the 'ecstasy' the nightingale's song is 'pouring forth' as the song of his own soul, which carries within it as 'high requiem' its own burial 'sod' ('Ode to a Nightingale' 55–60).

As one strain of the Romantic imagination, this highly idealized desire for death informs Shia Islam's intense focus upon the martyred Imams. This focus fully embraces the conviction that Muhammad's revelation has fallen into false Sunni hands, leaving Shia Islam outside of Persia with no sacred soil of its own. That is to say, Sunni Islam leaves Shia Islam outside of Iran in the condition of a soul denied its body. Martyrdom essentially transforms this condition into a refined spiritual state in which the body, having endured its death, is rewarded with its resurrection. At work in the imagination of the Romantic poet, who has confronted and presumably accepted the defeat of his creative power by a power alien to it, is a transcendental notion of conquest in which death becomes the soul's union with the object of its insatiable desire, which no earthly object, no matter how refined, can satisfy. Conquest under these psychological circumstances resides in a notion of death as union with the Beloved. For the mystically minded Shia, the reward is the unveiling by seventy-two Brides of inner meaning whose 'naked loveliness' fully transcends the limitations of the five senses as they remain in this world the 'chief inlets of soul.' The Islamic rejection of the incarnation of Allah as the ultimate blasphemy against Allah's unknowable essence thus opens the way to a soaring of the imagination into an abstraction or 'white radiance of Eternity' so pure that any 'Stain[ing]' of it had to be 'trample[d] [...] to fragments' in the name of Allah (*A* 463–4). For the incarnational West, this destruction has become a mounting source of terror. In its sheer excess of incarnation, the West has moved to the opposite extreme, the two worlds now become as far from each other as Hell in Milton's epic is 'from God and light of Heav'n / As from the Center thrice to th' utmost Pole.' 'O how unlike the place from which they fell!' (*PL* 1.73–5), exclaims Milton of the fallen angels, an exclamation resounding mightily as today Islam and the West confront each other in what would appear to be a life-and-death encounter in which the survival of both is at stake.

# 6

My dream's image of turning a somersault in the air and descending lightly as a feather remains an incongruous image of my mind, as incongruous as describing Blake's *Jerusalem* as a 'mild song.' The image finds me struggling against all odds to find within myself a 'Centre' that, far from separating Islam and the West as Milton separates Heaven from Hell, might perform between them a *hieros gamos* or sacred marriage grounded in what Blake calls 'the Spirit of Prophecy' (*CPP* 1) in which all religions are one. Blake enacts this apocalyptic marriage in *The Marriage of Heaven and Hell* when his highly unorthodox Jesus becomes 'the voice of the Devil' issuing from the 'depths of Hell' in Blake's 'Printing house,' where he luminously inscribes his 'infernal' scripture as a 'new heaven' of previously 'Unnam'd forms' (15). My gradual initiation into Blake's text in Frye's graduate class mentally enacted, as 'Allegory addressd to the Intellectual powers while it is altogether hidden from the Corporeal Understanding,' my unconscious somersault in the air, which landed me at the feet of the Báb (*CPP* 730). To take up residence in what Blake describes as the 'Grandest Poem that This World Contains' rather than in the literalist form of the Baha'i Faith, I awoke in my imaginative reading of Blake to find a more liberal enactment of its truth (730). I had been secularly trained in this truth, which was more richly confirmed by my agonized, sanity-threatening reading of *Milton* as Blake's vision of Christ's return. The figure of the Báb, as it took shape in the then-unknown operations of my unconscious, became the 'dark interpreter' of my reading of the Romantics, and of much else besides.

I say 'dark interpreter' because, given the culture in which I had been raised, the dream figure of the Báb mythically embodied the figure of Lucifer, the unfallen Light-Bearer who had, as Satan, fallen into the darkness of matter. For Shelley, Dante is 'the Lucifer of that starry flock which in the thirteenth century shone forth from republican Italy, as from a heaven, into the darkness of the benighted world. His very words are instinct with spirit; each is as a spark, a burning atom of inextinguishable thought; and many yet lie covered in the ashes of their birth, and pregnant with a lightning which has yet found no conductor' (*DP* 528). Shelley makes the same claim for Milton in seventeenth-century republican England. What still lies buried in the ashes of Satan's thought found its conductor in Shelley's Prometheus. Shelley considered Prometheus a 'more poetical character' because his Prometheus removed the 'direct moral purpose' that had 'interfere[d] with the interest' of Milton's Satan as hero (*SPP* 207; *DP* 527). Shelley thus sought to release Dante's *Divine Comedy* and Milton's *Paradise Lost* from the 'systematic form' these two works had 'conferred upon modern mythology,' a task he shared with all the Romantics, particularly Blake (*DP* 527). I embraced the figure of the Báb in the same way: as the Lucifer who ceaselessly renews the 'systematic form' or 'modern mythology' into which the Christian religion had settled. Blake affirmed this renewal in his first two tractates, *All Religions are One* and *There is No Natural Religion*, in which he identifies the Hebrew prophets as the founders of religion with 'the Poetic Genius,' whom he calls 'the true Man' (*CPP* 1). As my commitment to the 'true Man' within myself, I brought my dream of the Báb into this understanding of the 'Poetic Genius' as the unfolding revelation of the 'true Man['s]' 'Intellectual powers.' Jung calls this the Self.

I inherited this mythos as the gift of a liberal arts education I identify in particular with the University of Toronto, where I wrote my PhD thesis under the supervision of A.S.P. Woodhouse and Northrop Frye, published in 1964 as *The Apocalyptic Vision in the Poetry of Shelley*. In this study, as in Frye's graduate class, I was careful to distance myself from my dream of the Báb and the entire Persian world it constellated. I was also aware of the pregnancy of my silence, a silence Shelley describes as being so 'enamoured of [the Visionary's] voice' that it 'Lock[ed] [his] mute music in her rugged cell' (*Alastor* 65–6). The 'mute music' of the Báb, a figure comparable to the Visionary's 'veiled maid,' became for me the music of Romanticism in which my dream found its voice. Especially since retirement, I have been able to find the counterpart to my dream of the Báb in the unconscious source of inspiration endlessly explored by the Romantics in relation to the 'mind in creation,' less as a form of worship than as a poetic tale. Writing this book to sort out the distinction, I found Frye's work on religion, revelation, and myth of considerable help. Later in his career Frye focused upon the supernatural unveiling of the Word as *kerygma*, revelation or proclamation. He borrows the word from Rudolph Bultmann, who opposes it to myth, an opposition that would, Frye argues, 'obliterate' the Bible. While *kerygma* is 'a mode of rhetoric,' unlike almost all other forms of rhetoric it is 'not an argument disguised by figuration.' Rather, 'figuration' *is* the argument in the same sense that dream figures are not a disguise for meaning, but the meaning itself. Stripped of disguise, *kerygma* is 'the vehicle of what is traditionally called revelation,' though not in the popular sense in which it is commonly reduced to describe almost any 'conveying of information from an objective divine source to a subjective human receptor' (*Great Code* 29). This conveyance is problematic because 'information' may convey something like the 'literal truth' of the Bible, a literalness that depends upon myth to oppose it. If the Bible is literally true, then it no longer exists as myth. God as the author of what does not mythically exist is now, at least for those who believe in matter's literal existence, a God who is not only dead but has never, in the literal sense of physical existence, been alive. That is to say, God is neither alive nor dead. He simply does not exist. But *if*, as a 'willing suspension of disbelief for the moment,' He *does* exist as 'an objective divine source,' His existence *is* the existence of myth as His mode of communication. As myth this communication is called revelation, not in the sense of poetry but in the sense of a force coming from the supernatural rather than natural side of existence.

What then is myth? To varying degrees the Romantics I have dealt with throughout my career see myth as what Coleridge describes, with reference to the Logos, as the primary imagination. While this act issues from an 'objectively divine source,' it is immediately present to the finite mind as myth, without which the act exists only as 'the mere motions of my muscles and nerves.' For instance, the mechanical system that produces marks on my computer screen does not exist for my computer, in the same way that it does not exist for my muscles and nerves in terms of what I am now in the process of reading. What the computer does in producing the marks is not what I am doing in reading them. Between its marks and my reading of them a transformation has taken place so vast that it yet remains beyond our conscious understanding. Yet what emerges in the mind obviously exists. The difference between the computer marks and the mind's transformation of them into thought from which the marks emerged is the revelation of thought whose language is myth. We can best understand myth as the transformative operations of physical things in the human mind in which physical things come as hieroglyphics to exist as thought-things.

From the other side, as *kerygma*, divine things come into the human mind to exist as the mind's perception of them. Both the physical and the divine exist in human perception as myth. Here they meet, not to become the same thing, but to contain as myth the difference between them. This difference is myth's final complexity. If we cannot decipher this complexity as the mind's ultimate confrontation with its own operations, the complexity nevertheless offers itself to be deciphered by a consciousness that cannot fully reside there, nor anywhere else, short of the decipherment itself. I understand a 'willing suspension of disbelief' to be our willing acceptance of myth's offer of its decipherment. For some, this suspension is as close as the mind in the accepted circumstances of its existence can come to taking up its residence in its eternal home. In this spirit, I receive divine revelation into my life, not as my guest, but as my host whose gracious treatment of me as his guest – again, Blake's 'mild song' – allows me to understand something about his nature.


# 7


When in Shia Islam, as in all world religions, revelation takes up a permanent residence in each to the exclusion of the others, this exclusionary residence becomes a prison. In this state, religion desires what it cannot offer, no matter how hard the soul struggles to protect itself from invasion. In a global village, like the one that a soulless technology has built, religion thus becomes exceedingly fearful, knowing all too well the temptation to let the enemy in because religion secretly wants what the enemy has to offer. The more technology breaks down the material barriers that separate disparate cultures, the more the soul delusionally struggles to protect itself by building flimsy barriers in a futile effort to maintain the soul's isolation from what, as the 'motes of [its own] sick eye' (*Hellas* 781), it wantonly desires in what it sees.

It was at this point in *Hellas* that Shelley's Ahasuerus, though himself homeless, did his best to persuade Shelley to get out entirely, rather than further interfere in the name of freedom. As the release of Greece from Turkish tyranny, Christian pitted against Muslim, this freedom had already enacted its defeat in Shelley's recognition that freedom resided, if anywhere, beyond our mortal reach. That is to say, freedom existed only in the realm of endless speculation, which in a state of suspended disbelief had always been Shelley's home. In his Advertisement to *Epipsychidion*, in which he disposes of his earthly life through 'one annihilation,' Shelley writes: 'The Writer of the following Lines died at Florence, as he was preparing for a voyage to one of the wildest of the Sporades, [...] where it was his hope to have realised a scheme of life, suited perhaps to that happier and better world of which he is now an inhabitant, but hardly practicable in this' (*SPP* 392). Ahasuerus declares that

> this Whole
> Of suns, and worlds, and men, and beasts, and flowers
> With all the silent or tempestuous workings
> By which they have been, are, or cease to be,
> Is but a vision – all that it inherits
> Are motes of a sick eye, bubbles and dreams;
> Thought is its cradle and its grave, nor less
> The future and the past are idle shadows
> Of thought's eternal flight.                    (*Hellas* 776–84)

Here Shelley enacts the exhaustion that overtakes the soul in a world that has extinguished the soul without burial. This leaves Shelley to conduct the soul's funeral in a series of elegies that together mourn a self that, through the process of writing, has ceased to exist, the author becoming for the 'superincumbent hour' of composition his own spectre or ghost

(*A* 283). In his final fragment, found after his death, Shelley virtually performed this ectoplasmic feat. Since the death of the soul announces its resurrection, apocalypse lies waiting in the soul's constellation of its own death as the placenta upon which it prenatally feeds to be cast out as poisonous human waste at its birth. Like the placenta that poisoned Mary Wollstonecraft after the birth of Mary Shelley, this waste haunted Shelley's mind as humankind's earthly fate.

# 8

*The Dawn-Breakers*, which I had just begun to read when I fell asleep and had my dream of the Báb, begins this way, which may explain why I fell asleep:

> At a time when the shining reality of the Faith of Muhammad had been obscured by the ignorance, the fanaticism, and perversity of the contending sects into which it had fallen, there appeared above the horizon of the East that luminous Star of Divine guidance, Shaykh Ahmad-i-Ahsá'í. He observed how those who professed the Faith of Islám had shattered its unity, sapped its force, perverted its purpose, and degraded its holy name. His soul was filled with anguish at the sight of the corruption and strife which characterized the shí'ah sect of Islám. Inspired by the light that shone within him, he arose with unerring vision, with fixed purpose, and sublime detachment to utter his protest against the betrayal of the Faith by that ignoble people. Aglow with zeal and conscious of the sublimity of his calling, he vehemently appealed not only to shí'ah Islám but to all the followers of Muhammad throughout the East, to awaken from the slumber of negligence and to prepare the way for Him who must needs be made manifest in the fulness of time, whose light alone could dissipate the mists of prejudice and ignorance which had enveloped that Faith. (1–2)

In Persia, precisely at the same moment that the English Romantics were exploring their apocalyptic vision of the imagination, Shaykh Ahmad-i-Ahsá'í (1753–1826) and Siyyid Kázim (1793–1843) were reading the Qur'an with their chosen students in the same allegorical way that Blake was reading the Bible. Jung describes an acausal interpenetration of two otherwise unrelated events as *synchronicity*. Some such synchronous convergence marks the psychic space between Blake's apocalyptic vision of the Bible and Shaykh Ahmad's and Siyyid Kázim's apocalyptic vision of the Qur'an. For Blake this space is the spiritual form of the 'Vegetable Body,' and for Shaykh Ahmad it is the 'subtle' or 'diamond body' shaping as in a dream in the sleeping physical one. Blake describes this situation as Milton's Shadow moving through Blake's 'Vegetable Body,' a 'subtle body' that Keats in his feverish dream vision 'ached to see' as 'Language pronounc'd' (*Fall of Hyperion* 1.107), especially as this subtle body had already begun to take shape in the 'sullen entrails' of his decaying flesh. In my initial reading of Blake and the Romantics such a vision of the resurrected body unconsciously shaping in my dream of the Báb brought together these two worlds – Islam and the West – in a way henceforth impossible to separate no matter how hard I tried. If only for my own psychic survival, their vast and growing divide, which is outwardly assuming an ever-deepening abyss, serves to reinforce my need to bring forth, at a more fully conscious level, an unconscious convergence that has already taken shape in me, as indeed this convergence always already exists in 'the eternal act of creation' before its unfolding in time.

At stake in this new birth of consciousness is the freedom of the will, which Coleridge calls 'our only absolute *self*' (*BL* 1:114). Through their 'Visionary forms dramatic' (*J* 98.28), the Romantics set out to explore this freedom as the soul-making struggle against the apparent and oppressive omnipotence of matter. They did so to render matter's conquest of the external world answerable to the imagination as 'the living Power and prime Agent of all human Perception,' without which the material world does not exist, at least in relation to a *human* percipient. Judaism, Christianity, and Islam share in common revelation as the divine source of this fundamentally human struggle. The challenge that confronts me in relation to my dream of the Báb, which my unconscious now fully embraces, is the return to the divine source in order to release in the unconscious energies never previously tapped. To bring these energies to consciousness is another matter, which I now recognize as a global as much as a personal issue. However much I sought to avoid this recognition, it propelled me into the writing of this book. To the degree that it is conscious, I embrace it. To the degree that the process remains unconscious, I dissent. The result is my own ceaseless mental fight to impose upon this return to the divine source a Western orientation, which as a new consciousness meets the historical demands our new global situation imposes upon it. To which I would add: the surrender to revelation as my conscious acceptance of my unconscious experience of the Báb releases me from the ego's enduring infirmity, which is the ego's illusory struggle to realize what, as ego, it must reject. Release from the ego's tenacious grip is the struggle beyond which revelation remains as revelation sufficient unto itself because, as the 'I Am that I Am,' it is itself. Acceptance as surrender is, as Coleridge argues, the free act of the will. Though independent of all grounds, this act is received as 'not only coherent but identical, and one and the same thing with our own immediate self-consciousness' (*BL* 1:260). This 'immediate self-consciousness' is now a global consciousness.

# 2 Transcendent and Transcendental

The latter is exclusively the domain of PURE philosophy, which is therefore properly entitled *transcendental*, in order to discriminate it at once, both from mere reflection and *re*-presentation on the one hand, and on the other from those wanton flights of lawless speculation which abandoned by *all* distinct consciousness, because transgressing the bounds and purposes of our intellectual faculties, are justly condemned, as *transcendent*.

– Coleridge, *Biographia Literaria*

## 1

After writing *Sanity, Madness, Transformation*, I realized that I had unintentionally modelled the book on *Biographia Literaria*. Writing this companion volume has made me far more aware of the influence of Coleridge's text as a revelation of the brilliantly disturbed operations of Coleridge's own mind. Painfully abandoning his hope to write 'the FIRST GENUINE PHILOSOPHIC POEM' (*BL* 2:156), he turned the project over to Wordsworth. At the same time he realized, having read *The Excursion*, that Wordsworth, though 'capable of producing' it, would never write it. As a 'transcendental' philosopher himself, Coleridge realized a 'GENUINE PHILOSOPHIC POEM' could not yet be written for much the same reason that he could not write his proposed magnum opus, *Logosophia*, at least not in the 'immethodical' (*BL* 1:4) manner of *Biographia*. His hesitation was partly due to the fact that he had failed as a poet in the ideal or transcendental sense. In the spirit of a future deconstruction, he confronted in himself the inherent contradiction that separates a literary text from its transcendental claims to bring 'the whole soul of man into activity' by repeating rather than re-presenting 'the eternal act of creation.'

What Coleridge confronted in himself is what Derrida calls 'madness': the instantaneous act of the Cogito, which for Blake unconsciously occurs within 'a Pulsation of the Artery.' This moment, out of mind rather than within mind, imposes itself upon the work to become the rational disavowal of the work's 'historical guilt' (Derrida 35). As a disavowal, the 'primitive purity' (43) of madness becomes a crime against the order of language. As punishment for the crime, which Michel Foucault describes as the 'absence of the work' (Derrida 43), the grammatology of language acts as the jailer. Within this prison, a 'double monologue' of reason against madness takes place in which the 'two monologues, or the broken dialogue' envision within their opposition 'the historic liberation of a logos' (37). In this 'hyperbolical project,' which Derrida, quoting Glaucon in Plato's *Republic*, calls a '"marvelous transcendence,"' madness and sanity are for Derrida reconciled in theory rather than in fact (57). Their inherent differences are united by what for Coleridge is the mind's radical transformation of its operations. As a 'living Power,' these operations become the 'prime Agent' of the Cogito, whose act of creation as the 'infinite I AM' is instantaneous. Jung, as we shall see, hypothesizes this moment as a 'real zero point' without extension. 'Immediate are the Acts of God, more swift / Than time or motion,' declares Milton, 'but to human ears / Cannot without process of speech be told' (*PL* 7.176–8).

The issue for the poet is the '*process* of speech,' which as mythos or narrative separates it from the 'immediate.' As the slow but inevitable decline of 'inspiration,' this separation reduces the written text to 'a feeble shadow' of the poet's 'original conception.' Even when Milton's God commands His 'begotten Son' as His 'Word' to 'speak thou, and be it done,' what is done is circumscribed (*PL* 7.163–4). For Milton, speaking as an inspired poet, the Word as 'be it done' is the 'retire[ment]' of the 'uncircumscrib'd' God into Himself, where, 'free / To act or not,' He 'put[s] not forth [His] goodness' (7.170–2). Romanticism inherits its satanic dimension from Milton as the desire to stake an imaginative claim upon God's silence. In this 'Penetralium of mystery,' God forbids the pre-existent soul to awake from its dream of God's 'uncircumscrib'd' power. Halted by this power as the imagination's 'strength / Of usurpation,' Wordsworth must come to terms with it as grace, what Milton describes as 'deeds / Above heroic though in secret done.' Though as an epic poet Wordsworth, much to Blake's horror, felt he could pass

Jehovah 'unalarmed,' as a Christian, he had second thoughts: while 'Strong in herself,' the imagination's 'strength / Of usurpation' is stronger in the 'beatitude / That hides her.' As a 'beatitude' held 'in secret,' it is, 'like the mighty flood of Nile,' insufficient to 'fertilise the whole Egyptian plain' (Prospectus to *The Recluse* 35; *P* 6.613–16). With the help of laudanum, Coleridge perversely experiences this beatitude as a 'justly condemned' curse, which as the 'transcendent,' transgresses 'the bounds and purposes of our intellectual faculties' (*BL* 1:237). As beatitude, the 'transcendental' releases the mind from the heroic pursuit of the ego's 'spoils / That may attest [its] prowess' (*P* 6.610–11). The 'broken dialogue' between the 'transcendent' and the 'transcendental,' between 'fancy' and 'imagination,' the unconscious and consciousness, became for Coleridge the impossibility of writing 'the FIRST GENUINE PHILOSOPHIC POEM.'

Writing one hundred years before Freud's *The Interpretation of Dreams* (1900), Coleridge did not possess a science of the unconscious that treated its operations, not as the transgression of 'the bounds and purposes of our intellectual faculties,' but according to the legitimate use of biology as a science of the nervous system. Freud's psychology did not wallow in the delusional realm of the supernatural as a 'black tide of mud,' which Freud associates with the 'occult' psychology of Jung, finally dismissed by Freud as mad. Grounded in a biological notion of the sexual libido, Freud's psychology was, as Jung remarks, 'scientifically irreproachable and free from all religious taint' (*MDR* 151). For Jung, however, 'Yahweh and sexuality,' as 'two rationally incommensurable opposites,' nevertheless 'remained the same.' 'The name alone had changed,' Jung insists, 'and with it, of course, the point of view: the lost god had now to be sought below rather than above.' Jung continues:

> But what difference does it make, ultimately, to the stronger agency if it is called now by one name and now by another? If psychology did not exist, but only concrete objects, the one [Yahweh] would actually have been destroyed and replaced by the other [sexuality]. But in reality, that is to say, in psychological experience, there is not one whit the less of urgency, anxiety, compulsiveness, etc. The problem still remains: how to overcome or escape our anxiety, bad conscience, guilt, compulsion, unconsciousness, and instinctuality. If we cannot do this from the bright, idealistic side [Yahweh], then perhaps we shall have better luck by approaching the problem from the dark, biological side [sexuality]. (151–2)

Convinced that with the triumph of modern science Yahweh had fallen from 'above' to 'below,' Jung went in search of Him there. As Freud's *deus absconditus*, He had to be approached 'from the dark, biological side,' where, religiously perceived, the sexual libido is associated with Satan. In Jung's reading of the Book of Job, Satan infects Job's body, taking from him, as the extension of his body, all that Yahweh allowed Satan freely to access, warning him not to touch his soul.

Following Freud, Jung viewed the sexual libido as Yahweh's unfinished work of creation from which Yahweh, like Milton's God, had withdrawn. In Milton's account this vacuum left Newton's compasses to do the rest, which is why Blake attributes Newton's work to the fallen Yahweh, who as Urizen or natural religion turns His goodness to an evil end. As the operations of the divine imagination, God must be restored from his fallen to his original state, now consciously perceived as 'the human form divine.' In this sense, Jung saw that Freud's notion of the sexual libido was intimately bound to the unfinished biological work of evolution, which both Freud and Jung associated with the unconscious. Jung saw that the libido had assumed for the materialist Freud the role of Yahweh as the *deus absconditus*, whose hiddenness was His non-existence. Whereas as a biological psychologist Freud was interested in the 'sexual libido,' as an archetypal psychologist Jung was interested in the 'hidden or concealed god.' For Jung, in 'psychological experience' Yahweh and sexuality were two names for the same thing. Freud had only to allow Jung to extend sexuality to include, as libido, the spiritual. In Jung's archetypal understanding, Freud was the Moses who had already created this opportunity by appointing Jung the Joshua who would bring psychoanalysis to the promised land, which Freud could not enter. For Jung, this binding covenant tapped into the deepest reaches of Freud's Jewish nature and rendered Freud the author of a new revelation of Yahweh. Freud then buried this convenant's numinosity in a literal or biological interpretation that reduced psychoanalysis, as a new revelation of God, to a form of what Blake will call Priesthood.

Jung's future course announced itself to Freud physically in his study when the bookcase next to them threatened to explode under the impact of Jung's 'Thunder of Thought, & flames of fierce desire' (*J* 3.6). Jung writes: 'It was as if my diaphragm were made of iron and [like Los's forge in Blake's *Jerusalem*] were becoming red-hot – a glowing vault. And at that moment there was such a loud report in the bookcase, which stood right next to us, that we both started up in alarm, fearing the thing was going to topple over on us.' Freud rejected as '"sheer bosh"' Jung's explanation of the event as '"an example of a so-called catalytic exteriorization phenomenon [in which the inner state is the cause of the outer event rather than the other way around]."' Jung then predicted that '"in a moment there will be another such loud report!"' 'Sure enough,' writes Jung, 'not know[ing] what gave [him] this certainty,' 'no sooner had I said the words than the same detonation went off in the bookcase' (*MDR* 155–6). While composing his epic at Felpham, Blake experienced this phenomenon with similar certainty as divine dictation, which he further experienced as his descent into the collective unconscious. Like Jung, Blake associated this experience with Moses in 'Sinais awful cave,' an experience incrementally repeated by Muhammad in the cave on Mount Hira. Like Jung's, Blake's imagination as the Voice of God proclaiming the Word was the announcement of Jehovah's return. For both Jung and Blake, this instant of recognition closed the gap between the Cogito or 'infinite I AM' and 'the eternal act of creation' as the soul's metaphorical recognition of this act. In Blake's case, the silence of God was broken by a vast host of 'Persons & Machinery intirely new to the Inhabitants of Earth [...] written [...] from immediate Dictation twelve or sometimes twenty or thirty lines at a time without Premeditation & even against [Blake's] will.' This experience is strikingly similar to Jung's encounter with a vast crowd of souls who returned from Jerusalem, where they could not find what they were seeking. As we shall see in the next chapter, it may be argued that they were seeking the opening of the Eighth Eye, the soul's inner journey from Three to Four.

Though Coleridge responded to Wordsworth's chanting '*as if* it had then sprang forth at the first creative fiat,' his experience of the chanting drove him to discover this fiat's source as the 'living Power and prime Agent of all human Perception.' In Coleridge's imagination, the physical act of perception – the electrical sensations moving through the muscles and nerves as these sensations constitute the *massa confusa* of creation issuing from Wordsworth's body – became an *analogia visionis* of the Word newly released in every 'Pulsation of the Artery.' Coleridge was determined physiologically to trace this release back to its source as the site of an *incarnatio continua*. Part of this effort included a series of alchemical-like experiments that, as he confesses to Poole, so agitated the 'justly condemned' transcendent operations of his intellectual faculties that, like Christabel unsettled by Geraldine, he was unable to sleep:

But through her brain of weal and woe

So many thoughts moved to and fro,
That vain it were her lids to close;
[...]
To look at the lady Geraldine.                                  (239–44)

The sound of Wordsworth's voice awakened something forbidden in
Coleridge, the reality of which he had to know, but could not know
on the psychological level. Coleridge realized that, left to its own unruly resources, the psychological, rather than being transformed to become the transcendental, became, as the transcendent, forbidden. Like
Wordsworth, he thus found in his rational Christian system, which Blake
calls 'Priesthood,' a substitute for the 'poetic faith' he could no longer
psychologically sustain. His poems remained curiosities of the poet's unfinished psychological business, which continued to haunt him either
despite or because of his religious faith.

## 2

Coleridge distinguishes between the transcendent and the transcendental by comparing them respectively to the ancient Romans' division
of their northern provinces into 'Cis-Alpine and Trans-Alpine.' Coleridge tended to locate himself with the inhabitants of the 'Cis-Alpine,'
who are cut off from the 'higher ascents' of the 'Trans-Alpine,' inhabited by Wordsworth. Those in the 'Cis-Alpine' are immersed in 'mists
and clouds arising from uncultivated swamps,' which 'appear, now as
the dark haunts of terrific agents, on which none may intrude with im-
punity; and now all *a-glow*, with colours not their own, [. . .] gazed at, as
the splendid palaces of happiness and power' (*BL* 1:239). Here Coleridge
has in mind his own contribution to *Lyrical Ballads*, at least as the 'Trans-
Alpine' Wordsworth tended to diminish this contribution. 'The thought
suggested itself (to which of us I do not recollect),' Coleridge explains,

> that a series of poems might be composed of two sorts. In the one, the
> incidents and agents were to be, in part at least, supernatural; and the ex-
> cellence aimed at was to consist in the interesting of the affections by the
> dramatic truth of such emotions, as would naturally accompany such situ-
> ations, supposing them real. And real in *this* sense they have been to every
> human being who, from whatever source of delusion, has at any time be-
> lieved himself under supernatural agency. (*BL* 2:5–6)

Laudanum was likely the immediate reason Coleridge associated the 'supernatural' with 'delusion,' but the more urgent and comprehensive reason was his brief but intense addiction to Hartley's associationism. Emerging from the rise of modern science in the seventeenth century, this 'mechanical philosophy' used the mathematical tools provided by Islam. In Islam the mathematical order of nature as the human mind's engagement with it lay in an archetypal understanding of number as it exists in the mind of God, an understanding which as the Logos Islam derived from the Greeks. In the West the conception of nature as the revealed creation of God gradually became a secular concern conducting as modern science, if not at least initially to the Enlightenment dethroning of God, at least to the demystifying of God by identifying him with a natural rather than supernatural order. Newtonian physics, for example, aimed to offer new proof of God's existence and beneficence based upon the functioning of the natural world that science could now understand. As for the supernatural, in Newton, as later in Jung, it took the form of alchemy, which as an occult study of the mind of God Newton in the long haul paid more attention to than to physics. In this respect Newton's own alchemical studies, however indirectly, prefigured the Romantics' understanding of the alchemical power of the imagination. More than that, his intuitive powers developed in the study of alchemy may have psychically influenced his understanding of the laws of motion as a secret revelation of the soul, which he considered immutable.

The Romantic mission lay less in re-establishing God as the creator of nature than in a willing suspension of disbelief in God's enthronement as the imagination's feigning of it. In a psychological understanding of this feigning as a matter of poetic faith lay a new human revelation of the divinity that on one essential level supported the advancement of knowledge and did not as religious faith insult the mind's intellectual powers. Without such a poetic faith, the materialism of modern science, which put new sources of power into human hands, would be unable psychically to shape them to human ends. These ends depended on the shaping of a new myth. As the psychic embodiment of matter, this myth fully embraced as human the energy newly released by the scientific mind, an energy that left older, religiously bound mythologies exhausted, if not obsolete. It was hoped that such a myth would not constitute hubris or original sin, but would be the legitimate consummation of human energy described by Wordsworth as the marriage of the newly conceived human mind with the newly conceived natural universe. The product of this marriage would be the imaginative vision of the earthly kingdom of the newly revealed God of the imagination, the earth itself becoming His enlightened bride.

Coleridge added the marginal gloss to *The Ancient Mariner* in order to correct the poem's 'flights of lawless speculation [...] abandoned by *all* distinct consciousness' (*BL* 1:237). He thus sought to release the soul from the repetition compulsion into which, without 'beatitude,' its transcendental operations are doomed to sink. In his 'Hymn Before Sunrise' Coleridge likewise sought to avoid what Shelley calls the dangers of the 'dizzy Ravine' in which the passive mind, as 'One legion of wild thoughts,' is overwhelmed by 'fast influencings' of the 'clear universe of things around' ('Mont Blanc' 41, 38, 40). Coleridge in his 'Hymn' focuses less upon the ravine of Arve than on the 'dread and silent Mount' (13) as the voice of God, which Shelley rejects by naming this voice an unknown 'Power dwell[ing] apart in its tranquillity / Remote, serene, and inaccessible' ('Mont Blanc' 96–7). To impose God's voice on the mountain, Coleridge explains, the visible mountain had first to 'vanish from [his] thought,' allowing him to worship 'the Invisible alone' as if 'entranc'd in prayer' ('Hymn' 15–16). 'Hast thou a charm to stay the Morning-Star / In his steep course?' (1–2) he asks the mountain, as in the opening line his soul takes up residence in an 'entranc'd' state. The river Arve, which 'Rave[s] ceaselessly' at the foot of Mont Blanc, becomes the prayer of 'some sweet beguiling melody, / So sweet, we know not we are listening to it' (5, 17–18).

Coleridge may have in mind the 'ceaseless music' of Wordsworth's river Derwent, which 'loved / To blend [its] murmurs with [his] nurse's song' so that they 'flowed along [his] dreams,' 'compos[ing] [his] thoughts / To more than infant softness' (*P* 1.270-1, 274, 277–8). This sound Coleridge first heard in Wordsworth's chanting 'as if all had then sprang forth at the first creative fiat,' which convinced him that Wordsworth was capable of writing the 'FIRST GENUINE PHILOSOPHIC POEM.' For Coleridge, this poem would be transcendental rather than transcendent, would present rather than *re*-present the 'eternal act of creation' as it logocentrically unfolds in the action of the primary imagination, which action however unconsciously 'brings the whole soul of man into activity.' Upon that act of perception, as half Wordsworth's own, the creation becomes Wordsworth's consciousness of it. 'Of genius, power, / Creation and divinity itself / I have been speaking,' declares Wordsworth of his 1798–9 version of *The Prelude*, inspired in part by Coleridge's high estimation of his poetic power, 'for my theme has been / What passed within me' (*P* 3.175–6). In 'Hymn Before Sun-rise' Coleridge wants to deploy the same transcendental operations he experienced in Wordsworth's mind, but his attempt to reach an *'artificial consciousness'* (*BL* 1:236) is forced. Indebted to Schelling, Coleridge argues that this consciousness is actualized as a *'philosophic consciousness'* by 'an effort of freedom' creatively shaping a distinctly intellectual consciousness, 'which lies beneath or (as it were) *behind* the spontaneous consciousness natural to all reflecting beings' (1:236). For Coleridge, freedom belongs exclusively to the *'esemplastic'* power of the creative imagination 'to shape into one' (1:168), the spontaneous consciousness of the 'transcendent' into 'transcendental' oneness.

While Coleridge's philosophical account of the imagination in *Biographia Literaria* is directly influenced by his response to Wordsworth's poetry, it also contains a recognition of this poetry's philosophical limitations. Coleridge realized that Wordsworth's psychological enactment of the imagination lacked a genuine philosophical understanding of its 'transcendental' power. Wordsworth, in turn, had reason to fear the overtaxing of the brain inherent for him in Coleridge's 'transcendental' pursuits, an overtaxing that could lead to 'despondency and madness' ('Resolution and Independence' 49). The relations between them were not entirely unlike the relations between Coleridge's Mariner and the Wedding Guest. The psychological counterpart of Coleridge's philosophical notion of an *'artificial consciousness'* is Wordsworth's vision of the 'infant Babe' who 'sinks to sleep / Rocked on his Mother's breast; who with his soul / Drinks in the feelings of his Mother's eye!' (*P* 2.232–7). Wordsworth calls this instinctual constellation 'the first / Poetic spirit of our human life' (2.260–1), an instinctual constellation that Freud will take up in the first decades of the twentieth century. Drawing upon German idealism, which he was among the first to introduce to England, Coleridge, especially with Schelling in mind, philosophically accounts for what Wordsworth 'Felt in the blood' ('Tintern Abbey' 29) in this way:

> They and they only can acquire the philosophic imagination, the sacred power of self-intuition, who within themselves can interpret and understand the symbol, that the wings of the air-sylph are forming within the skin of the caterpillar; those only, who feel in their own spirits the same instinct, which impels the chrysalis of the horned fly to leave room in its involucrum for antennae yet to come. They know and feel, that the *potential* works in them, even as the *actual* works on them! In short, all the organs of sense are framed for a corresponding world of sense; and we have it. All the organs of spirit are framed for a correspondent world of spirit; tho' the

latter organs are not developed in all alike. But they exist in all, and their first appearance discloses itself in the *moral* being. How else could it be, that even worldlings, not wholly debased, will contemplate the man of simple and disinterested goodness with contradictory feelings of pity and respect? 'Poor man! he is not made for *this* world.' Oh! herein they utter a prophecy of universal fulfilment; for man *must* either rise or sink. (*BL* 1:241–2)

Wordsworth at his mother's breast, her 'eye' lovingly fixed upon him, is drinking in the 'sacred power of self-intuition.' In its archetypal dimension, the mother, as the Logo-Sophia (*Logosophia*), makes her divine infant 'an agent of the one great Mind' (*P* 2.257). In its instinctive intercourse with the mother, this infant is 'creator and receiver both' (2.258). In his parting of the way with Freud, Jung describes this divine incest as the gods' prerogative, an inner marriage or *hieros gamos* that enacts their consciousness of themselves as gods, an enactment repeated for Coleridge in the finite mind as the act of perception itself. This 'self-intuition' or divine marriage with the sacred mother was instinctively present to Wordsworth, particularly in his personal relations with his sister. It was not for Coleridge except as an '*artificial consciousness*' requiring a near impossible act of the will to assert the will's freedom. Coleridge's experience of opium as incest or the 'milk of Paradise' meant that he was possessed by rather than in possession of his creative powers. Put another way, the imagination that came naturally to Wordsworth came artificially to Coleridge as his struggle not to be possessed by this imagination's incestuous power.

This struggle became Coleridge's unfinished *Logosophia*, which as a metaphysical work extending Milton's Christian achievement, Coleridge turned over to Wordsworth, thus defeating his own poetic freedom, even though he knew after reading *The Excursion* that Wordsworth, though capable, would never produce such a work. 'No man was ever yet a great poet, without being at the same time a profound philosopher,' Coleridge writes in his analysis of Shakespeare's poetic power. 'In Shakespeare's *poems*,' he argues, 'the creative power, and the intellectual energy wrestle as in a war embrace. Each in its excess of strength seems to threaten the extinction of the other.' 'At length, in the DRAMA,' he then goes on, 'they were reconciled, and fought each other with its shield before the breast of the other. Or like two rapid streams, that at their first meeting within narrow and rocky banks mutually strive to repel each other, and intermix reluctantly and in tumult; but soon finding a wider channel and more yielding shores blend, and dilate, and flow on in one current and with one voice' (*BL* 2:25–6). This 'war embrace,' in which 'creative power' and 'intellectual energy' contend for control, becomes in the end a single vision in which, as an '*artificial consciousness*,' 'creative power' *is* 'intellectual energy.' In their profound bonding Coleridge and Wordsworth each carried the other's needed strength, not as an inner marriage or *hieros gamos*, but as a deficiency of 'creative power' in Coleridge and 'intellectual energy' in Wordsworth. As a result, their relations turned poisonous with absence and robbed them of the joint labour their astonishing relationship had constellated as the proposed *Recluse*, to which at the end of *The Prelude* Wordsworth refers as an act of 'deliverance, surely yet to come' (14.445).

Coleridge saw that Wordsworth's 'creative power' was too bound to his myth of the divine child, a dependence that radically stalled the development and release of Wordsworth's 'intellectual energy.' This interference was nowhere more evident than in Wordsworth's account of Coleridge's six-year-old son Hartley as a 'Mighty Prophet! Seer blest! / On whom those truths do rest, / That we are toiling all our lives to find' ('Intimations of Immortality' 115–17). Coleridge asks:

> In what sense is a child of that age a *philosopher*? [...] In what sense is he declared to be '*for ever haunted* by the Supreme Being? or so inspired as to deserve the splendid titles of a *mighty prophet, a blessed seer*? By reflection? by knowledge? by conscious intuition? or by *any* form or modification of consciousness?' These would be tidings indeed; but such as would pre-suppose an immediate revelation to the inspired communicator, and require miracles to authenticate his inspiration. Children at this age give us no such information of themselves; and at what time were we dipt in the Lethe, which has produced such utter oblivion of a state so godlike? (*BL* 2:138–9)

The 'miracles' required to 'authenticate his inspiration' are, Blake suggests, in Blake's case provided by the 'immediate Dictation twelve or sometimes twenty or thirty lines at a time sometimes forty lines at a time without Premeditation & even against [his] Will.'

Yet although Coleridge's philosophical mind questions Wordsworth's 'intellectual energy,' he nevertheless remains in awe of what in Wordsworth was to him immediately present as 'the postulate of philosophy and at the same time the test of philosophic capacity': the 'heaven-descended KNOW THYSELF!' (*BL* 1:252). Inscribed over the temple at Delphi, this postulate was the instinct and command of Wordsworth's own nature, one that, though affirmed by a true metaphysics, was in

Wordsworth's case psychologically *a priori.* That is to say, for Coleridge what Wordsworth knows from experience as something acted upon from without he also knows 'must have pre-existed, or the experience itself would have been impossible' (1:293). So long as a poet lived in an age in which he had the objective support of a true metaphysics, Coleridge believed, the poet's task is to wed her 'creative power' to her 'intellectual energy' and present rather than re-present a true metaphysics as the 'FIRST GENUINE PHILOSOPHIC POEM,' the metaphysics of which *is* the act of its creation.

But, Coleridge concludes, Wordsworth could not do this, precisely because his poetry's expression of 'intellectual energy' lacked a metaphysics worthy of this expression. Indeed, by not distinguishing between fancy and imagination, as we saw in the previous chapter, Wordsworth failed to realize that the soul pre-exists any experiential consciousness of it as the condition of experience itself. While he could deal with this understanding as myth in his 'Intimations' ode, philosophically he dismissed this knowledge as 'far too shadowy a notion to be recommended to faith.' Thus, Coleridge lays the groundwork for his theory of imagination in chapter 13 of *Biographia Literaria* by concluding the previous chapter with the argument that in his 1815 Preface Wordsworth failed to distinguish the fancy as '*the aggregative and associative power*' from the imagination (*BL* 1:294). 'I continue to deny, that it belongs at all to the imagination,' Coleridge declares; 'and I am disposed to conjecture, that he has mistaken the co-presence of fancy with imagination for the operation of the latter singly. A man may work with two very different tools at the same moment; each has its share in the work, but the work effected by each is distinct and different' (1:294).

Even at this point, I suggest, Coleridge is still at work with Wordsworth on the 'FIRST GENUINE PHILOSOPHIC POEM,' which he fears Wordsworth has, for lack of 'intellectual energy,' abandoned. 'This has been my Object, and this alone can be my Defence,' he writes, concluding his *Biographia Literaria* with a hymn to 'Night, sacred Night!', which reaches as true religion well beyond the limits of his carefully constructed 'Scheme of Christianity':

> and O! that with this my personal as well as my LITERARY LIFE might conclude! the unquenchable desire I mean, not without the consciousness of having earnestly endeavoured to kindle young minds, and to guard them against the temptations of Scorners, by shewing that the Scheme of Christianity, as taught in the Liturgy and Homilies of our Church, though not

discoverable by human Reason, is yet in accordance with it; that link fol-
lows link by necessary consequence; that Religion passes out of the ken of
Reason only where the eye of Reason has reached its own Horizon; and that
Faith is then but its continuation: even as the Day softens away into sweet
Twilight, and Twilight, hushed and breathless, steals into the Darkness. It is
Night, sacred Night! the upraised Eye views only the starry Heaven which
manifests itself alone: and the outward Beholding is fixed on the sparks
twinkling in the aweful depth, though Suns of other Worlds, only to pre-
serve the Soul steady and collected in its pure *Act* of inward Adoration to
the great I AM, and to the filial WORD that re-affirmeth it from Eternity to
Eternity, whose choral Echo is the Universe. (2:247–8)

Here, Coleridge moves well past the poetic embodiment of the 'living
Power and prime Agent of all human Perception,' as the mythical form
of the universe, to a religious embodiment in which the soul is preserved
by the 'Liturgy and Homilies' of the Anglican Church. He has moved,
link by logocentric link, from the less than 'pure' finite repetition of 'the
eternal act' toward this act's transcendental object. As the superhuman
action of grace or 'beatitude,' this approach releases the fallen soul from
a delusional host of ghostly temptations, the 'dramatic truth' of which
only reinforces their 'fond illusion.' In short, he has moved from a willingly suspended disbelief in the 'infinite I AM' to a 'steady and collected
pure *Act* of inward Adoration toward the great I AM.'

What Coleridge celebrates as the true 'Object' of his 'LITERARY
LIFE' mirrors in a Christian context what Shelley celebrates in a pagan
context in *Adonais* as 'the One,' which is for Shelley neither an 'infinite
I AM' nor an individual or finite one. Coleridge's 'aweful depth' as the
soul's 'pure *Act* of inward Adoration' is Shelley's 'void circumference' (*A*
420). Coleridge's 'Liturgy and Homilies' are, at best for Shelley, 'Frail
spells – whose uttered charm might not avail to sever, / From all we hear
and all we see, / Doubt, chance, and mutability' ('Hymn to Intellectual
Beauty' 29–31). As incarnation they are, at worst, Jupiter's 'antique empire insecure, though built / On eldest faith, and Hell's coeval, fear' (*PU*
3.1.9–10), a dominion Jupiter is about to make secure by having

> begotten a strange wonder,
> That fatal Child, the terror of the Earth,
> Who waits but till the destined Hour arrive
> Bearing from Demogorgon's vacant throne
> The dreadful might of ever living limbs

Which clothed that awful spirit unbeheld –
To redescend and trample out the spark.                    (3.1.18–24)

In *Adonais* the 'spark' is the 'fire for which all thirst,' which as the act of composition 'Consume[s] the last clouds of [Shelley's] cold mortality.' In this demonic context, poetry does Jupiter's work by trampling out the 'spark,' just as in *The Triumph of Life* the 'shape all light' 'thought by thought, / Trampled [the mind's] fires into the dust of death' (387–8).

## 3

When Shelley gazes at the 'Dizzy Ravine' rather than Mont Blanc, he 'seem[s] as in a trance sublime and strange / To muse' on his 'human mind' as his 'own separate phantasy' (35–7). His passive mind is no longer 'Holding an unremitting interchange / With the clear universe of things around' as this mind unconsciously renders and receives 'fast influencings' (38–40). In this state, what he appears to be writing, to cite Coleridge's rejection of Hartley, 'may be as truly said to be written by Saint Paul's church' as by the poet himself (*BL* 1:118). In 'On Life' Shelley writes that the mind reduced to 'fast influencings' 'dispenses [materialists] from thinking.' Shelley describes his 'moveless' mind 'as a long-forgotten lyre / Suspended in the solitary dome / Of some mysterious and deserted fane' awaiting the 'breath' of the 'Great Parent' so that its 'strain / May modulate with murmurs of the air, / And motions of the forests and the sea / And voice of living beings' (*Alastor* 42–8). He follows this passage with a long account of the breath of the 'Great Parent,' not as the *pneuma* of the Holy Spirit – Wordsworth's 'sweet breath of heaven' stirring within as a 'correspondent breeze' (*P* 1.33, 35) – but as a 'remote, serene and inaccessible' Power whose 'intelligence' is so dissimilar to his own that 'intercourse' with it is impossible (*SPP* 73). Any intercourse with the 'Great Parent,' described by Coleridge as an '*artificial consciousness*,' therefore becomes a 'generous error,' instigated by a 'sacred thirst of doubtful knowledge,' or the willing dupe of 'illustrious superstition' (73).

On one level, Shelley agrees with Wordsworth when he argues that the 'infant Babe' is the 'first / Poetic spirit of our human life,' particularly when Wordsworth goes on to expand the power emanating from the mother 'through the growing faculties of sense' (*P* 2.256) into a creative power, which acts 'like an agent of the one great Mind' to become 'creator and receiver both.' In 'On Love' Shelley writes:

> We are born into the world and there is something within us which from the instant that we live and move thirsts after its likeness. It is probably in correspondence with this law that the infant drains milk from the bosom of its mother. This propensity developes itself with the development of our nature. We dimly see within our intellectual nature a miniature as it were of our entire self, yet deprived of all that we condemn or despise, the ideal prototype of every thing excellent or lovely we are capable of conceiving as belonging to the nature of man. (*SPP* 504)

At the same time, this 'thirst' does not find its 'antitype' in the maternal 'prototype.' For Shelley, the poetic conviction that it does is a 'fond illusion' that reduces poetry to what 'seems,' rather than revealing what 'is.' 'Seems, madam? Nay, it is. I know not "seems"' (1.22.76), Hamlet declares to his mother, deception by the mother thereby becoming the birth of a modern psychology.

Realizing that a biological account of 'the first / Poetic spirit' (Freud's sexual libido) does not, even as a 'fond illusion,' remain 'Through every change of growth and of decay, / Pre-eminent till death' (*P* 2.264–5), both Wordsworth and Shelley recognized that inspiration had a deeper source than the personal unconscious, what Shelley calls the 'Abysm' (*PU* 2.4.114). Indeed, if it did not, Jung will later argue, 'Culture would then appear as a mere farce, the morbid consequence of repressed sexuality' (*MDR* 150). (To which Freud replied, '"Yes, [...] so it is, and that is just a curse of fate against which we are powerless to contend."') The deeper source, in which the poet becomes 'an agent of the one great Mind' and all poetry the 'episodes to that great poem, which all poets, like the co-operating thoughts of one great mind, have built up since the beginning of the world' (*DP* 522), becomes in Jung the 'collective unconscious' as the 'living Power and prime Agent of all human Perception.' The act of perception as a psychic act becomes a symbol of the physical object in which the physical object itself contains, in the act of perceiving it, what as the human act of perception this object symbolizes. 'For, in the last analysis,' Jung writes in *The Archetypes of the Collective Unconscious,* 'psychic life is for the greater part an unconscious life that surrounds consciousness on all sides – a notion that is sufficiently obvious when one considers how much unconscious preparation is needed, for instance, to register a sense-impression' (27). Romanticism examines the mind's creative process in terms of this 'unconscious preparation' required 'to register a sense impression.' As symbol, this supremely human act of sense impression is both subject and object. Wordsworth describes this act as the marriage of the mind to 'this goodly universe / In love and holy passion' (Prospectus to *The Recluse* 53–4).

# 4

To consummate this marriage ceaselessly in every 'Pulsation of the Artery,' like the ceaseless coitus of Shiva and Shakti, places huge demands on the mind. Quoting Wordsworth, Keats calls this labour 'the Burden of the Mystery,' which ultimately he could not bear (*KL* 92). This burden is why Shelley's 'mind in creation is as a fading coal which some invisible influence, like an inconstant wind, awakens to a transitory brightness' that wanes the moment composition begins (*DP* 531). Here Shelley psychologically describes a state of post-coital depression in which the act of creation becomes 'a feeble shadow of the original conception of the poet' (531). It is no surprise, then, that when the gods fall, as Jung argues, they fall into human psychosis. The human psyche cannot bear the reality of the gods, which is the reality of the archetypal imagination explored by the Romantics, unless this awareness is radically mediated by the human mind's logocentric operations, of which Descartes' logic is a pre-eminent example. 'So that, to come back to Descartes,' Derrida writes,

> any philosopher or speaking subject (and the philosopher is but the speaking subject par excellence) who must evoke madness from the *interior* of thought (and not only from within the body or some extrinsic agency), can do so only in the realm of the *possible* and in the language of fiction or the fiction of language. Thereby, through his own language, he reassures himself against any actual madness – which may sometimes appear quite talkative, another problem – and can keep his distance, the distance indispensable for continuing to speak and to live. But this is not a weakness or a search for security proper to a given historical language (for example, the search for certainty in the Cartesian style), but is rather inherent in the essence and the very project of all language in general; and even in the language of those who are apparently the maddest; and even and above all in the language of those who, by their praise of madness, their complicity with it [Foucault], measure their own strength against the greatest possible proximity to madness. Language being the break with madness, it adheres more thoroughly to its essence and vocation, makes a cleaner break with

madness, if it pits itself against madness more freely and gets closer to it: to the point of being separated from it only the 'transparent sheet' of which Joyce speaks, that is, by itself – for this diaphaneity is nothing other than the language, meaning, possibility, and elementary discretion of a nothing that neutralizes everything. (54–5)

Romanticism invokes madness as the interior or unconscious ground of thought to which thought is answerable. As we have already seen, for Derrida the Cartesian 'Cogito, ergo sum,' thought as the purest form of thought or 'I AM,' is madness. At its point of madness, the Cogito is humanly uninhabitable as thought. Jung describes this impossible moment as a 'real zero point' without extension, Blake's 'Pulsation of the Artery.' To become humanly inhabitable, what Derrida calls 'the attempt-to-say-the-hyperbole,' the poet must submit to the 'historical enunciation' of language that 'tranquilizes itself and excludes madness' (Derrida 62). In this tranquilization, what Shelley in his translation of Plato's Ion calls the 'divine insanity' of the poet 'betrays itself (or betrays itself as thought)' and 'enters into a crisis and a forgetting of itself that are an essential and necessary period of its movement' as mythos. 'I philosophize only in terror,' writes Derrida, 'but in the confessed terror of going mad. The confession is simultaneously, at its present moment, oblivion and unveiling, protection and exposure: economy' (76).

Romanticism confronts this 'economy,' in which the Cogito becomes a 'feeble shadow' of itself, as a betrayal of the Cogito's pure creativity – Milton's 'uncircumscrib'd' God who 'retire[s]' into himself and 'puts not forth His goodness' (PL 7.140–1). In this 'crisis,' Derrida argues, 'reason is madder than madness – for reason is non-meaning and oblivion – and madness is more rational than reason, for it is closer to the wellspring of sense, however silent or murmuring' (62). 'One song they sang,' Wordsworth writes of his 'Communing [...] through earth and heaven / With every form of creature, as it looked / Toward the Uncreated with a countenance / Of adoration, with an eye of love.' '[A]nd it was audible, / Most audible,' he then continues, 'when the fleshly ear, / O'ercome by humblest prelude of that strain, / Forgot her functions, and slept undisturbed' (P 2.412–18; my italics). When Wordsworth compares the sound of his own voice to the river Derwent's 'murmurs' blended with his 'nurse's song' in sleep, it is the voice of 'some other Being' rather than himself, a voice he associates with the 'eagerness of infantine desire' as a 'Union that cannot be' (2.33, 26, 24). Plato's 'divine insanity' becomes for Shelley an enchanted cave in which, 'Like human babes in their brief innocence,' Prometheus is united with the three Oceanides, Asia, Panthea, and Ione, whose home is the bottomless caverns of the sea (*PU* 3.3.33). There they weave spells, which are 'the progeny immortal / Of Painting, Sculpture and rapt Poesy / And arts, though unimagined, yet to be' (3.3.54–56). Wordsworth further identifies his song with 'all that glides / Beneath the wave, yea, in the wave itself, / And mighty depth of waters' (*P* 2.407–9). 'My soul is an enchanted Boat / Which, like a sleeping swan, doth float / Upon the silver waves of thy sweet singing,' declares Shelley's Asia. 'Till like one in slumber bound,' she continues, 'Borne to the Ocean, I float down, around, / Into a Sea profound, of ever-spreading sound' (*PU* 2.5.72–4, 82–4).

'I used to brood over the stories of Enoch and Elijah [like Blake dining with Isaiah and Ezekiel in *The Marriage of Heaven and Hell*], and almost to persuade myself,' writes Wordsworth in the Fenwick note to his 'Intimations of Immortality' ode,

> that, whatever might become of others, I should be translated, in something of the same way, to heaven. With feelings congenial to this, I was often unable to think of external things as having external existence, and I communed with all that I saw as something not apart from, but inherent in, my own immaterial nature. Many times while going to school have I grasped at a wall or tree to recall myself from this abyss of idealism to the reality. At that time I was afraid of such processes. In later periods of life I have deplored, as we have all reason to do, a subjugation of an opposite character, and have rejoiced over the remembrances, as it is expressed in the lines
>> Obstinate questionings
>> Of sense and outward things,
>> Fallings from us, vanishings, etc.                    (*Fenwick Notes* 61)

Neither fearing the 'abyss' nor deploring an opposite 'subjugation,' Shelley moved dialectically toward the 'Uncreated.' Jung pursued an empirical 'subjugation' as the dialectical opposite of the Uncreated necessary to the intuition of the *ignotum per ignotius*. In the end he surrendered to the *ignotum*, less as the ego's defeat than as the true measure of the ego's strength. As a transcendental philosopher who rejects the transcendent's lawlessness, Coleridge insists that, while the pure transcendence of the 'Uncreated' can be intuited as a fact of experience, it remains in itself independent of the soul's intuition of it. If it were not, this intuition would be the soul's extinction as the 'Uncreated' itself, the terror of Milton's 'uncircumscrib'd' God described by Blake as 'Unknown, unprolific, / Self-closd, all repelling' ([*First*] *Book of Urizen* 3.2–3). In Jung's case, this 'Unknown' is the 'black tide of mud' Freud was determined to suspend in its course as it made its way through the occult detours of Jung's otherwise brilliant mind. For Coleridge in *Christabel*, associating inspiration with addiction, this fear of 'divine insanity' amounted to a near-paralysing terror.

'The authors of those great poems which we admire,' Plato writes in Shelley's translation, 'lose all control over their reason in the enthusiasm of the sacred dance, and, during this supernatural possession, are excited to the rhythm and harmony which they communicate to men' (*Complete Works* 8:230). This terror, amounting finally to panic, is the fear of madness in which the god who takes possession of the mind becomes an evil spell, the poem itself becoming this spell's exorcism. 'The challenge that is present in all texts and that *The Triumph of Life* identifies, thematizes, and thus tries to avoid in the most effective way possible,' writes de Man, 'is here [in the fragment found after Shelley's drowning] carried out in a sequence of symbolic interruptions [narratives enacting their own dissolution], and is in its turn interrupted by an event [Shelley's literal drowning] that is no longer simply imaginary or symbolic. The apparent ease with which readers of *The Triumph of Life* have been able to dispose of this challenge demonstrates the inadequacy of our understanding of Shelley, and beyond him, of romanticism in general' (67). 'What we have done,' de Man continues, 'is bury them in their own texts made into epigraphs and monumental graves.' Like Wordsworth's chanting of *The Prelude*, which Coleridge experienced as 'but Flowers / Strew'd on my corse, and borne upon my Bier / In the same Coffin, for the self-same Grave!' ('To a Gentleman' [William Wordsworth] 73–5), this burial, rather than repress the threat of burial, can 'state the full powers of this threat in all its negativity' (de Man 67). In Shelley's case the sheer power of this 'negativity' awakened in de Man 'the suspicion that the negation is a *Verneinung*, an intended exorcism' (68).

In *The Triumph of Life* Shelley watches the 'mask / Of darkness' fall away as the 'Sun sprang forth / Rejoicing in [its] splendour' (2–4), as if he no longer rejoices in the spell of language conjured in *Prometheus Unbound*. Now he sees language's 'mysterious doom' as '"Figures ever new [that] / Rise on the bubble"' only as quickly to pass away because, '"paint them how you may,"' he explains to the ghost of Rousseau, they are a delusion (*TL* 248–9). Thus, while he agrees in 'On Life' that 'Nothing exists but as it is perceived,' we as perceivers '*I*, and *you*, and *they* are grammatical devices invented simply for arrangement and totally devoid of the intense and exclusive sense usually attached to them.' To assume 'the existence of distinct individual minds similar to that which is employed in now questioning its own nature, is likewise found to be a delusion' (*SPP* 508). The 'arrangement' of language merely throws our shadows on a '"false and fragile glass"' (*TL* 247). 'Considered performatively,' de Man explains, 'figuration (as question ['Then, what is Life?']) performs the erasure of the positing power of language,' which for de Man constitutes the 'madness of words' exorcism cannot erase (64). Nothing short of silence can.

While for Derrida silence is 'the absence of a work,' it is also 'the work's limit and profound resource' (54). In this anagogical sense, of which Shelley was the most conscious, the ultimate meaning of a Romantic poem lies in its 'Uncreated' non-existence. Nourished by the 'Vitality of poison,' Byron knew, as neither Shelley nor Rousseau did, that if Earth as a 'purer nutriment' had 'supplied' rather than extinguished the 'spark' with which Heaven lights the spirit, he could never have written the poetry whose unprecedented success lay in mirroring the age rather than breaking the mirror. Shelley and Rousseau confront the shattered fragments of 'Heaven's light [which] forever shines' (*A* 461). They realize they have brought this destruction upon themselves instead of using it to flee back 'to their native noon,' although Rousseau suggests that it is not too late for Shelley, who can still choose 'thoughts which must remain untold' (*TL* 21). Coleridge confronts the same issue in *Christabel*. Trapped in an evil spell, he must either escape or become hopelessly enmeshed in the 'transcendent.' That is to say, he must choose silence more as 'the work's limit and profound resource' than as the 'absence of the work.' Coleridge gradually came to understand the difference between spell or incantation and the 'Liturgy and Homilies' of the Anglican Church. Geraldine is 'A sight to dream of, not to tell!' writes Coleridge, as if struggling to resist the spell of Geraldine as she takes Christabel in her arms, knowing that any resistance only feeds the spell: 'In the touch of this bosom there worketh a spell / Which is lord of thy utterance, Christabel!' (247, 255–6). To which he quickly adds, 'But vainly thou warrest' (259), unable to admit fully to himself that the spell is the demonic perversion of the primary imagination. A similar fate overcomes the Visionary in *Alastor* when he is irresistibly enfolded in the dissolving arms of the veiled maid:

Now blackness veiled his dizzy eyes, and night
Involved and swallowed up the vision; sleep,

Like a dark flood suspended in its course
Rolled back its impulse on his vacant brain.                    (188–91)

Quoting Plotinus, Coleridge writes: "'Should any one interrogate [Nature], how she works, if graciously she vouchsafe to listen and speak, she will reply, it behoves thee not to disquiet me with interrogatories, but to understand in silence, even as I am silent, and work without words.'" 'Likewise,' Coleridge continues,

> in the fifth book of the fifth Ennead, speaking of the highest and intuitive knowledge as distinguished from the discursive, or in the language of Wordsworth,
>     The vision and the faculty divine; [Plotinus] says: 'It is not lawful to enquire from whence it sprang, as if it were a thing subject to place and motion, for it neither approached hither, nor again departs from hence to some other place; but it either appears to us or it does not appear. So that we ought not to pursue it with a view of detecting its secret source, but to watch in quiet till it suddenly shines upon us; preparing ourselves for the blessed spectacle as the eye waits patiently for the rising sun.' (*BL* 1:240–1)

Coleridge rejects the pursuit of the primary imagination in order to find its 'secret source,' the intended subject of his *Logosophia*. He is now prepared to embrace this 'source' as the revealed Word and the true object of religious faith, 'the IMMEDIATE, which dwells in every man as an original intuition, or absolute affirmation of it.' But the psychic fact that it 'does not in every man rise into consciousness' does not mean that we should go down into the unconscious and bring it to consciousness (*BL* 1:243). Shelley attempts to do so in *Adonais* by 'compelling there, / All new successions [of the 'dull dense world'] to the forms they wear; / Torturing th'unwilling dross that checks its flight / To its own likeness, as each mass may bear' (*A* 382–5). But Coleridge feared the absence of Nature, especially under the effects of opium. Instead, he sought metaphysically to transform the delusional presence of Nature embraced by the mechanical philosophy into the Christian God theologically understood by the poet's severely disciplined use of his 'intellectual energy.' Yet while this transformation alleviated the nightmare of delusion, it cruelly restricted his 'creative power.' Like Wordsworth grieving over his brother's drowning in 1805, Coleridge, grieving far more ominously over his own addiction, submitted his 'creative power' to a 'new control' ('Elegiac Stanzas' 34). At first Wordsworth and Coleridge could fancy 'that the

mighty Deep / Was even the gentlest of gentle Things.' But as their relations darkened, they gradually realized that without a Christian God the
'mighty Deep' became, like Peele Castle, a 'hoary Pile' ('Elegiac Stanzas'
11–12, 17). Both found in the Anglican faith an 'unfeeling armour of old
time' (51) with which to brave the diminishment of creative power. They
were distinctly unlike Blake, who alone among the Romantics could affirm the Word by subjecting Nature to a radical and ruthless interrogation. This interrogation brought natural law to Judgment by compelling
this law, as Milton's false God wearing the moral disguise of the Word, to
'Defend a Lie, that he may [as Satan] be snared & caught & taken' (*M*
8.47–8). Blake released himself from the Word as 'Priesthood,' which
Coleridge and especially Wordsworth (in Blake's view) falsely embraced
as 'forms of worship.' By radically renewing the living Word as the divine
imagination through his own inspired poetry, Blake struggled to restore
Christianity to its original life as a 'poetic' tale.

# 5

For many of the Romantics, the mechanical philosophy had reduced the
soul to the ghostly form or epiphenomenon of matter. In the 'still cave of
the witch Poesy,' Shelley viewed the 'dizzy' rush of sensations through his
brain as the 'shadows' of his soul ('Mont Blanc' 44, 45). He hoped to restore these ghostly forms of soul-sensations to their source as soul, rather
than to their 'phantom' form or 'faint image' as physical sensations or
the 'Ghosts of all things that are.' Only when and if he can do this will
Mont Blanc be there as other than what Wordsworth describes as a 'soulless image on the eye / That usurped upon a living thought / That never
more could be' (*P* 6.526–8). Shelley's task, like Coleridge's and Wordsworth's, is to restore Nature to its true form as a 'living thought,' rather
than 'a *something-nothing-every-thing*, which does all of which we know, and
knows nothing of all that itself does.' 'All knowledge,' Coleridge insists,
'rests on the coincidence of an object with a subject. [...] For we can
*know* that only which is true: and the truth is universally placed in the
coincidence of the thought with the thing, of the representation with the
object represented' (*BL* 1:252–4).

In the long history of thought, understood as the soul's transforming
operations that restore the fallen nature of things to their soul place of
origin as unfallen nature, religion has served as the divine container of
this soul process. For this reason, thought as soul process is, for religion,
the likeness and image of God by which God is known. All true knowl-

edge is, therefore, the knowledge of God. What is not the knowledge of God is not knowledge; it is superstition. Coleridge's distinction between the transcendent and the transcendental is his distinction between what, as knowledge, is God and what is not God. His task, as a transcendental philosopher, is to restore the mind to the knowledge of God as the 'coincidence of the thought with the thing.' This 'coincidence,' he argues, occurs in the action of the mind as the act of perception itself. The primary imagination does not create a copy of the object, it is the object itself: 'It is the table itself, which the man of common sense believes himself to see, not the phantom of a table, from which he may argumentatively deduce the reality of a table, which he does not see' (*BL* 1:261–2). For Coleridge, Wordsworth's genius lay in this 'truest and most binding realism,' which 'is far elder and lies infinitely deeper than [the] hypothetical explanation of the origin of our perceptions, an explanation skimmed from the mere surface of mechanical philosophy' (1:261).

This explanation is also what Coleridge means when he argues that Wordsworth is capable of writing the 'FIRST GENUINE PHILOSOPHIC POEM.' *The Recluse* would dispense with supernatural machinery by replacing the supernatural with the 'binding realism' whose source is 'infinitely deeper' than the 'transcendent' realm 'That ever was put forth in personal form – / Jehovah – with his thunder, and the choir / Of shouting Angels, and the empyreal thrones.' Wordsworth thus declares that

> Not Chaos, not
> The darkest pit of lowest Erebus,
> Nor aught of blinder vacancy, scooped out
> By help of dreams – can breed such fear and awe
> As fall upon us often when we look
> Into our Minds, into the Mind of Man.    (Prospectus to *The Recluse* 32–40)

Wordsworth and Coleridge made this domain their 'haunt, and the main region of [their] song' (41). Fiercely holding on to supernatural machinery of his own devising, which Coleridge would dismiss as delusion, Blake despised this 'new' natural religion. For Wordsworth and Coleridge, however, it offered a way of subjecting the transcendental philosophy to a psychological analysis for which Coleridge invented the term 'psychoanalytical' in 1805 (*Notebooks* 2:2670). The identification of God with the soul and the soul with the true knowledge of Nature (as human nature), while not pantheism, is the metaphysical-psychological ground of something like pantheism. For Coleridge, this ground had been prepared by

Shakespeare and Milton. While not possessed by the Holy Spirit, each was in his own way in possession of it, their poetical works becoming the first Protestant fruits of the Holy Spirit as natural revelation. Therefore, when Keats suggests that Soul-making is a 'grander scheme of salvation than the chrysteian religion,' he has in mind something like Wordsworth and Coleridge's plan for *The Recluse*, which project demonstrated what Keats calls the 'grand march of Intellect' (*KL* 96) to which the Romantics were committed. Coleridge associated this 'Grand march' with the Biblical descent of the 'New Jerusalem' as the culmination of the prophetic vision. For him, this vision had to be released from the fancy's law of association in order that association could be truly understood as the imagination's coincidence of subject and object as distinct from the copy of this union. 'The formation of a copy is not solved by the mere pre-existence of an original,' he explains; 'the copyist of Raphael's Transfiguration must repeat more or less perfectly the process of Raphael,' which is to say the actual or original act of transfiguration that constitutes the work of the primary imagination (*BL* 1:137). For Coleridge, the human ground of the co-incidence of subject and object as the 'more than magic' transfiguration of both constitutes the freedom of the will that all humans share in common as their 'only absolute *self*.'

Coleridge writes that Shakespeare and Milton occupy 'the two glory-smitten summits of the poetic mountain,' Milton being the 'compeer not rival' of Shakespeare (*BL* 2:27). The difference between them – Keats's difference between '*Negative Capability*' and the 'egotistical sublime' (*KL* 157) – is that, as the 'Proteus of the fire and the flood,' Shakespeare 'darts himself forth, and passes into all the forms of human character and passion,' whereas Milton 'attracts all forms and things to himself, into the unity of his own IDEAL' (*BL* 2:27–8). For Milton, the Restoration enacted the defeat of the Puritan Revolution, after which he took his revenge in the name of his Puritan God (Blake's Urizen). Milton's blindness confronted him with a 'Universal blanc,' 'Nature's works' being 'expung'd and ras'd, / And wisdom at one entrance quite shut out' (*PL* 3.48–50). He was then left torn between his 'creative power' and his 'intellectual energy.' His Puritan Christ rejected the pagan models of his two epics and final drama because they represented the temptation of Satan's world. Milton overcoming the world became, as a final show of 'creative power,' Milton's Agonistes, the blind Samson who brings the world down in a final terrorist act that leaves Milton 'calm of mind,' his Puritan passion finally 'spent,' just as Samson 'Pull'd down the same destruction on himself' (1758, 1658).

Shakespeare's 'darting forth' engages a radically different action. Declaring 'here is my space,' Antony, embracing Cleopatra, can casually assert, 'Let Rome in Tiber melt and the wide arch / Of the rang'd empire
fall! '(1.1.33–4). In overcoming the world, his characters are searching
out new ways of engaging it. 'I'll set a bourn how far to be belov'd,' declares Cleopatra. 'Then must thou needs find out new heaven, new earth'
(1.1.16–17), Antony replies, knowing 'There's beggary in the love than
can be reckon'd.' Shakespeare's 'creative power' embraced a world that
cannot be 'reckon'd,' his 'intellectual energy' refusing to set a 'bourn'
upon this energy. Far from working against each other, his 'creative
power' and 'intellectual energy' propelled each other toward a unity that
contained a new understanding (or, to borrow Harold Bloom's term,
'invention') of human nature as a 'new heaven, new earth.' As noted
earlier, Coleridge sees in Shakespeare a 'war embrace' between 'creative
power' and 'intellectual energy' that eventually intermixes 'reluctantly
and in tumult' to 'blend and dilate, and flow in one current with one
voice.'

In Romanticism the poet discovers an inner marriage or *hieros gamos*.
'One song, they sang, and it was audible,' writes Wordsworth, rendering
the 'audible' answerable to the inaudible, which Shakespeare explores
as death. Cleopatra images this death as 'my babe at my breast, / That
sucks the nurse asleep.' Far from fearing it, she describes 'the stroke of
death' as 'a lover's pinch, / Which hurts, and is desir'd.' Associating the
dead Iras, poisoned by Cleopatra's farewell kiss, with the infant sleeping
at the nurse's breast, Cleopatra further ruminates: 'Dost thou lie still? /
If thus thou vanishest, thou tell'st the world / It is not worth leave-
taking.' And yet, this death is worth the effort:

> If she first met the curled Antony
> He'll make demand of her, and spend that kiss
> Which is my heaven to have. Come, thou mortal wretch,
>     [*To an asp, which she applies to her breast.*]
> With thy sharp teeth this knot intrinsicate
> Of life at once untie, O, couldst thou speak,
> That I might hear thee call great Caesar ass
> Unpolicied!                                          (5.2.299–310)

In this astonishingly erotic enactment of death ('Husband I come! Now
to that name my courage prove my title!' [5.2.289–90]), Shakespeare
in the image of the babe asleep at the nurse's breast pre-figures Words-

worth's blessed 'infant Babe' at the breast of the mother as 'the first /
Poetic spirit of our human life.' The sucking asleep becomes for Wordsworth the movement of mind beyond the created to the 'Uncreated' in
which 'the fleshly ear, / O'ercome by humblest prelude of that strain,
/ Forgot her functions, and slept undisturbed.' Lead by Wordsworth,
the Romantics sink deeper into an unconscious realm, constructing an
'*artificial consciousness*' to explore it ('Nature wants stuff / To vie strange
forms with fancy; yet, t'imagine / An Antony were nature's piece 'gainst
fancy, / Condemning shadows quite' [*Antony and Cleopatra* 5.2.97–9]). In
doing so, they open the 'Uncreated,' which is for Shakespeare, as it became for Shelley, the desire to 'break [his] staff, / Bury it certain fadoms
in the earth, / And deeper than did ever plummet sound / [...] drown
[his] book' (*The Tempest* 5.1.54–6).

The 'Uncreated' is also the terror of 'madness.' This terror confronted
Wordsworth in his dream of the crazed Bedouin as Wordsworth's dream
of Coleridge, whom he was partly compelled to follow, knowing that 'in
the blind and awful lair / Of such a madness, reason did lie couched.'
Overcome by the 'strong entrancement' of such a madness, he knew
that he could share the 'maniac's fond anxiety,' and, like 'Shakespeare,
or Milton, labourers divine,' go with Coleridge 'Upon like errand.' The
'like errand' is to bury the immortal book by placing it in a 'Poor earthly
casket of immortal verse,' as if only there could it be preserved (*P* 5.165).
'On whom those truths do rest, / Which we are toiling all our lives to
find,' writes Wordsworth of the child who,'deaf and silent, read'st the
eternal deep,' which lies, except for the 'Mighty Prophet! Seer blest,' 'In
darkness lost, the darkness of the grave' ('Intimations of Immortality'
112–18).

The Christian orthodoxy into which Wordsworth and Coleridge
settled is their burial of the book, the intellectual abatement or suppression of a 'creative power' of which Shakespeare in his work left no
apparent evidence. Between opening and sealing, Shakespeare and Milton, the Romantics shaped their vision of the potentially human. In the
opening they feared the excess to which it may conduct, much as Milton
feared the Satan whom Shelley declared the hero of *Paradise Lost*, insisting that the epic contained within it the 'strange and natural antithesis'
of the religious system for which 'it has been a chief popular support'
(*DP* 526). Working with his 'strange and natural antithesis' dialectically essential to the poet's 'creative power,' Milton, for Blake, was 'of the
Devils party without knowing it' (*MHH* 6). This return in Blake's 'Vegetable Body' became the process in which he brought the Devil in him-

self to consciousness, which awareness constitutes the 'true Friendship' of 'Opposition' (*MHH* 20). While this recognition does not render Satan the true hero of Milton's epic, it does release Milton from Urizen's tyranny, Milton's Puritan God who sought to paralyse Milton's 'creative power.' Blake's reading of Milton radically realigns Milton's 'intellectual energy' to support rather than restrict his 'creative power.' Concluding his chapter comparing Shakespeare to Milton, Coleridge quotes Wordsworth, who describes Shakespeare and Milton as the English poet's 'first blood' from which 'In every thing we are sprung' and in which 'We must be free or die' ('It is not to be thought of' 11–14).

# 6

At the end of the Second World War, which followed fast upon the dropping of the atomic bomb on Hiroshima and Nagasaki, the Japanese not knowing there were no further bombs waiting to drop, Roy Daniells, the Chairman of the English Department at the University of Manitoba, offered me, to my considerable amazement, a job teaching a course in world literature, about which I knew next to nothing, to a class for veterans that was about to begin. I was offered the job for three reasons: I was still in my air force officer's uniform when Daniells interviewed me; I had done well in Sedgwick's well-known Shakespeare course at the University of British Columbia, from which Daniells had graduated, having done equally well in it; and Daniells had found no one else to teach the course.

The first work on the course was Euripides' *Electra* in Gilbert Murray's translation. Daniells handed me a copy, printed in stiff, grey, recycled wartime, paper and told me to take it home and read it. Two weeks later I found myself at eight o'clock on a forty-below-zero Monday morning in January in a converted army hut facing a motley crew of veterans, many of them in cast-off uniforms sprawled out at individual desks ill-fitted to their clearly restless bodies that had for me the familiar smell of steamy flesh and melting snow. When the bell sounded, I got up from behind my desk as if rising from my bunk, and, holding my borrowed copy of Euripides' *Electra* in my hand as a shield between myself and them, I said: 'What we are about to do is far more real than anything we have yet done.' The look they gave me matched, I knew, the look I gave them. I instantly knew that if we failed to hold it until we mutually registered what had just been said we would be in imminent danger of losing it forever in the silence of an irremediable disconnect. We held it until I sensed a certain relaxation spreading through the converted hut as if, rather than missing its target, it had struck. There issued from them, as well as from me, no acknowledged agreement. It was something entirely different from anything I had experienced before, which, as it turned out, would in an as-yet-unforeseeable future become the basis upon which I would conduct my English classes: 'a willing suspension of disbelief for the moment, which constitutes poetic faith.'

Unknown to me in the instant of its utterance, some other being had spoken, introducing me to the stranger who became the fictional form of myself. He, as it turned out, gradually absorbed the totality of my experience in a way that I instinctively knew I could absorb in no other way. I had in the first utterance issuing from my mouth in a converted army hut against a backdrop of sizzling radiators and fluorescent lights made a covenant with a group of sceptical veterans in which fiction rather boldly became a greater reality than we, some wearing the lifetime scars of warfare, had ever known.

Having read the play that Daniells loaned me, I explained that it was about Agamemnon, who returns from the Trojan War to find his wife, Clytemnestra, in an adulterous relationship with Aegisthus, who then proceeds to murder Agamemnon for the sacrifice of his daughter Ephigenia. Electra, Agamemnon's other daughter, yearns for the return of her brother, Orestes, in order to avenge her father's murder, which they subsequently commit, with dire consequences, including madness. This brief synopsis led to the more immediate question: 'So what have you returned to?' That question was our shared entrance into Greek tragedy, which, by not making it our own, released us from it by, at a more profound level, allowing us to enter it in that willing state of suspended disbelief, which contained within it an otherwise unfamiliar knowledge of ourselves. In my first class on Euripides I had unknowingly entered the career that gradually, with the help of the Romantics, became my life.

So what in that first class had I returned to? The answer to that question I did not share that morning, though it increasingly informed, like the ghost of a life returning, my (our) exploration of a literary world, which imposed a global perspective upon our suspended disbelief in who or what we were fictionally becoming, upon a time rather than in it, a reality that could not otherwise be.

I refer to my dream of the Báb, the consequences of which I sought to escape on a purely personal level by joining the Royal Canadian Air Force as a way of restoring myself to reality. The processing that I could not at the time (1941) of the dream perform, the parade square and what followed apparently releasing me from it, I now returned to in a veteran's class in a converted army hut, the dawn rising up out of the January darkness during the eight o'clock classes as a greeting of the spirit announcing its return. The place I was in I would later associate with a *temenos,* two psychically spaced chairs facing each other as the Jungian site of analysis.

It was in this site, the classroom, a mandala in whose centre I stood, that I discovered in myself the Romantics and began my more serious work, always with that first class of veterans in mind as a fiction approximating the real, from which it was our, particularly my own, psychological responsibility to protect ourselves, lest it take possession of us. Here it became Sedgwick's class on Shakespeare that both launched and protected me. And here, too, at Manitoba, studying Milton under Malcolm Ross, Satan, as the victim of possession, or Milton's act of exorcism performed upon himself, became the subject of my MA thesis, which I intended to expand into a doctorate at the University of Toronto until I registered in Northrop Frye's first graduate course on Blake. That course imposed upon me an act of self-intuition that, in the name of fiction, I had taken elaborate precautions to avoid. It almost cost me my sanity, which, as the opening of an abyss, confronted me with an archetypal knowledge of myself, which the personal mirrors rather than invents, a knowledge the Romantics exhaustively explored.

Jung calls the God image of this archetypal knowledge the Self. Revealed to me in my dream of the Báb, it showed me who, in the sight of God, I am, in something of the same way that Coleridge first listened to Wordsworth chanting his poem aloud as if it had, like 'the ANCIENT of days and all his works, [...] then sprang forth at the first creative fiat.' As we have seen, the effects on Coleridge were alarming: Wordsworth descended to him as the 'Know Thyself' from heaven, showing Coleridge what true poetry is in a way that made Coleridge know 'that he himself was no Poet' (*Collected Letters* 2:714). In sheer desperation, Coleridge decided to finish and publish *Christabel,* which Wordsworth had rejected for the second edition of *Lyrical Ballads.* At the time, Coleridge was fully occupied with other matters: overthrowing 'the doctrine of Association [...] and with it all the irreligious metaphysics of modern Infidels'; and solving 'the process of Life & Consciousness' by deducing '*one sense*' from the 'five senses' (706). The latter especially made Wordsworth fear for Coleridge's sanity. Seeking release, Coleridge returned to his unfinished poem, which dealt with the same metaphysical issues, Christabel symbolizing the '*one sense*' and Geraldine the tyranny of the 'five senses' divorced from them. Not surprisingly, however, when Coleridge returned to the poem to finish it for independent publication as if in defiance of Wordsworth, Christabel became confused in his mind with Geraldine. '[Y]et I dared behold my Image miniatured in the pupil of her hollow eye, so steadily did I look her in the Face! – for it seemed to me a Suicide of my very soul to divert my attention from Truths so important, which came to me almost as a Revelation,' he explains to Poole. 'Likewise, I cannot express to you, dear Friend of my heart! – the loathing, which I once or twice felt, when I attempted to write, merely for the Bookseller, without any sense of the moral utility of what I was writing. – I shall there-fore, as I said, immediately publish my CHRISTABEL, with two Essays annexed to it, on the Praeternatural – and on Metre' (*Collected Letters* 2:707). This he would do, Coleridge implies, to show Wordsworth that, as a poet of the fancy, Coleridge is 'no Poet' compared to Wordsworth as a 'poet of the imagination.'

In something of the same state of mind that led Coleridge to get on with *Christabel* – he never finished it – I decided after the war to get on with processing my dream of the Báb, not sure whether it belonged to fancy or the imagination. 'Fanatics have their dreams, wherewith they weave / A paradise for a sect,' Keats begins *The Fall of Hyperion* (1.1–2). 'Whether the dream now purposed to rehearse / Be poet's or fanatic's will be known / When this warm scribe my hand is in the grave,' he con-cludes his introduction, as if indeed he is holding his 'warm scribe' from the grave toward the reader, warning him that upon his response will the poem live or die (1.16–18). I extend no such warning to my reader, though I have carefully reflected upon Keats's warning to me in the com-position of this book. It is, in truth, a warning I have received in different ways from all the Romantics as I move back and forth between the claims of truth in relation to the dream of the Báb and the 'willing suspension of disbelief' that affords me the psychic space in which to bring it to con-sciousness. This consciousness is inherent in the energy of the intellect when wedded to the shaping power of the imagination, the organ of the uncreated soul by which the soul gradually becomes conscious of itself as the 'I Am that I Am.'

Coleridge, who witnessed this process in its '*ideal* perfection' (*BL* 2:15) in Shakespeare, describes it best in his account of the 'sacred power of self-intuition.' The 'SUM or I AM,' he writes, '[...] is a subject which becomes a subject by the act of constructing itself objectively to itself; but which never is an object except for itself, and only so far as by the very same act it becomes a subject. It may be described therefore as a perpetual self-duplication [*artificial consciousness*] of one and the same power into object and subject, which presuppose each other, and can [dialectically] exist only as antitheses' (*BL* 1:272-3). He further insists that the 'SUM OR I AM' is '*Hysteron-Proteron*,' for which he coined the verb 'hysteroproterize' to describe the normal order in which the latter becomes the former and the former the latter, and in which the 'I AM' starts out as an accomplished fact, otherwise it could not develop toward a consciousness of it. The accomplished fact is the precondition of the search for it. In this sense, one has to be already there (self-intuition) if one wants to get there. The Báb (literally 'Gate') becomes this logical sense of being there, the dream metaphor of the 'SUM,' necessary to the process of getting there.

# 3 'The Furnaces the Stomach for digestion'

'The crooked horn mellows the hoarse raving serpent, terrible, but harmonious.'

– Blake, *Milton*

## 1

The previous chapter was partially concerned with the written fragments of Coleridge's *Logosophia* as their transcendental philosophy conducts to religious faith. After their parting of the ways in 1810, Coleridge was anxious to differentiate himself from Wordsworth, whom he still considered the greater poet, although Coleridge knew he was the greater philosopher. Hearing that Byron shared his negative view of *The Excursion*, Coleridge asked Byron to recommend his poems for publication. Preferring Coleridge's poetry to Wordsworth's, Byron agreed, particularly because Coleridge offered to write a general Preface 'on the Principles of philosophic and genial criticism relatively to the Fine Arts in general; but especially to Poetry: and a Particular Preface to the Ancient Mariner and the Ballads, on the employment of the Supernatural in Poetry and the Laws which regulate it' (*Collected Letters* 4:561). Assured of Byron's support, Coleridge now identified himself as an author with his own 'sacred power of self-intuition,' a transcendental philosopher whose interest in the supernatural, according to his 1817 marginal gloss to *The Ancient Mariner*, was no longer bound to delusion but rather grounded in Christian faith. Fall and redemption, rather than crime and punishment, were now his focus.

But Coleridge remained troubled by a more urgent spiritual issue:

surrendering the pressing demands of his frail ego to a higher, providential Christian end. He was now fully aware of how, under the influence of opium as the lawless operations of the transcendent fancy, the ego usurps the lawful work of the transcendental imagination. He also knew that this delusional binding of the fancy to its 'justly condemned' operations is the tyranny of mechanical association, which robs the eternal soul of its sacred identity. Fancy, as opposed to the imagination, was Satan's work, the demonic parody of the transcendental. Coleridge was still struggling within his satanic, opium-addicted self against the materialism of the mechanical philosophy. His ambivalent desire to part from Wordsworth becomes more apparent when we read *Biographia Literaria* as suspended uneasily between the ego's 'biographia' and the soul's 'autobiographia.' By analysing Wordsworth's poetic genius, Coleridge, with the help of German idealism, was also moving beyond Wordsworth dialectically to explore his own mind in a way that anticipates Hegel's advancement past the phenomenological limitations of Kant. That is to say, he was exploring a new metaphysical ground upon which the Christian revelation, rejected by materialism, could psychologically establish itself as Wordsworth's immediate or primary act of perception.

Still haunted by Wordsworth's 1810 dismissal of him, Coleridge's transcendental philosophy became indirectly bound to a psychological analysis of his 'supernatural' poems that, within a Christian framework, indirectly related madness to divine madness. Coleridge sees this madness being 'philosophically as well as sublimely embodied in the Satan of [Milton's] Paradise Lost.' He associates this sublimity with 'the COMMANDING GENIUS' of the 'mechanical philosophy,' which 'will have no obstacles, but those of force and brute matter' (*Lay Sermons* 65–6). Coleridge's fear of this satanic influence partly led him to publish *The Statesman's Manual.* With Napoleon in mind, but also projecting his own addicted abuse of the 'infinite I AM' onto external events, he was inwardly persuaded that modern nations were falling under Satan's 'COMMANDING GENIUS.' In response he calls for redemption in the Anglican Church, a display of the 'egotistical sublime' that, as we have seen, made Keats regret a lack of '*Negative Capability*' that turned Coleridge from poet to priest. But Coleridge increasingly feared the subjective or 'psycho-analytical' dangers of the ego as both devourer and expander. The ego appeared to act on behalf of the transcendental, what Freud would call the superego. But the ego also subjected the transcendental to a willing suspension of disbelief that, from whatever source of 'delusion,' turned the transcendental into the 'semblance of truth' (*BL*

2:6). By treating the soul as drama, psychoanalysis reduces the soul to fiction.

By expanding *Biographia Literaria,* Coleridge struggled to find a *modus vivendi* between the personal and the universal, aware that the age was more interested in the entertainment value of the personal or anecdotal, what Wordsworth called its 'degrading thirst after outrageous stimulation' (*William Wordsworth* 599), than in the alien nature of the universal. But he would never fully reconcile the 'sacred power' of his 'self-intuition' with the more immediate psychoanalytical awareness that he considered this power's rather feeble shadow. That is to say, he could not confront the fact that the unconscious act of self-intuition, as the action of the primary imagination, is readily unveiled at the conscious level as an 'infinite I AM' whose infiniteness is the work of the inflated ego, which Byron saw as Coleridge's messianic delusions. Vacillating between the ego of Freudian psychoanalysis and the Self of Jungian depth psychology, I found myself caught in a similar struggle. When in the name of the Báb the inflated ego takes possession of the will, the conscious work of the secondary imagination can take a demonic turn, as Coleridge well knew. Here the 'infinite I AM' becomes Satan or Geraldine as 'the fearful resolve to find in itself alone the one absolute motive of action, under which all other motives from within and from without must be either subordinated or crushed' (*Lay Sermons* 65).

In *Answer to Job* (1959) Jung confronted the Shadow of Yahweh, the *deus absconditus* whom Blake identifies as Urizen or Satan. Hidden in his limited, arrested perfection, Yahweh does not realize he has reduced the human condition to the 'circumscrib'd' creation of Newton's compasses, what Coleridge calls the mechanical philosophy's 'force of brute matter.' In Jung's account of the myth, Yahweh's elder son Satan is envious of his younger brother's election as the 'only begotten.' With Yahweh's permission, Jung argues, Satan thus inflicts upon humanity the suffering that is the psychological requirement for their redemption. For Jung, the divine act of resurrection that vicariously atones for original sin becomes a fully human act necessary for the individuation process, the archetypal pattern of which he identifies with Satan's rebellion against Yahweh. In the service of the ego rather than the Self, the Promethean energy of this Satan archetype can produce a Napoleon or, worse, Hitler.

It is a psychological rule that when an archetype has lost it metaphysical hypostasis, it becomes identified with the conscious mind of the individual, which it influences and refashions in its own form. And since an archetype always possesses a certain numinosity, the integration of the numen generally produces an inflation of the subject. It is therefore entirely in accord with psychological expectations that Goethe should dub his Faust a Superman. In recent times this type has extended beyond Nietzsche into the field of political psychology, and its incarnation in man has had all the consequences that might have been expected to follow from such a mis-appropriation of power. ('Foreword' 315)

Exploring 'how and why the devil got into the consulting-room of the psychiatrist' ('Foreword' 315), Jung, unlike Freud, mythically identifies the return of the repressed with what has not yet reached consciousness rather than with what consciousness abjects. For him the unconscious is thus a creative source, what Shelley describes as 'The everlasting uni-verse of things / Flow[ing] through the [one] mind' ('Mont Blanc' 1–2). Always resisting institutionalization, this potentially limitless energy is the ceaselessly unfolding God image whose mythical goal is the *hieros gamos* or inner marriage of masculine and feminine, which Shelley cele-brates as the reunion of Asia and Prometheus. Following his heart attack in 1944, Jung in a hallucinatory state experienced this inner marriage at an unconscious level as the Jewish Kabbalistic marriage of Malcuth and Tifereth or as Revelation's Marriage of the Lamb in Jerusalem. Both scenarios unveil the hidden God and Jung himself becomes the inner marriage, dictated to him in the veiled language of the Kaballa in what he described as *The Seven Sermons to the Dead written by Basilides in Alexan-dria, the City where the East toucheth the West*. The first sermon begins: 'The dead came back from Jerusalem, where they found not what they sought. They prayed me let them in and besought my word, and thus I began my teaching' (cited in *MDR* 378). At the end of the seventh sermon the hu-man soul, confined in a transitory space, opens itself to the *pleroma*, its in-finite space in which glows a single star, which becomes the soul's eternal home after it leaves its transitory life. Known or unknown to itself, the soul, collectively named Abraxas (Shelley's Adonais), has been inwardly moving toward this eternal home as the creator and destroyer of all gods and demons. As the soul departs from its temporal home, these gods and demons, like the dissolution of a spell, go up in flame as fantasy, burned by the very fire for which the soul thirsts. The One that eternally remains is the single star inhabiting empty or neutral space as the infinite, which for Wolfgang Pauli, as we shall see in the next chapter, becomes the long-sought quantum equation uniting into one the psychophysical motions of the cosmos as its unveiled fourth dimension.

The painted veil, by those who were, called life,
Which mimicked, as with colours idly spread,
All men believed or hoped, is torn aside –
The loathsome mask has fallen                              (*PU* 3.4.190–3)

declares Shelley's 'Spirit of the Hour.' 'All Human Forms identified even
Tree Metal Earth & Stone,' declare Blake's more charitable 'Four Living
Creatures Chariots of Humanity Divine Incomprehensible,' which 'In
beautiful Paradises expand,'

                                          all
Human Forms Identified, living going forth & returning wearied
Into the Planetary lives of Years Months Days & Hours reposing
And then Awaking into his Bosom in the Life of Immortality
And I heard the name of their Emanations they are named Jerusalem.
                                   (*J* 99.1, 98.24–5, 2–5)

# 2

For Derrida, madness is at once the 'absence of a work' and the immediate presence of the Cogito, which the mind's sanity must betray.
Redeeming this betrayal, what he calls 'protection,' comes with the re-
fusal to intern madness by acknowledging it as the mind's 'limit and
profound resource.' With Derrida's help, I have come to the conviction
that my dream of the Báb embraces rather than rejects my mind as the
dream's 'limit and profound resource.' In this sense I have come to know
my mind as 'the sacred power of self-intuition' that, 'while it exists in
all, does not in all rise to consciousness.' For Coleridge this meant repeating on the 'finite' level the 'eternal act of creation in the infinite
I AM,' the unconscious model for my previous book that informs the
current book's more conscious effort. Coleridge found his model in the
Christian scheme of salvation that, 'though not discoverable by human
Reason, is yet in accordance with it.' For him, thought moves toward the
'filial WORD [...] whose choral Echo is the Universe.' Confronted by a
satanic addiction that restrained the spell cast by the incantation of his
verse, Coleridge replaces the spell with the ecclesiastical chant of 'Liturgy and Homilies.' But he also thus sacrificed his poetic power, which
he paradoxically experienced as freedom. Opium usurped Coleridge's
God-given identity by submitting the mind to the mechanical philoso-

phy. But this passivity also opened the mind to an apocalyptic power that gradually overwhelmed Coleridge in a way that the weapons of mass destruction resulting from quantum physics may yet overwhelm us all.

If I was first tempted to embrace the Báb as a revelation of the 'filial WORD,' I gradually came to accept my unconscious and speechless somersault in the air as the 'limit and profound resource of my mind.' But I also became aware of the dangerous inflation that comes with viewing my dream of the Báb in terms of the ego's demonic embrace. For this reason, among others, I have been aware of the arduous labour this dream imposes upon my 'Intellectual powers,' as distinct from my 'Corporeal Understanding,' in order to avoid psychosis. My struggle to read Blake, mirroring his own struggle in his 'Printing house in Hell,' and accompanied by my reading of Jung as a psychological commentary on the creative process, made Blake my chief poetic rather than religious mentor. For indeed I had no lasting religious mentor to help process my dream. I feared – and continue to fear – the impact of religion upon Blake's understanding of the creative imagination when its inherently 'poetic' nature settles into a form of worship, as it did in Coleridge and Wordsworth. At the same time, I recognize the psychic fact that by writing this book the creative process that is struggling to impose a shape upon my dream is becoming increasingly difficult. *Biographia Literaria* rather arbitrarily concludes with Coleridge's Anglican processional, first into twilight and then into 'Night, sacred Night.' Knowing that night is a psychological blackness, he is presumably able to transform blackness into light through the action of grace. I have not yet reached that state of darkness. When and if I do, I will not predict in advance the outcome, lest I receive it as the product of my own conscious devising.

# 3

Prefacing his revised version of *Wandlungen und Symbole der Libido* (1912), first translated into English as *The Psychology of the Unconscious* (1916), and eventually as *Symbols of Transformation*, Jung writes in 1950: 'Old age and illness released me at last from my professional duties and gave me the necessary time to contemplate the sins of my youth' (*Symbols* xxiii). Jung was unhappy with the first edition because 'There was no opportunity to let my thoughts mature. The whole thing came upon me like a landslide that cannot be stopped.' Only in the final chapters did he realize that the landslide was his break with Freud and his theory of sexuality

based in the Oedipal dimension of incest. Jung describes the effects of
this break as an 'explosion [described in his memoirs as taking place in
his red-hot diaphragm] of all those psychic contents which could find no
room, no breathing-space, in the constricting atmosphere of Freudian
psychology and its narrow outlook.'

A key influence on the writing of *Wandlungen* was Théodore Flournoy's
*From India to the Planet Mars: A Case of Multiple Personality with Imaginary
Languages* (1899), which Jung read while working with schizophrenics at the Burghölzli Clinic. On several occasions Jung discussed his
troubled relationship to Freud with Flournoy, who 'put his finger on
Freud's rationalism, which made much of him understandable, as well
as explaining his onesidedness' ('Théodore Flournoy'). Whereas Jung
was earlier drawn to Freud's scientific positivism, which always found
what it was expecting, Flournoy 'wanted nothing' from his cases. Or as
Jung explains, 'Under the influence of Freud I acquired knowledge, but
nothing became clear.' Nothing became clear, I suggest, because in the
schizophrenic, especially Miss Miller, whose fantasies form the matrix
of *Wandlungen*, the fantasy is all too clear – that is to say, absolutely real.
Hence, the chances of dislodging the fantasies from the schizophrenic's
mind are analytically remote, if not impossible. Flournoy's advice to Jung
was invaluable in approaching these fantasies: 'he taught me to maintain
a distance between myself and the object, and supported me in my efforts to classify and maintain things in a broad horizon. His method was
more descriptive, without letting in suppositions, and in spite of a warm
and lively interest in the patient, he always held himself at a considerable
distance. Thus he never lost sight of the whole' ('Théodore Flournoy').

Jung came to know this 'whole' as the archaic ground of all consciousness whose immediacy became evident to him in his work with schizophrenics. For Jung the growth of consciousness depended upon the
conscious mind's access to this collective unconscious. By embracing the
collective unconscious, Donald Winnicott argues, Jung healed his own
'childhood schizophrenia' (491), though by constructing a fortress to
keep reality out (or as Wolfgang Giegerich argues, Bollingen became
Jung's Disneyland.) Jung saw things differently. In *Symbols of Transformation* he describes the supposedly 'unintelligible' hallucination of a schizophrenic patient who 'told me he could see an erect phallus on the sun.
When he moved his head from side to side, he said the sun's phallus
moved with it, and *that was where the wind came from*'. (101). Only once
Jung found out that similar 'visions' occurred in 'Mithraic liturgy' did he
see an 'astonishing' parallel between schizophrenia and religion: 'it is

not a question of a specifically racial heredity, but of a universally human characteristic. Nor is it a question of *inherited ideas*, but of a functional disposition to produce the same, or very similar, ideas. This disposition I later called the *archetype*' (102). By confronting this archetypal reality, Jung was able to break free of Freud's dogmatic and wholly Oedipal emphasis on sexuality.

This break at once left Jung with a myth and revealed to him the archetypal dimension of what he saw as Freud's own myth of sexuality:

> Myth, says a Church Father, is 'what is believed always, everywhere, by everybody'; hence the man who thinks he lives without myth, or outside it, is an exception. He is like one uprooted, having no true link either with the past, or with the ancestral life which continues within him, or yet with contemporary human society. He does not live in a house like other men, does not eat and drink like other men, but lives a life of his own, sunk in a subjective mania of his own devising, which he believes to be the newly discovered truth. This plaything of his reason never grips his vitals. It may occasionally lie heavy on his stomach, for that organ is apt to reject the products of reason as indigestible. The psyche is not of today; its ancestry goes back many millions of years. Individual consciousness is only the flower and the fruit of a season, sprung from the perennial rhizome beneath the earth; and it would find itself in better accord with the truth if it took the existence of the rhizome into its calculations. For the root matter is the mother of all things. (*Symbols* xxiv)

In Freud's materialistic psychology, in which the soul is conceived as the biological libido or 'root matter,' Jung experienced what Coleridge and Shelley experienced in the mechanical philosophy: a 'subjective mania' of Freud's own devising, like Hartley's associationism, by which Jung had been at first seduced. According to Shelley, the Romantics were trapped in a culture in which 'the accumulation of the materials of external life exceed the quantity of the power of assimilating them to the internal laws of human nature. The body has then become too unwieldy for that which animates it' (*DP* 531). What animates the body is the 'one Spirit's plastic stress,' which, as the operation of the imagination, is indeed something divine.' Shelley continues:

> It is at once the centre and circumference of knowledge; it is that which comprehends all science [as, for Jung, the psyche contains all science], and that to which all science must be referred. It is at the same time the root

and blossom of all other systems of thought; it is that from which all spring, and that which adorns all; and that which, if blighted, denies the fruit and the seed, and withholds from the barren world the nourishment and the succession of the scions of the tree of life. (531)

The struggle to bring to consciousness this 'tree of life,' Jung's 'perennial rhizome beneath the earth' where the archetypes dwell, propels the Romantic quest to construct a myth able to contain this collective unconscious as the spiritual form of the 'Vegetable Body.' As Asia declares to Panthea,

> The fragments of the cloud are scattered up –
> The wind that lifts them disentwines my hair –
> Its billows now sweep o'er mine eyes – my brain
> Grows dizzy – I see thin shapes within the mist.

Among these shapes Panthea describes 'A countenance with beckoning smiles – there burns / An azure fire within its golden locks – / Another and another – hark! they speak!' What speaks is a chorus of spirits, not unlike those that flooded Jung's home. 'To the Deep, to the Deep,' they cry,

> Down, Down!
> Through the shade of Sleep,
> Through the cloudy strife
> Of Death and of Life;
> Through the veil and the bar
> Of things which seem and are,
> Even to the steps of the remotest Throne.
> Down, Down! (*PU* 2.3.47–62)

The 'remotest Throne' is Demogorgon, about to be vacated as the mind, like Derrida's Cogito, becomes divine madness. 'I see a mighty Darkness / Filling the seat of power,' Panthea announces;

> and rays of gloom
> Dart round, as light from the meridian Sun,
> Ungazed upon and shapeless: – neither limb
> Nor form nor outline, yet we feel it is
> A living Spirit. (2.4.2–7)

The 'light' from the 'meridian Sun' is the unrefracted light of the 'white radiance of Eternity.' As soon as the 'sacred few' touch the world with its 'living flame,' they fly 'back like eagles to their native noon.' As the 'living flame' fades, all that is left are 'rays of gloom.'

Shelley's vision stages Jung's encounter with the collective unconscious of the unmediated schizophrenic mind, which Jung learned objectively to perceive rather than to become possessed by. Whereas for Winnicott the collective unconscious was Jung's barrier (as if all children were not schizophrenic), for Jung the collective unconscious was what Derrida calls 'economy,' not merely as the source of consciousness but as 'the work's limit and profound resource,' 'from which all spring.' Again, this is what Coleridge means by the primary imagination as the 'living Power and prime Agent of all human Perception,' the sheer impossibility of which likely became the underlying 'rhizome' of his addiction. Like mania, addiction has no 'economy'; it experiences economy only as 'betrayal.' Confronted by the nightmare that perception became, Coleridge had, short of madness, no alternative but religion.

But the 'Corporeal Understanding' remains. For Jung and the Romantics before him, myth and its entire psychic machinery as the soul's immemorial record of itself had been reduced to Keats's fond believing lyre/liar. If it was any longer possible to revive myth as a living reality, the poet needed to descend into some untrodden region of the mind. When in *Alastor* Shelley describes the Narrator's mind as 'a long-forgotten lyre, / Suspended in the solitary dome / Of some mysterious and deserted fane,' he likely had in mind the post-*Excursion* Wordsworth, who for Shelley used his Christian faith to repress his suspended disbelief in the creative imagination. Like Coleridge, Wordsworth could no longer allow himself to be 'duped' by the 'awful doubt' and 'dramatic truth' of 'illustrious superstition,' or 'deluded' by the frail spells of the imagination's 'generous error.' Shelley *can* because he refuses to believe that Christ's sacrifice releases humanity from its fallen state. When the Furies confront Prometheus, otherwise committed to what Shelley calls the 'intellectual philosophy' (*SPP* 508), with an image of himself as the crucified Christ, he cries: 'Oh horrible! Thy name I will not speak, / It hath become a curse' (*PU* 1.603–4).

# 4

Jung feared the inflationary dangers of the Romantic imagination partly because he was so strongly attracted to them. In his first rather violent encounter with his inner feminine or anima, whom he identified with 'the "soul," in the primitive sense,' he resisted her apparent determination to persuade him that what he was doing in writing down and even painting his fantasies was art. Catching hold of her, he shouted: '"No, it is not art! On the contrary, it is nature."' When she did not reply, Jung 'reflected' that the '"woman within [him]" did not have the speech centers [he] had. And so I suggested that she use mine.' While Jung does not record the 'long statement' she 'came through with,' he does say that it was 'full of a deep cunning,' or at least it 'seemed' to be. 'If I had taken these fantasies of the unconscious as art,' Jung goes on, 'they would have carried no more conviction than visual perceptions, as if I were watching a movie. I would have felt no moral obligation toward them. The anima might then have easily seduced me into believing I was a misunderstood artist, and that my so-called artistic nature gave me the right to neglect reality. [...] Thus the insinuations of the anima, the mouthpiece of the unconscious, can utterly destroy a man' (*MDR* 186–7).

In the anima Jung confronted his own psychotic corner. After ten years of working with schizophrenics at the Burghölzli, he had every reason to fear the 'woman within [him].' 'In the final analysis the decisive factor is always consciousness, which can understand the manifestations of the unconscious and take up a position toward them,' he concludes, determined to silence the poet in himself who, in 'Nietzsche, Hölderlin, and many others' insane drove them insane (*MDR* 187, 177). Terrified of the anima, what his mother in his phallic dream between the ages of three and four called the 'man-eater,' Jung, 'enduring these storms,' knew 'from the beginning' that there was a 'demonic strength' in him (12, 177). This left him in 'no doubt' that, in searching for their 'meaning,' he 'was obeying a higher will.' '[T]hat feeling,' he asserts, 'continued to uphold me until I had mastered the task' (177). But the mastery did not come easily, for the anima could be overpowering. The sound of her voice, as the archetypal unconscious expressing itself through him, grated on his nerves, 'as when someone draws his nails down a plaster wall, or scrapes his knife against a plate' (178). When she took possession of his own vocal chords, he 'had no choice but to write everything down in the style' she 'selected.' 'Sometimes it was as if I were hearing it with my ears,' Jung explains, 'sometimes feeling it with my mouth, as if my tongue were formulating words; now and then I heard myself whispering aloud' (*MDR* 178). In the Greek myth, King Tereus rapes Philomel and cuts out her tongue so that she cannot tell. Transformed into a nightingale, she struggles in vain to articulate the source of her grief.

'The change of Philomel, by the barbarous king / So rudely forced,'
Eliot writes in *The Waste Land*;

> yet there the nightingale
> Filled all the desert with inviolable voice
> And still she cried, and still the world pursues
> 'Jug Jug' to dirty ears.                                    (99–103)

In Jung's fantasy, Philomel becomes Philemon, who first appeared to
Jung in a dream in which the sky is 'covered not by clouds but by flat
brown clods of earth' (*MDR* 182). Out of these clods ('"Jug Jug" to dirty
ears') appeared Philemon as 'a winged being sailing across the sky' holding 'four keys, one of which he clutched as if he were about to open a
lock' (182–3). The lock he was about to open was to the gate of Jung's two
towers at Bollingen over which he inscribed the words '*Philemonis Sacrum
– Fausti Poemitentia,*' or 'Shrine of Philemon – Repentance of Faust.' The
latter referred to Goethe's Christian redemption of Faust by disposing of
Mephistopheles, whom, in the same way that Blake or Shelley redeemed
Milton's Satan, Jung saw as Goethe's real hero and Jung's 'personality
No. 2,' his 'daimon of creativity' (45, 358). At Bollingen, Jung returned
to Mephistopheles as the womb of the Great Mother as the Fourth or
eternal feminine, who in Goethe had taken the hermaphroditic form of
the unresolved *hieros gamos* rather than the true androgynous form as the
inner union of masculine and feminine. Goethe's disposal of Mephistopheles thus became the unfinished work not only of Jung but of the
entire Christian aeon, a labour bestowed upon Jung as the 'illegitimate
son' to Goethe's Great Father (234). This 'daimon of creativity' would
raise Jung to his true legitimacy, a transformation that would redeem
Goethe's disposal of Mephistopheles by opening the fourth gate, the
feminine Fourfold.

To do so, Jung remained obedient to the unconscious, willing to be
duped by its illustrious superstition. In his immediate experience of
schizophrenic patients, or in his devotion to alchemy, Jung became aware
that the psychic operations of the unconscious are 'instigated' by what
Shelley calls a 'sacred thirst of doubtful knowledge.' Just as my reading
of the Romantics made me the willing victim of this 'sacred thirst,' Jung
willingly suspended his disbelief by endowing the imagination with a
'semblance of truth' borrowed from his 'inward nature' as the 'shadows'
of it (*BL* 2:6). This nature's real truth – if it is real – one cannot know. My
own dream of the Báb instantly confronted me with apparitions of this

truth, but for years remained too unabsorbed for me to endow it with the reality it instantly imposed. What I was in fact confronting was what Wolfgang Pauli confronted in his alchemical dreams, some forty of which Jung analysed in *Psychology and Alchemy* (1944). In these dreams, which Pauli refers to as 'background physics,' he confronts the unconscious or anima as the highly problematic or indeterminate observer who at the microphysical level influences what is observed. Both Bohr and Pauli had observed this subjective aspect of quantum physics, even though Einstein rejected it 'as a *regressive* tendency,' an aberration in quantum theory, which would eventually be corrected by 'a return to the old ideal of the detached observer.'

As Pauli explains to Jung,

> I remarked to Bohr at the time that Einstein was regarding as an imperfection of wave mechanics within physics what in fact was an imperfection of physics within life. Mr. Bohr readily agreed with this statement. Nevertheless, I had to admit that there was an imperfection or incompleteness somewhere, even if it was outside the realm of physics, and since then Einstein has never stopped trying to bring me around to his way of thinking. (*Atom* 121)

For Einstein there could be no such imperfection in nature, because for him God does not play with dice. But Pauli's radical challenge to Einstein, which eventually won Pauli a 1945 Nobel Prize, had confronted him with 'problems of feelings' that brought on a severe personal crisis, which in 1931 had 'led to [his] becoming acquainted with analytical psychology' (121). Out of this crisis he realized within quantum physics 'an imperfection of life' or principle of indeterminacy that, via his work with Jung, he identified with the unconscious in the uncertain grip of the anima, which struggle was nevertheless necessary to life's desire for completeness.

Put another way, this feminine confronted the 'perfection' of Pauli's otherwise masculine desire for a scientific objectivity beyond subjective observation with its own '*Negative Capability*,' which in quantum mechanics is the potential work of the soul, and of soul-making, in bringing the subatomic world to the light of consciousness. Without the anima, quantum physics was suspended between the contrary motions of particle and wave, caught at the subatomic level in what Shelley in 'On Love' calls 'the chasm of an insufficient void' (*SPP* 503), which 'void' the mind, in the name of love, is compelled to penetrate and inhabit as its long sought home. '*Just as physics seeks completeness, your analytical psychology seeks a home,*' Pauli explains to Jung. 'For there is no denying the fact that psychology, like an illegitimate child of the spirit, leads an esoteric, special existence beyond the fringe of what is generally acknowledged to be the academic world.' To which he adds: '*But this is how the archetype of the* coniunctio *is constellated.* Whether and when this *coniunctio* [or inner marriage of masculine and feminine] will be realized I do not know, but I am in no doubt at all that this would be the finest fate that could happen to both physics and psychology' (*Atom* 122).

Like Wordsworth and Coleridge, Jung and Pauli believed that physics and psychology, body and soul, might merge in the divine marriage or New Jerusalem as the Kingdom of God on earth. '[L]ong before the blissful hour arrives,' writes Wordsworth, '[I][w]ould chant, in lonely peace, the spousal verse / Of this great consummation' (Prospectus to *The Recluse* 56–8). But also like Wordsworth and Coleridge, the relations between Jung and Pauli deteriorated, after which Jung, in declining health, struggled to hold onto his psychology, in particular by releasing the prophetic voice of the anima. The brutal loss of her tongue had caused in Jung a major heart attack that brought him in a hallucinatory state to the Marriage Feast of the Lamb where, in the presence of the heartbroken anima, Jung himself became the healing marriage. His life revived and renewed, he was then taken over by an altered state of consciousness that produced *Answer to Job*, a feverish act of dictation in which the raped Philomel becomes the released *dea abscondita* who tells her terrifying tale, which in the telling becomes the anima's or Sophia's recovery of her tongue. As Eliot writes in *The Wasteland*, echoing the Elizabethan onomatopoeia for the nightingale's song,

Twit twit twit
Jug jug jug jug jug jug
  So rudely forc'd.
Tereu.                                                    (*The Wasteland* 203–6)

As we have already seen, in his youth Jung, under the influence of his mother's No. 2 personality, had recognized Mephistopheles as Goethe's unacknowledged hero. Now Mephistopheles was vindicated as the redeemer of Jung's dark feminine. As Lamia, she is the serpent woman now become Lucifer, Satan's eternal form as his union with the feminine in himself. Though not in a fully conscious state, Jung had mythically enacted the move from Three to Four, which he argued still required quantum physics to be rationally understood.

Jung recognized that 'the Christian idea of sacrifice' had 'led in the course of a few centuries to a development of consciousness which would have been quite out of the question but for this training [in the transcendence of human nature].' 'Developments of this kind,' he goes on to argue, 'are not arbitrary inventions or mere intellectual fantasies; they have their own inner logic and necessity.' For Jung, belief in the Christian dogmas, which affirm the divine enactment of transcendence in the crucifixion, constitutes a renunciation as opposed to a mere taming of man's animal instincts 'for the sake of a spiritual goal beyond this world.' 'This ideal,' he insists, 'is a hard schooling which cannot help alienating man from his own nature and, to a large degree, from nature in general' (*Symbols* 435). The 'inner logic and necessity' of this Christian ideal lies in its teleological imperative, which, as the eternal providence of Eros, governs the operations of the psyche to produce a 'development of consciousness' otherwise impossible. Jung believed he had found this development in alchemy, which took the projected form of a fantasy unavailable to consciousness until the projection was first withdrawn and then absorbed by the scientifically disinterested mind. But Jung also realized that subjecting psychic phenomena to such rational scrutiny could rob them of their unconscious container as fantasy before they are ready to leave. That is to say, if unconscious contents are rudely forced before they have reached full term, they may not survive as living phenomena under the laboratory conditions of objective perception.

Jung describes this dilemma in the archetypal terms of his upbringing, in which he is a '"dumb" Parsifal' forced to witness in silence his father, stricken as Amfortas, the Fisher King, with a wound that would not heal (*MDR* 215). Jung's father studied Oriental languages at the University of Göttingen and wrote his dissertation on the Arabic version of the Song of Songs, the quintessential biblical account of the anima even more extravagantly elaborated in its Arabic version, which for the Sufi poets became an erotic model of the *hieros gamos*. In Europe it became an Arabic source of courtly love, in which, Shelley argues,

Love became a religion, the idols of whose worship were ever present. It was as if the statues of Apollo and the Muses had been endowed with life and motion and had walked forth among their worshippers; so that earth became peopled by the inhabitants of a diviner world. The familiar appearances and proceedings of life became wonderful and heavenly; and a paradise was created as out of the wrecks of Eden. (*DP* 525)

Jung's mortally wounded father lived as a country parson in 'the wrecks of Eden' in something of the same way that Keats in *The Fall of Hyperion* finds himself in an 'arbour with a drooping roof' where a feast is spread out, 'Which, nearer seen, seem'd refuse of a meal / By angel tasted, or our mother Eve' (1.25, 30–1). As if struggling in vain to inhabit the Arabic paradise of the Song of Songs, that is to say, Jung's father was poisoned by its Protestant remainders. 'But, as once Gilgamesh, bringing back the magic herb from the Western Land [...] was robbed of his treasure by the demon-serpent,' Jung writes of Hölderlin's *Hyperion*, 'so Hölderlin's poem dies away in a painful lament, which tells us that his descent to the shadows will be followed by no resurrection in this world' (*Symbols* 413–14). The same fate confronts Keats's Lamia when fixed by the philosopher Apollonius's eye: she returns to her serpent form. Vanishing from Lycius's creating mind, she leaves his 'arms [...] empty of delight,' his marriage robe becoming his winding sheet (*Lamia* 307). Except for Blake, Romantic poetry is at best suspended between resurrection and death; at its darkest level, as in Keats or Shelley, poetry enacts its own burial.

Analysing the fantasies of a schizophrenic in *Symbols of Transformation*, Jung concludes that it might be best to let the hero of the fantasies die as 'not much more than the personification of a regressive and infantile reverie, having neither the will nor the power to make good his aversion from this world by fishing up another from the primeval ocean of the unconscious, which would truly have been an heroic act.' Jung then continues:

Such a sacrifice can only be accomplished through whole-hearted dedication to life [which, Jung believed, Freud lacked because ultimately he was dedicated to *thanatos*]. All the libido that was tied up in family bonds [the Oedipus complex] must be withdrawn from the narrower circle into the larger one, because the psychic health of the adult individual, who in childhood was a mere particle revolving in a rotary system, demands that he should himself become the centre of a new system. That such a step includes the solution, or at least some consideration, of the sexual problem is obvious enough, for unless this is done the unemployed libido will inevitably remain fixed in the unconscious endogamous relationship to the parents [family romance] and will seriously hamper the individual's freedom. [...] For if he allows his libido to get stuck in a childish milieu, and does not free it for higher purposes, he falls under the spell of unconscious compulsion [repetition compulsion]. Wherever he may be, the unconscious will then recreate the infantile milieu by projecting his complexes, thus reproducing all over again, and in defiance of his vital interests, the same dependence and lack of freedom which formerly characterized his relations with his parents. (*Symbols* 414–15)

Although Coleridge constructed a Christian identity to resolve this 'lack of freedom,' in his poetry this effort remains an infantile compulsion in which the Wedding Guest, bound to the Mariner's 'strange power of speech,' 'listens like a three years' child' (587, 15). As if to break free of Freud's similar hold on Jung's psyche, Jung, for two months contemplating in silence the terror of the break, eventually concluded *Symbols of Transformation* with the following statement: 'To the extent that the world and everything in it is a product of thought, the sacrifice of the [sexual] libido that strives back to the [Oedipal] past necessarily results in the creation of the world' (415). More firmly grounding himself in this new world by extensively revising and expanding his original 1912 text of *Symbols* in 1950, Jung also more firmly grounded himself in the world itself by confronting and resolving his own fear of schizophrenia embodied in the fantasies of his schizophrenic patients – which is also to say in his own psychosis.

Jung continues: 'For him who looks backwards the whole world, even the starry sky, becomes the mother who bends over him and enfolds him on all sides, and from the renunciation of this image, and of the longing for it, arises the picture of the world as we know it today. This simple thought is what constitutes the meaning of the cosmic sacrifice, a good example being the slaying of Tiamat, the Babylonian mother-dragon, from whose body heaven and earth were made' (415). The slaying of Tiamat was symbolized in Jung's dream, shortly after his break with Freud in 1913, in which Jung kills Siegfried, the unconscious hero of his mother's Teutonic myth. Like Jung's binding to Freud, this binding to the mother was no longer life affirming:

It was before dawn; the eastern sky was already bright, and the stars fading. Then I heard Siegfried's horn sounding over the mountains and I knew that we [he was accompanied by an unknown, brown-skinned savage] had to kill him. [...] Then Siegfried appeared high up on the crest of the mountain, in

the first ray of the rising sun. On a chariot made of the bones of the dead
he drove at furious speed down the precipitous slope. When he turned the
corner, we shot at him, and he plunged down, struck dead. (*MDR* 180)

A similar killing occurred in a dream Jung had the night before his
mother's death:

> Suddenly I heard a piercing whistle that seemed to resound through the
> whole universe. [...] Then there were crashings in the underbrush, and a
> gigantic wolfhound with fearful, gaping maw burst forth. [...] It tore past
> me, and I suddenly knew: the Wild Huntsman had commanded it to carry
> away a human soul. [...] [T]he next morning I received the news of my
> mother's passing. (313)

The symbolic killing of Siegfried and the Wild Huntsman carrying off
his mother to the *sälig Lüt*, 'Wotan's army of departed souls' (231), pre-
figure Jung's later troubled relations with the Third Reich. The dream
figures of Siegfried as the rising sun, his chariot made of the bones of
the dead, and the gigantic wolfhound of Wotan taking his mother to
her ancestral home, belong to an energy released by his 'daimon of creativity,' which 'ruthlessly' had its way with Jung, its higher purpose or
meaning not always immediately discernible (358). With the dropping
of the atomic bomb on Hiroshima in August 1945, however, Jung makes
it clear that 'far beyond the borders of Germany [now in ruins],' a 'most
pernicious schism that has ever beset Christianity' was taking place: an
ultimate schism within the Godhead itself, which is, or may be, about to
end the world ('Why I Am Not a Catholic' 647). The highest intellectual
achievement of the human mind in quantum physics had released into
motion a new world. But its first offspring was also the instrument of its
destruction. Enacting a similar *enantiodromia*, Mary Shelley, with her husband in mind, who himself participated in its creation, wrote the dream-
inspired novel *Frankenstein*, which she subtitled *The Modern Prometheus*.


# 5


In Blake's *Milton*, the sleeping Milton is dreaming *Paradise Lost*, which
Urania dictates to him 'unimplor'd' as 'unpremeditated Verse' (*PL* 9.22,
24). The dreaming Milton enters Blake's body as a Spectre or Shadow at
the metatarsus of Blake's left foot. Having been imprisoned in his epic

for 'One hundred years, pondring the intricate mazes of Providence,' Milton as its unfulfilled author has, like the poem itself, assumed 'A mournful form double; hermaphroditic: male & female / In one wonderful body' (*M* 2.17, 14[15].37–8). This grotesque shape is the result of the way the poem was inscribed by his 'Sixfold Emanation' or 'Selfhood,' 'those three females whom his Wives, & those three whom his Daughters / Had represented and contain' (17[19].1–2). Their containment is a demonic parody of his true Emanation or bride, Urania, who in *Paradise Lost* remains bound to the 'Almighty Father' (*PL* 7.11). This binding contorts the Father, the tyrant Urizen or God of natural religion. In this tormented shape Milton's 'Sixfold Emanation' inscribes 'Him' as an 'Almighty Power' (*PL* 1.44) as they unwillingly receive the blind Milton's dictation 'in blood & jealousy / [...] dividing & uniting without end or number' (*M* 17[19].7–8). The God of *Paradise Lost* becomes a kind of Ixion wheel binding Urania to tongueless silence.

This bound Urania is heard in Blake's voice as he reads *Paradise Lost* aloud to his trembling, strangely unconsummated wife Catherine. That is to say, in *Milton* Urania enters in fear and trembling into Blake's garden at Felpham as the twelve-year-old virgin Ololon, who searches for Milton in order to fulfil what was left unfulfilled in *Paradise Lost*. Their torturous consummation, enacted by first casting off the 'rotten rags of Memory,' largely constitutes the psychic action of Blake's epic, which as 'wondrous [...] acts' remained 'unknown' to him, 'Except remotely' (40[46].2–3). 'Obey thou the Words of the Inspired Man,' Blake's Milton cries 'in terrible majesty' to Ololon. 'All that can be annihilated must be annihilated / That the Children of Jerusalem may be saved from slavery' (40[46].28–31). Milton's voice is alarmingly like Jung's in *Answer to Job*, for what 'must be annihilated' in *The Seven Sermons to the Dead* is the historical record of Jerusalem as the 'Corporeal Understanding' of the visionary city. This record must be cast out, which is to say transformed by the imagination into its true form as 'Allegory addressd to the Intellectual powers.' Or as the dead say in *Seven Sermons*, 'We have come back from Jerusalem where we found not what we sought.'

At the trumpet sound of Blake's voice Ololon, like Milton, has left the unhappy heaven of Milton's epic and descended into Blake's garden where Milton's poem is being recreated. Here is how Blake describes what is happening within him as he reads Milton's epic aloud:

Suddenly around Milton on my Path, the Starry Seven
Burnd terrible! my Path became a solid fire, as bright

As the clear Sun & Milton silent came down on my Path.
And there went forth from the Starry limbs of the Seven: Forms
Human; with Trumpets innumerable, sounding articulate
As the Seven spake; and they stood in a mighty Column of Fire
Surrounding Felpham's Vale, reaching the Mundane Shell, Saying

Awake Albion awake! reclaim thy Reasoning Spectre. Subdue
Him to the Divine Mercy, Cast him down into the Lake
Of Los, that ever burneth with fire, ever & ever Amen!
Let the Four Zoa's awake from Slumbers of Six Thousand Years.

(39[44].3–13)

The casting down of Milton's 'Selfhood' into 'the Lake of Los' is the
work of Blake's incisor on the copper plate in his 'Printing House in
Hell.' With the help of 'corrosives,' 'salutary and medicinal,' this process
will melt away 'the apparent surfaces' of Milton's epic and display 'the
infinite which was hid.' That is to say, Blake is melting away the hermaphroditic body of *Paradise Lost*, which he describes as

the Rock Sinai; that body,
Which was on earth born to corruption: & the Six Females
Are Hor & Peor & Bashan & Abarim & Lebanon & Hermon
Seven rocky masses terrible in the Desarts of Midian.    (17[19].14–17)

From the retrospect of sixty-five years, I can now see in Blake's vision of
the sleeping Milton who enters Blake's 'Vegetable Body' at the metatarsus of his left foot to begin the arduous journey of progressive revelation
to Blake's brain, from which Ololon proceeds down the nerves of Blake's
right arm into his writing hand, an analogue in my dream vision of a
somersault in the air that landed me at the feet of the Báb. At that moment, though unknown to myself, just as Milton moved metaphorically
through the body of Blake, I began an equally arduous metaphorical
journey through the body of the Báb's revelation. Put another way, like
Jung confronting the psychotic corner inhabited by his 'daimon of creativity,' I struggled to bring the dream to a consciousness that my brain
could absorb. I was obviously not conscious of making such a journey in
the way I here describe it. By writing this book as some conscious recognition of the dream's largely unconscious process, I have released myself
from the schizophrenic fantasy the dream otherwise is, in Jung's sense

of being released from a split-off other who has taken possession. Blake's apocalyptic description of himself 'outstretchd upon the path / A moment' as Milton's 'clear Sun' suddenly appears and silently comes down the path, is an accurate account of my experience of the dream in the instant of my awakening from it. I have described this instant in terms of Derrida's notion of the Cogito: an instant of madness, which had to be betrayed in order to return to consciousness. Without Blake's account, I might have failed to keep my dream 'within the world' in the way that Blake kept his. Assuming that madness is 'deranged and excessive,' Derrida explains, 'it implies the fundamental derangement and excess of hyperbole which opens and founds the world as such by exceeding it' (57). Without Blake's hyperbolic treatment of this moment, my dream – if remembered at all – might have 'rolled back its impulse on my vacant brain' and so split off from my consciousness of it to live a schizophrenic life of its own. The highest poetry descends into the 'Abysm' of madness to recreate rather than abandon the world.

In a poet like Blake, 'a voice / Is [not] wanting' (*PU* 2.4.115–16). For other Romantics, the descent is darker. When Jung's Siegfried swiftly appears driving the chariot of the rising sun, Jung slays him (though Germany did not). When Keats's Hyperion mounts his chariot, 'Fain would he have commanded, fane took throne / And bid the day begin, if but for change. / He might not: – No, though a primeval God' (*Hyperion* 1.290–2). 'Prometheus shall arise / Henceforth the Sun of this rejoicing world,' Shelley's Asia tells Demogorgon (*PU* 2.4.126–7). 'When shall the destined hour arrive?' she asks. 'Behold!' declares Demogorgon, pointing to the approaching chariots, each driven by 'rainbow-winged steeds' in each of which 'there stands / A wild-eyed charioteer, urging their flight,' 'As if the thing they loved fled on before' (2.4.128–37). In his final fragment, a blinded, Janus-faced Chariot of Life extinguishes in its path everything that is mortal within a lunatic spectacle that Byron, to Shelley's mind, saw in the annual Venice carnival. Only the 'sacred few' escape this masque of death, a demonic parody of the crucifixion reduced to a 'curse.' Having 'touched the world with living flame,' a 'flame' that serves finally only to extinguish itself, the 'sacred few' have 'Fled back like eagles to their native noon.' Unlike Blake, Shelley's descent into madness extinguishes the world: the One split off from the Many, leaving the Many trampled to fragments. The Chariot of Death, which those 'lost in stormy visions' mistakenly call Life, awakens them from 'the dream of life' as that dream darkens into a nightmare. For

Jung in *Symbols of Transformation,* this is the archetypal schizophrenic scenario, which in himself he sought to rescue from the absoluteness of its
own internal dialectic.

Yes, it takes one to know one! More than that of any other Romantic,
Blake's poetry addresses itself to our immediate situation in ways that
provide an objective measure of our understanding of this situation. Rejecting as a 'Delusion / Of Ulro' (*M* 26[28].45–6) the natural causality
that materialism assigns to behaviour at every level, Blake argues for this
materialism's quantum acausality understood as the discontinuity of energy charges as they leap back and forth from one orbit of action to another: Beulah, Generation, Ulro, Eden. All four levels or states of energy
engage each other so that their complex operations become relative
to each other as the shifting conditions that bind, unbind, and rebind
them without number. That is to say, their harmonious integration as
the 'Fourfold,' which Blake insists is the 'Human,' is always in process/
on trial, 'living going forth & returning wearied / Into the Planetary lives
of Years Months Days & Hours reposing / And then Awaking into his
bosom in the Life of Immortality.' This 'bosom' is not Jung's archetypal
mother at the core of Freud's Oedipus complex, who is 'the whole world,
even the starry sky' enfolding him 'on all sides.' It is 'he, who dwells in
flaming fire' (*MHH* 6) and who, as pure energy, is perpetual 'Forgiveness of Sins' (*J* 98.23), which is love. The 'comforter or Desire,' whom he
sends 'that Reason may have Ideas to build on,' is his Emanation, who is
named Jerusalem (*MHH* 6). As his consort or bride, she weaves the fourfold or four-square garment, 'the Four Arts: Poetry, Painting, Music, /
And Architecture which is Science.' In 'Eternity,' Blake explains, these
are 'the Four Faces of Man' woven by New Jerusalem as the apocalyptic
bride of Jehovah (*M* 27[29].55–6). In his fully human form as the operations of the imagination, Jehovah is the 'One Man' whose 'Head,'
'Heart,' 'Loins & Seminal Vessels,' and 'Stomach & Intestines' are the
four gates that stand open to each other, giving and receiving in endless
circulation their shared energies (34[38].14–16). Together these constitute the 'Pulsation of the Artery' in which 'the Poets Work is Done: and
all the Great / Events of Time start forth & are concievd' (29[31].1–2).
When all four gates stand open, the 'whole soul of man into activity' can
'view all these wondrous Imaginations' (34[38].18), Blake's 'Visionary
forms dramatic.'

In *Milton,* Ololon, looking for Milton in order to consummate their
marriage, has to visit each of the four gates in order to open them again

to one another, the doors having been sealed from each other. The result of this sealing is Milton's hermaphroditic body. Its tormented forms – 'the Double-sexed; / The Female-male & the Male-female, self-dividing' (19[21].32–3) – occupy the perverse positions of the fallen four Zoas, who stand before Milton as, for 'one hundred years,' he ponders the 'intricate mazes' of his epic, which keep 'dividing & uniting without end or number.' First explored in the eight nights preceding the apocalypse of Blake's unengraved *Four Zoas*, this is the psychic scene that Ololon enters as Milton ascends up the left side of Blake's body, she descending down his right side from his brain into his writing hand. Step by step this hand must, as *Milton*, record all that is going on. Blake confesses that he cannot account for much of this activity because it lies beyond his power of description. He can only name this activity's readiness to happen as the immediacy of what, as 'Comminglings: from the Head even to the Feet,' is, in the disentangling of its rich perversity, always happening.

Much of this action takes place through animals that in dreams, as Jung explores in *Psychology and Alchemy*, enact the operations of the unconscious. In *Milton* 'terrific Lions & Tygers' especially constellate the energies of the collective unconscious, which as 'All Animals upon the Earth, are prepar'd in all their strength / To go forth to the Great Harvest & Vintage of the Nations.' That is to say, Blake's unconscious is ready as prophet to sound the trumpet of the Resurrection, in which all the atoms of the cosmos will assemble at a newly constellated spiritual centre. As 'Divine Mercy,' this trumpet, Blake's 'Eight Immortal Starry-Ones' (the Eighth Eye as Eden), reverses Newton's Trumpet of Judgment, which proclaims the immutable laws governing the physical motions of matter, because this Trumpet 'drove in fury & fire' the human spirit 'into Ulro dark' (34[38].3–4). Having entered Blake's 'Vegetable Body,' Ololon, given the condition of Blake's 'Loins & Seminal Vessels' as well as his 'Stomach & Intestines,' enters Ulro as a 'void Outside of Existence' in order to release Milton's imagination from its reduction to Newton's compasses.

As a result of Ololon's descent to open the four gates, Blake's Los declares:

Fellow Labourers! The Great Vintage & Harvest is now upon Earth
The whole extent of the Globe is explored: Every scatterd Atom
Of Human Intellect now is flocking to the sound of the Trumpet
All the Wisdom which was hidden in caves & dens, from ancient

Time; is now sought out from Animal & Vegetable & Mineral
The Awakener is come. outstretchd over Europe: the Vision of God is
  fulfilled.
The Ancient Man upon the Rock of Albion Awakes.          (25[27].17–23)

The awakening of the 'Ancient Man upon the Rock of Albion' as a 'Couch
/ Of Death' is, in Blake, the move from the 'Threefold' as the 'Sexual'
('Loins and Seminal Vessels') to the 'Fourfold' (15[17].10–11, 4.5) This
is the marriage of masculine (head) and feminine (heart) as the *hieros
gamos* or 'Human,' all four functions working together as the 'whole soul
of man in activity.' In *Psychology and Alchemy* Jung also describes a powerful mandala dream of the 'World Clock' (205) in which, to cite Blake in
*Jerusalem,* all its 'Years Months Days & Hours' are assembled to a single
point as the mandala's invisible centre or Self. Jung relates this clock to
the 'alchemical hermaphrodite' as the masculine Trinity in his unconscious longing for the feminine Quaternity. This longing is the alchemical hermaphrodite's desire to be released from the time of its agonized
sexuality into the eternity of its resolution as the androgyne, the inner
marriage of the masculine and feminine.

  'Since the figure [of the mandala] has a cosmic aspect – world clock – ,'
Jung writes, analysing one of Pauli's recurrent dreams, 'we must suppose
it to be a small-scale model or perhaps even a source of space-time, or at
any rate an embodiment of it and therefore, mathematically speaking,
four dimensional in nature although only visible in a three-dimensional
projection' (*Psychology and Alchemy* 205). Jung associates this three-dimensional realm with existence itself, what Freud associates with the sexual
libido. Beyond that, however, is the inner marriage that resolves and transcends the outer marriage, like the Papal Bull of Pius XII (1950), which
promulgates the physical ascent of the Virgin Mother to the wedding
chamber of her Son. In the fourth act of Shelley's lyrical drama, the Chorus of the Hours enact this ascension in which, 'drink[ing] the hot speed
of desire' (*PU* 2.5.5), they dissolve into their destined home in Eternity,
which is the soul's 'native noon.' 'The sun will not rise until noon. – Apollo / Is held in Heaven by wonder,' declares Shelley's 'Spirit of the Hour.'
Keats, whose imagination was unequal to holding Apollo in Heaven until the soul had first risen to its 'native noon,' had to reverse the direction of Shelley's action, however painfully. Apollo held in Heaven must
shed his wings and 'with fierce convulse / Die into life' (*Hyperion* 3.129–
30).

# 6

The imagination of the Romantic poet is haunted by the apparitions of the abandoned soul, which spectres the mechanical philosophy dismisses as phantoms of the overheated brain. Yet this haunting compels them to restore the phantoms to their objects as their symbolic form. Blake describes this restoration as the symbol imaginatively transforming rather than mechanically corresponding to its object. As Coleridge argues, the latter reduces symbols as the 'Reality' of matter to the 'empty echoes which the fancy arbitrarily associates with apparitions of matter' and thus reduce the primary imagination to delusion (*Lay Sermons* 30). In his Annotations to Wordsworth's Preface to *The Excursion*, Blake argues that Wordsworth's mind, by passing Jehovah unalarmed, had fallen 'into the Abstract Void' (*CPP* 666). That is to say, rather than releasing Prometheus, Wordsworth cast his imagination, as Shelley cast Jupiter, into the abyss with Satan.

Tilottama Rajan has analysed how in his early prophecies Blake's imagination is haunted by its 'Spectre,' leaving his visionary figures – Thel, Oothoon, Bromion, Theotormon – suspended in a series of indeterminate and conflicting states: 'by placing Christ at the centre of his phenomenology of spirit, [the later] Blake represents imagination as typological, [which] demands, for the representation to be sustained,' an archetypal reading that translates individual experience into a central paradigmatic story.' The 'cultural imperialism that informs such a reading' is why Rajan restricts herself to Blake's early poems, post-structurally affirming what 'the "romantic imagination" tries to dismiss.' 'But,' she argues, 'the early poems are too close to their social referents not to be aware of the cultural imperialism [sheep and goats rather than men and women] that informs such reading as a will-to-power over the text's own uncertainties' ('En-gendering' 90). I take Rajan's point about the 'cultural imperialism' that results when the poetic tale of 'individual experience' is turned into a 'central paradigmatic story' whose myth hardens into a religious system. Latent in all Romantic authorship is this psychic demand to confer identity upon itself, a tendency to truth-claims that post-structuralism rejects as nothing more than a fiction that has forgotten that it is a fiction and needs to be reminded. This rejection becomes especially urgent when the tyranny of truth-claims becomes a mounting and fearful state of fanatical worship whose spectral terrors now constitute a global plague threatening humanity with extinction.

This mounting contemporary plight informs Rajan's position, and its immediate effect – insofar as it can be described as immediate – is to subject culture to a critical investigation of its dangers as a warning against them. But this warning also tends to drain culture itself of its inherent, life-affirming numinosity. Like most post-structuralists, Rajan fails to perceive the process of recreation as a ceaseless mental fight to build Jerusalem by rejecting the fixed and definite qualities of its formalized construction, particularly as they tend to bind the mind to a literalist reading of them. So fearful is she of the tyranny of imperial edifices that the creative evidence of their cultural construction is dismissed at their dangerous, if not delusional, unconscious or transconscious, source.

In Blake's address to the reader of *Jerusalem* in Plate 2, the sheep and goats as distinct from men and women is his declaration of the 'plastic stress' of the imagination's dialectic, which as perpetual 'forgiveness of Sins' is the making of what he calls a 'Divine Body,' understood as the imaginative resurrection of a dead one. Originally excised over the right side of the door Los is about to enter, but later expunged, is the statement, 'Half Friendship [a poem neither dead nor alive] is the bitterest Enmity said Los / As he enterd the Door of Death for Albion's sake Inspired' (*J* 1.8–9). Incised and then expunged on the left side in reverse or mirror writing is the statement, 'Every Thing has its Vermin O Spectre of the Sleeping Dead!' (1.11). Above the archway incised and then expunged appeared 'There is a Void, outside of Existence, which if enterd into / Englobes itself & becomes a Womb' (1.1–2). Los, 'for Albion's sake Inspired,' is entering the 'Void, outside of Existence,' carrying in his right hand the globe, which becomes with his entrance an impregnated (Inspired) 'Womb,' dialectically dividing as the 'long sufferings of God' (1.10). Because 'there is a Judgment,' however, the 'sufferings,' as crucifixion, are 'not for ever there' (1.10). As the 'mind in creation,' they come to an end in what Blake calls 'Divine Mercy.' The 'Judgment' that dialectically informs this process becomes the Resurrection that ultimately contains the 'Judgment.' That is to say, Blake imaginatively perceives the 'Door of Death' as the eternal life of the imagination. The 'Vermin,' which 'Every Thing has,' is not simply cast into the 'Void,' but dialectically participates in the Void's pregnancy (englobing) as dialectically essential to this potentiality. It is in this sense that, in the full use of their 'Intellectual powers,' all true poets belong to 'the Devils party.'

Ololon descending from 'the Portals of [Blake's] Brain' down 'the Nerves of [his] right arm' (*M* 2.6–7) into his writing hand enacts in his 'Vegetable Body' the complex motions of the 'mind in creation.'

The operations of his 'Vegetable Body' are not the mere motion of his muscles and nerves, dismissed by Coleridge as the delusion of the mechanical philosophy. In the transformation of these 'Corporeal' motions by means of the 'Intellectual powers,' the imagination gradually and painfully shapes them to an apocalyptic end as the imagination moves through the realms of the 'Daughters of Beulah! Muses who inspire the Poets Song,' which Blake describes as 'Realms / Of terror & mild moony lustre, in soft sexual delusions / Of varied beauty' (*M* 2.1–4). Because the Daughters of Beulah cannot enter the fourfold realm of Eden, they remain bound to the threefold realm of the sexual, where for Jung Freud remained bound. 'But to / The Sons of Eden,' Blake explains, 'the moony habitations of Beulah, / Are from Great Eternity a mild & pleasant Rest' (30[33].12–14). For the Daughters of Beulah, Eden, as the 'life of Man,' is 'too exceeding unbounded' so that they require a 'Temporal Habitation' (30[33].22, 29). 'I would give / All that I am to be as thou now art! / But I am chained to Time, and cannot thence depart!' (*A* 232–4), Urania laments as she attempts in vain to restore the dead Keats to life.

The actual creative process blurs Blake's distinction between the Daughters of Beulah and the Sons of Eden. As Milton in Blake's vision travels through Blake's 'Vegetable Body' during Blake's reading of *Paradise Lost* aloud to his trembling wife Catherine, the 'Spectres of the Dead,' which is the body's automatic motion of muscles and nerves, described by Blake as a 'Polypus of soft affections without Thought or Vision' (*M* 24[26].38), are restored to life by the 'ministry' of the Daughters of Beulah, as distinct from Milton's three daughters. The 'Spectres of the Dead [...] take sweet forms / In likeness of' the 'Eternal Great Humanity Divine' (*M* 2.8–10). Thus, when Milton enters Blake's sleeping body, 'the Spirits of the Seven Angels of the Presence' enter with him. In dream, they rise up 'as an Eighth / Image Divine tho' darken'd; and tho walking as one walks / In sleep; and the Seven comforted and supported him.' This 'Eighth Image Divine' inhabits the Eden the Daughters of Beulah cannot enter because this state is 'too exceeding unbounded.' At the same time, the Sons of Eden who inhabit Eden as the 'Eighth Image Divine' cannot in the temporal sense arrive there without the aid of the 'Seven' who, as an unfolding process described by Shelley as 'Torturing th'unwilling dross that checks its flight,' comfort and support the poet (as well as lure and tempt him) along the arduous epic way. For Blake, Milton in the composition of *Paradise Lost* remained trapped in the threefold sexual, the Daughters of Beulah becoming in the temporal dictation of the epic his 'Sixfold Emanation,' his three wives and three daughters, who in 'their Bodies remain clos'd / In the dark Ulro till the Judgment' (*M* 17[19].4–5). The 'Judgment' is Blake's *Milton*, in which, 'By giving up of Selfhood,' Milton's wives and daughters from a 'distàn[ce] view'd [Milton's] journey / In their eternal spheres, now Human' (17[19].3–4). This distant viewing becomes the 'wondrous' acts of Milton and Ololon, which remain in *Milton* 'unknown' to Blake, 'Except remotely.'

Dismissing this complex dreaming state, which exceeds the rational limits of natural causality, as the 'Phantom of the over heated brain,' Blake's materialistic 'reasoner' reduces the psychic action of Los to a 'false appearance' (*M* 29[31].15). All that Blake's 'reasoner' sees with his five senses is 'a Globe rolling thro Voidness' (*M* 29[31].16), rather than the visionary globe, which Los holds in his right hand in the Frontispiece to *Jerusalem*. The 'Globe rolling thro Voidness,' Blake insists, 'is a delusion of Ulro,' which is supported rather than rejected by the microscope and telescope:

> The Microscope knows not of this nor the Telescope. They alter
> The ratio of the Spectators Organs but leave Objects untouched
> For every Space larger than a red Globule of Mans blood.
> Is visionary: and is created by the Hammer of Los
> And every Space smaller than a Globule of Mans blood. opens
> Into Eternity of which this vegetable Earth is but a shadow:
> The red Globule is the unwearied Sun by Los created
> To measure Time and Space to mortal Men. every morning.
> Bowlahoola & Allamanda are placed on each side
> Of that Pulsation & that Globule, terrible their power.    (*M* 29[31].16–26)

Blake's epic vision enacts the complex motions of the 'Vegetable Body' as Los recreates them to become what they are in eternity: the motions of a 'Divine Body.' Blake does not ignore their 'Vegetable' motions as they constellate themselves in Ulro in an infinite variety of ways, manifesting themselves in the perverse behaviour of the natural man. In his earlier Lambeth books, haunted by the spectral form of the Orc-Urizen cycle, Deism or natural religion threatens to bind man to nature's law. Blake's later poetry enacts one giant 'Divine Body' taking shape in space and time by transforming the infinite perversity of this natural man. In some similar fashion I increasingly identified my dream encounter with the Báb with Blake's one giant body as the imaginal operations of my material body. Los entering the Door of Death 'for Albions sake Inspired' became, as my understanding of Blake's vision of the Second Coming in his garden at Felpham, a model or prototype upon which my dream of the Báb began to take shape. The Los who entered Blake by stooping down and putting on his sandal found its anagogical counterpart in my landing at the feet of the Báb. My 'Corporeal Understanding,' that is to say, gradually became answerable to my 'Intellectual powers.'

# 7

Among other things, this book attempts to bring to our increasingly endangered world, a global battlefield where ignorant armies clash by day and night, a figurative perspective that respects rather than dismisses the metaphorical nature of the human act of perception described by Shelley as 'the poetry of life' (*DP* 530). Shelley argues that poetry 'is connate with the origin of man' (511). Shelley was born into a metaphorical world always in danger of hardening into a system that reduces the metaphorical to the literal. He thus argues that the imagination, as the presiding organ of the 'Intellectual powers,' must maintain the vitality of metaphor as this energy continues to mark 'the before unapprehended relations of things' in order to perpetuate them as the consciousness of them (512). If this perpetuation is arrested in fixed form, however, the metaphoricity of the human world becomes a prison. When this happens, 'language will be dead to all the nobler purposes of human intercourse' (512). Language becomes 'the Spectres of the Dead.'

Echoing Dante's account of the soul in Limbo, the first circle of Hell, T.S. Eliot describes the spectral world to which human intercourse is there reduced:

> I had not thought death had undone so many.
> Sighs, short and infrequent, were exhaled,
> And each man fixed his eyes before his feet.
> Flowed up the hill and down King William Street,
> To where Saint Mary Woolnoth kept the hours
> With a dead sound on the final stroke of nine.      (*The Waste Land* 63–8)

The 'dead sound' announces the Day of Judgment, Limbo becoming Blake's 'Void Outside of Existence' in which, illustrating Dante's Inferno at the end of his life, Blake was still fully engaged in the ceaseless 'Mental Fight' to release himself from Ulro. Human culture as the endless 'Mental Fight' against the tyranny of its closure must never give way to the fear of closure, which can undermine from within what it seeks to support from without.

This fear becomes the ultimate temptation facing Shelley's Prometheus bound to the precipice of his own frozen Will, personified by the Furies sent by Jupiter to unbind the Will:

> The good want power, but to weep barren tears.
> The powerful goodness want: worse need for them.
> The wise want love, and those who love want wisdom;
> And all best things [goodness, wisdom, love, and power] are thus confused
>    to ill.                                                (PU 1.625–8)

What Shelley seems to have in mind is the collapse of the Human Fourfold, Blake's fall of the four Zoas into their demonic parody, over which Urizen, like Shelley's Jupiter, presides. For Jung and Pauli in their work together, the demonic form of this collapse is the dropping of the atomic bomb on Hiroshima. 'Lo! I unfold my darkness,' declares Blake's Urizen, 'and on / This rock, place with strong hand the Book / Of eternal brass, written in my solitude.' To release Milton and himself from the 'solitude' of closure, Blake wrote *Milton*.

At the same time, I should also note, lest the point be forgotten, the release from closure. We can call this release – which keeps the text open to its indeterminacy in the same way that quantum physics keeps the motions of matter, at least at the subatomic or unconscious level, open to indeterminacy – the feminine: a state of willing suspension in which the possibilities are not subjected to a premature foreclosure. In its relation to the fourfold as the human, the feminine yet remains to be creatively resolved. Fundamentally informing this study is the unresolved presence of the feminine as the indeterminate, which locates the human in the ceaseless 'Mental Fight' of its impossible creation, but an impossibility that also protects this creation from closure while at the same time threatening the human with foreclosure. In the context of indeterminacy, the dream figure of the Báb remains suspended between the masculine and feminine, a hermaphrodite who, as the inner marriage or *hieros gamos*, ideally becomes the androgyne. Following the biblical account of the descent of the New Jerusalem apparelled as a bride to meet the bridegroom, Blake presumably has this latter figure in mind when he describes Jesus descending into his garden, his limbs enfolded in the 'Clouds of Ololon,' which, as 'a Garment dipped in blood / Written within & without in woven letters,' is Blake's own illuminated text inspired by the 'Daughters of Beulah' (*M* 42[49].12–13). Calling upon them to come into his hand to record Milton's journey through Blake's body, Blake recognizes that their vision includes its dark side: a 'False Tongue,' which turned Milton's journey in *Paradise Lost* as recorded by his physical daughters into a demonic vision of Jesus as 'a curse, an offering, and an atonement' (*M* 2.13). This same 'False Tongue' confronted Blake at Felpham in the form of Satan (his patron Hayley), to whom he was tempted to submit. To overcome the dangerous limitations of the Daughters of Beulah, Blake recognizes that he will need, however 'darken'd,' a greater guide: an 'Eighth Image Divine,' which descends in the final plate as 'the Starry Eight.' In Shia Islam the 'Starry Eight' is the 'Eighth Climate' or Heaven from which, as the prophetic imagination, the Hidden Imam descends as the return of Jesus. 'Surely I come quickly. Amen. Even so, come, Lord Jesus,' the Bible ends. Jesus coming as an eternal process of human becoming is, for Blake, *The Everlasting Gospel*, which is subject to the human imagination's ceaseless renewal as what he calls the 'Great Code of Art' (*CPP* 274).

# 4 The Fourfold

The Sexual is Threefold. The Human is Fourfold.

– Blake, *Milton*

## 1

Blake's 'Fourfold' mythopoeic vision enacts the awakening of Albion, asleep upon a 'Couch / Of Death,' to a full consciousness of himself as the 'human form divine.' Albion has fallen from this consciousness into what Blake calls the limit of 'Contraction [...] named Adam' (*M* 13[15].21), below which Satan dwells in Ulro as the limit of 'Opacity,' a 'Void Outside of Existence.' 'Opacity' is the endless dividing of 'Contraction' into demonic parodies or negation of the fallen creation, which divide 'without end or number.' At the end of the Bible, the 'Fourfold,' which Blake names the four 'Zoas,' are the four living beasts 'full of eyes before and behind' (Revelation 4.6). These four – Urthona, Tharmas, Luvah, and Urizen – surround the throne of God as a four-faced charioteer driving God's chariot. Their counterpart in Jung are the four human functions: *instinct*, comparable to Urthona as creative fertility; *feeling*, comparable to Luvah as the anima, bringing instinct to consciousness; *thought*, comparable to Tharmas as the creative realization of instinct; *intuition*, comparable to Urizen as wisdom or sense of form. These Zoas or functions constitute the 'whole soul of man in activity,' Coleridge's 'poet, described in *ideal* perfection' (*BL* 2:15). While Coleridge tends to arrange these functions hierarchically, Blake and Jung tend to treat them as equals, which Coleridge *does* describe as a fifth or imagination, a 'synthetic and magical power' that 'diffuses a tone, and spirit of unity, that blends, and (as it were) *fuses*, each into each' (2:16). All four Zoas or faculties dissolve 'as it were' into one, to become in Shelley 'the One.' In Revelation, John of Patmos, like Blake after him, sees this 'One' when, as John describes the vision, 'a door was opened in heaven and the voice which [he] heard was as it were a trumpet talking with [him]; which said, "Come up hither, and I will shew thee things which must be hereafter"' (4.1).

At the end of his life, Shelley also saw a door opening in heaven as the 'fire for which all thirst' consuming the last clouds of his mortality, a consummation that John of Patmos describes as the end of the world. The four-faced charioteer has now become the demonic form of the four Zoas: 'one whom years deform / Beneath a dusky hood and double cape / Crouching within the shadow of a tomb' (*TL* 88–90). '[A]ll that is, has been, or will be done' was barely seen as the chariot, with 'solemn speed,' majestically extinguished everything in its mindless path, the earth becoming the charnel of those who rule it as worms 'monarchize' a corpse (104, 106, 504). Blake describes this nightmare as 'the Sleep of Ulro,' which he further attributes to Newton's compasses used by Milton's Messiah to circumscribe chaos as the natural or fallen creation. 'May God us keep / From Single vision & Newtons sleep,' Blake writes to his patron, Thomas Butts (*CPP* 722). Newton's sleep is Satan's rule of the 'Void Outside of Existence' whose circumscribed form is *Paradise Lost* over which Urizen presides as the 'Zenith' of Milton's constricted imagination. 'Then first I saw him in the Zenith as a falling star' (15[17].47), declares Blake describing Milton's fall into Newton's world in which Satan becomes Milton's cast-out energy, Jung's *deus absconditus*.

Blake's Urizen is the God of *Paradise Lost* who, retiring into his own sterile perfection, leaves Satan 'at large to his own dark designs' (*PL* 1.213). In *Answer to Job*, Satan's 'dark designs' on Job in the end confront Satan with 'How all his malice serv'd but to bring forth / Infinite goodness, grace and mercy shown' to Job (*PL* 1.217–18). In Jung's treatment of him, Job thereby transforms Yahweh from a tyrant into what Coleridge describes as the 'poet, described in *ideal* perfection," or what Jung calls Yahweh's continuous 'creaturely incarnation,' as distinct from His arrested incarnation in Christ. For Jung, this arrested incarnation, Blake's 'Priesthood,' sacrifices 'instinctive desire, or libido,' to produce instead the 'infinite-sexual fantasies' of Freud's incest theory that 'reveal the shadow' (*Symbols* 431, 419).

Jung explains, however, that if viewed in terms of the collective rather than personal unconscious, the incestuous regression to the mother's body is 'usually effected not through the natural channels but through the mouth, through being devoured and swallowed [as the infant Jung feared being devoured and swallowed by the Jesus of the prayer his mother taught him].' As a result, the regression reaches back 'to a deeper layer of the nutritive function, which is anterior to sexuality' – a '"Jonah-and-the-Whale" complex' as distinct from the 'so-called Oedipus complex.' Jung continues:

> Even there it does not make a halt, but in a manner of speaking continues right back to the intra-uterine, pre-natal condition and, leaving the sphere of personal psychology altogether, irrupts into the collective psyche where Jonah saw the 'mysteries' ('*représentations collectives*') in the whale's belly. The libido thus reaches a kind of inchoate condition in which, like Theseus and Peirithous on the journey to the underworld, it may easily stick fast. But it can also tear itself loose from the maternal embrace and return to the surface with new possibilities of life. (*Symbols* 419–20)

'What actually happens in these incest and womb fantasies,' Jung continues,

> is that the libido immerses itself in the unconscious, thereby provoking infantile reactions, affects, opinions and attitudes from the personal sphere, but at the same time activating collective images (archetypes) which have a compensatory and curative meaning such as has always pertained to the myth. Freud makes his theory of neurosis – so admirably suited to the nature of neurotics – much too dependent on the neurotic ideas from which precisely the patients suffer. This leads to the pretence (which suits the neurotic down to the ground) that the *causa efficiens* of his neurosis lies in the remote past. In reality the neurosis is manufactured anew every day, with the help of a false attitude that consists in the neurotic's thinking and feeling as he does and justifying it by his theory of neurosis. (*Symbols* 420)

Here Jung makes an implicit distinction between the personal unconscious as the seat of neurosis and the collective unconscious as the much more dangerous seat of psychosis – a psychosis Jung embraces in the same way that Derrida embraces the Cogito. Over this distinction, Jung and Freud came to a parting of the ways. Jung describes the radical regression that leaves Blake's 'rotten rags of Memory' far behind, so that in the inspired space of madness, which the imagination enters, described by Blake as 'Inspiration,' the archetypal world comes into play. While the soul may get stuck in the archetypal realm as a full-blown psychosis, as Jung well knew from his work with schizophrenics, there are some who can find their way back, bringing with them the healing treasure they found. This radical return was Coleridge's experience of Wordsworth's poetry, particularly when listening to Wordsworth chanting it aloud. Until personal matters seriously interfered to confront Coleridge with Wordsworth's neurosis as mere repetition rather than the psychosis as a radical renewal of 'the ANCIENT of days and all his works,' Coleridge experienced in Wordsworth's recitations what he calls 'the prime merit of genius and its most unequivocal mode of manifestation': 'that freshness of sensation which is the constant accompaniment of mental, no less than of bodily, convalescence' (*BL* 1:80–1).

Working with Jung on his dreams, Pauli feared that Jung was becoming stuck in the collective unconscious, unable to find a way out of the labyrinth in which Jung, like Blake's Milton, found himself in his mounting illness. Given that the psyche represents 'the "irrational aspect of reality,"' Pauli believed that the psyche's operations cannot be rationally discernible unless given 'the definition "*neutral*" and *not the definition "psychic."*' That is to say, the psyche had to be treated with the willing suspension of disbelief that comes with scientific objectivity so that one didn't get trapped in the archetypal realm, or, put another way, so that one saw the psyche from the point of view of the Self rather than the ego. 'But I wish to make it quite clear that my hope that you might agree with this general point of view is based on the impression that some of the *pressure needs to be removed* from your analytical psychology,' Pauli explains. 'The impression I have is of a vehicle whose engine is running with overloaded valves (expansion tendency of the concept "psyche"); that is why I should like to relieve some of the pressure and let off steam' (*Atom* 106). Pauli continues:

> I would venture to make the following diagnostic and prognostic conjecture: The 'steam' mentioned [...] turns out to be unconscious physics, which has accumulated over a period of time in your analytical psychology without you having intended it. Under the influence of the flow of unconscious contents directed away from psychology, future development must entail such an *extension of physics*, possibly together with biology, so that the psychology of the unconscious can become part of this development. But it is not capable of development on its own and when left to its own devices. (I

would suspect that your work always brings on your heart condition when-
ever you unwittingly swim against this current). (*Atom* 109–10)

Jung could not change the flow of his unconscious away from psychology, nor was he willing to agree that its future lies in 'an *extension of
physics,* possibly together with biology.' He would agree, perhaps, that
his heart condition was increasingly aggravated by his work with Pauli
as it took him away from his own. But that would mean that he should
leave Pauli to pursue it without his interference. As Jung later writes to
Pauli,

> Your work is highly stimulating and creditable. It is to be hoped that your
> train of thought will also have an enhancing effect on your own special
> field. Psychology at the moment is lagging so far behind that there is not
> much of value to be expected from it for quite a while yet. I myself have
> reached my upper limits; and am consequently hardly in a position to make
> any contribution of note. (*Atom* 133)

When in 1930 Jung turned to a serious study of alchemy, its rich store
of long-abandoned, psychically projected materials largely took the
place of the schizophrenic patients he had daily studied for ten years
in his medical practice at the Burghlözli. When the young Pauli with
a severe anima problem brought to Jung a host of alchemical dreams,
a 'background physics' directly related to Pauli's theoretical work as a
quantum physicist, Jung believed he had found an Archimedean point
outside the psyche by which objectively to know it. Without this point,
he writes, 'I do not imagine for a moment that I can stand above or beyond the psyche, so that it would be possible to judge it, as it were, from
some transcendental Archimedean point "outside." I am fully aware that
[without it] I am entrapped in the psyche and that I cannot do anything
except describe the experiences that there befall me' (*Practice* 124).
And when Jung realized that quantum physics distinguished itself from
classical physics by introducing into the laws of subatomic motion the
unconscious observer of those motions as an acausal or indeterminate
influence upon them, he knew that in the analysis of Pauli's dreams he
was working with the acausal factor quantumly at work in the new physics. This factor would allow him to treat dreams in the same objective
way that a physicist treats the observed motions of matter. Jung's depth
psychology thus became as necessary to Pauli as a quantum physicist as
Pauli's quantum physics became necessary to Jung as a depth psycholo-

gist. Their importance to each other lay in their shared recognition that the future of both psychology and physics resided, not in their separate fields, but in their joint labours.

## 2

Pauli called Jung's depth psychology 'unconscious' or 'background physics' because it was grounded in the anima, which as 'the mouthpiece of the unconscious, can utterly destroy a man,' as it nearly destroyed Pauli. In his relations with Pauli, whose abstract skill as a mathematician was unmatched by any of his brilliant colleagues, including Einstein, Jung increasingly focused on the archetypal numinosity of numbers, which impacted Pauli's mind even more than his admittedly highly wrought sexual libido, associated with a Catholic mother who committed suicide. Jung fully realized Pauli's mathematical genius, though to the end of his life Jung stubbornly dismissed mathematics as 'a downright lie or a fraud' (*MDR* 28). To explain this genius, Jung concluded that in Pauli incest, understood in Freudian terms, had descended far below the level of infantine desire to the 'Mysteries' read by Jonah in the belly of the whale. Numbers as the 'Mysteries' became, for the mathematician Pauli, '*représentations collectives.*' Understanding these phenomena as the archetypes of the collective unconscious, Pauli was able not only to raise them to consciousness, but *as* consciousness rationally to use mathematics scientifically to prove some previously unknown and unmeasured motions of matter. This ability radically changed science's growing understanding of the psychophysical universe and the energy that propelled it. In the operations of Pauli's uncanny mind, energy could either destroy or transform the world. Such an energy became known as 'the Pauli effect,' whose most extravagant manifestation was when the entire cyclotron at Princeton University, which was conducting experiments with which Pauli entirely disagreed, was destroyed by a fire of unknown origin.

In Jung's memoirs, revised in 1959 at the age of eighty-four, he never quite explains his rejection of mathematics. But he does relate this rejection to the weapons of mass destruction that mathematics had by that time produced: 'Least of all did I understand my own *moral* doubts concerning mathematics,' Jung writes (*MDR* 28). For Jung as for Pauli, dropping the atomic bomb on Hiroshima was a radical betrayal of the mathematical mind as the highest and noblest manifestation of its numinous operations. This mind's reduction to what Pauli considered a

schizophrenic fantasy in which divine madness becomes mere madness
– always a danger facing a mathematical genius – led him to leave Princeton and return to Zurich where with Jung he could analyse his own
despair.

Archetypally understood, Pauli's anima problem lay in the obvious inability of his sexual libido to gratify the numinous demands of his spiritual libido, intimately connected to the numinosity of numbers. Largely
for this reason he realized that both he and Jung, whose fear of the
anima was evident, had to lower the pressure imposed upon them by
the unconscious operations of the psyche by treating them in a '*neutral*'
rather than highly charged manner, which produced in Jung 'bouts of
tachycardia and arrhythmia' (*Atom* 101). Jung was prepared to agree, but
he explained to Pauli that he was now too old and too unwell to shift his
ground. He therefore turned the work he could not perform over to his
colleague Marie-Louise von Franz, as he had long been in the habit of
doing. As we shall see, von Franz knew, in a way that neither Pauli nor
Jung knew, how deeply connected the anima is to the archetypal realm
of numbers. For her, the anima was this realm's numinosity. So when
Pauli came to her with his dreams, which he believed contained the unconscious solution to various mathematical problems still perplexing
him as a quantum physicist, she was *a priori* persuaded that the solutions
he sought depended upon him falling madly in love. By working his way
through this dilemma to some rational understanding of it, presumably
with her, he might find there the mathematical solutions he was seeking.
That is to say, Pauli had to confront the anima in the way that he best
negatively knew it in order mathematically to find his way out of destruction to its quantum resolution.

'After C.G. Jung had completed his work on synchronicity in "Synchronicity: An Acausal Connecting Principle" [which he published with
Pauli's paper, 'The Influence of Archetypal Ideas on the Scientific Theories of Kepler,' in *The Interpretation of Nature and the Psyche*],' von Franz
explains,

> he hazarded the conjecture, already briefly suggested in his paper, that it
> might be possible to take a further step into the realization of the unity
> of psyche and matter through research into the archetypes of the natural
> numbers. He even began to note down some of the mathematical char-
> acteristics of the first five integers on a slip of paper. But, about two years
> before his death, he handed this slip over to me with the words: 'I am too
> old to be able to write this now, so I hand it over to you.' For a long time I

was uncertain whether I ought to undertake this task, or simply keep the idea in mind, in order to pass it on to someone more competent than I. But after Jung's death the problem allowed me no rest. [...] This work has thus come into being over a period of more than six years. (*Number and Time* ix)

As what she calls 'a first attempt to clarify a few questions on this difficult subject,' the 'difficult subject' on its tragically subjective level becomes the role of the anima as it played itself out in von Franz's relations with Pauli, and above all with Jung. Pauli explored these relations in part in his active fantasy, *The Piano Lesson* (1953), dedicated to von Franz. In this work, as we shall see in the next chapter, Pauli, rejecting von Franz's erotic intentions as the anima, tries in vain to persuade her to distance herself from her master, Jung.

For Jung, the alchemical hermaphrodite is the anima as spiritual yearning 'fettered fast' in the sexual libido, longing for freedom. 'Insofar as the two bridges [synchronicity and numbers] linking psychology and physics are of such a singular nature and so difficult to grasp – with the result that no one dares to tread them – ,' Jung writes to Pauli,

> psyche and its science have been suspended in a bottomless room, and, as you so rightly say, 'homeless.' You suppose that it is through this that the archetype of the *coniunctio* is constellated. That is true inasmuch as precisely for the past 10 years I have been more or less exclusively preoccupied with this subject. [...] We may safely interpret [the *Unus Mundus*, the one world], as the one which the unconscious sees and seeks to produce, [as] more or less corresponding to that synthesis [a Platonic prior or primeval world which is also the future of the *eternal world*] which your dreams aspire toward. The final chapter of my book *Mysterium Coniunctionis* is the representation of this alchemical endeavour. [...] Oddly enough, the problem is still the same 2,000-year-old one: How does one get from Three to Four? (*Atom* 128–9)

Jung first faced this '2,000-year-old' problem in his 1912 *Wundlungen und Symbole der Libido*: How does one get from the sexual libido to the spiritual libido without falling into the 'bottomless room' of schizophrenia? How does one remain 'suspended' over the abyss, 'Nietzsche, Hölderlin, and many others' having failed to bridge it? Suspension as Coleridge's 'willing suspension of disbelief' would not, for Jung and Pauli, suffice. The poet, Jung argues, is not answerable to reality. His 'willing suspension of disbelief' allows the poet to neglect reality by attending to the dangerous, sometimes black magic of spell and incantation – the spell of Coleridge's Geraldine, Keats's Lamia, Shelley's Urania, or Blake's 'Female Will' (*J* 30[34].31). To bind oneself, however unknowingly, to one of these numinous figures constellates the hermaphrodite as the tortures inflicted by the sexual libido in its resistance to the larger demands of the spiritual libido. 'There was something else that seemed to me significant at that first meeting,' Jung writes about Freud:

> It had to do with things, which I was able to think out and understand only after our friendship was over. There was no mistaking the fact that Freud was emotionally involved with his sexual theory to an extraordinary degree. When he spoke of it, his tone became urgent, almost anxious, and all signs of his normally critical and sceptical manner vanished. A strange, deeply moved expression came over his face, the cause of which I was at a loss to understand. I had a strong intuition that for him sexuality was a sort of *numinosum*. [...] Although I did not properly understand it then, I had observed in Freud the eruption of unconscious religious factors. Evidently he wanted my aid in erecting a barrier against these threatening unconscious contents. [...] He gave me the impression that at bottom he was working against his own goal and against himself; and there is, after all, no harsher bitterness than that of a person who is his own worst enemy. (*MDR* 150–2)

Blake hears in the 'unpremeditated Verse' Milton is dictating to his unwilling daughters the 'harsh bitterness' of a poet 'who is [as Satan] his own worst enemy.' In Blake's reading of Milton's text, Milton enters the sepulchre of Blake's 'Vegetable Body' in this Satanic form in the hope of resurrection. In his hermaphroditic self-torment, in which the spiritual is at war with the demonic as a 'mournful form double,' Milton enters Blake's equally sexually tormented body. Together they set out to transform the 'Vegetable Body' into a site of 'Resurrection & Judgment.'

Bearing the Freud within himself as his own psychological version of Milton's Satan whom Blake sets out to transform, in *Symbols of Transformation*, as we have seen, Jung launched his own journey that in his 1944 heart attack culminated in a hallucinogenic vision of the Marriage Feast of the Lamb, a vision Blake hyperbolically describes in the final apocalyptic plates of *Milton* and *Jerusalem*. '"Lord! What demonic hyperbole?"' Socrates's Glaucon cries out in *The Republic*, 'planting us,' as Derrida explains, 'in the light of a hidden sun which is *epekeina tes ousias* ['beyond being']' (57). Like the light of Asia interpenetrating Prometheus, this sun exceeds the light of the physical sun and thus opens and founds another world by returning the old one to the madness of the Cogito. For Blake, this interpenetration is the descent of Ololon into 'the Fires of Intellect that rejoic'd in Felphams Vale / Around the Starry Eight.' This apocalyptic constellation assembles as the 'Starry Eight' in Blake's brain while he is reading *Paradise Lost* aloud to his wife. In its archetypal form, this constellation is a 'Pulsation of [Blake's] Artery' in which Blake's bones tremble at the 'immortal sound' of 'Four Trumpets' applied to the mouths of the 'Immortal Four' (the Four Zoas) whose breath is the 'Four winds.' In this 'moment,' Blake's soul leaves his 'Vegetable Body' (as in his heart attack Jung's soul for a moment left his). Blake's return to this Body becomes the engraving, printing, and illuminating of his out-of-body experience in and as the 'Judgment & Resurrection' of his 'Vegetable Body' in his 'Printing House in Hell.'

The counterpart of Blake's 'Printing House' is Jung's writing and revision of his major works in what he calls the three dimensional world, which became in its vegetable essence the artificial 'little box' of his heavily laden library where he sat at his desk alone. The spectral form of this 'little box' is Freud's library where in Vienna Jung and Freud once sat together, Jung's abdomen becoming a red-hot forge, the explosion of which was powerful enough to bring Freud's bookcase tumbling down on top of both of them. Beginning with *Wundlungen und Symbole der Libido*, Jung writes in the shadow of this experience, the energy there released as 'Judgment' becoming in what followed its resurrected form: the release of a new revelation of Yahweh from the sexual box in which Freud had buried it. 'Why open all gates?' Jung asked himself. One of Jung's most vivid accounts of this three-dimensional box in which he sought to describe a new four-dimensional world is, as we have seen, his analysis of Pauli's mandala dream of the world clock in *Psychology and Alchemy* (treated in greater detail in his 1937 Terry Lectures at Yale University, published a year later as *Psychology and Religion*). In this dream, two circles, one vertical, the other horizontal, share a common centre. In Jung's interpretation, which Pauli experienced as the '"most sublime harmony,"' the vertical circle is the Fourfold and the horizontal circle is the Threefold, the space/time motions of which enact the historical realization of the Fourfold (*Psychology* 66). As Jung explains, however, the centre, unlike traditional mandalas, is now empty (just as the throne of Demogorgon in Shelley's Zoroastrian mandala, *Prometheus Unbound*, is left empty). Describing a series of mandalas, Buddhist, Christian, and Hindu, Jung notes that they all 'seem to have been made in order to express the importance of the central figure' (*Psychology and Religion* 67). In the case of Pauli's mandalas, 'the centre is empty. It consists only of a mathematical point,' what Jung describes as 'a point without extension – a real zero-point' where psyche and matter 'touch and do not touch' (*Psychology and Religion* 67; 'On the Nature' 215). It was this 'mathematical point,' what Jung calls the 'psychoid archetype,' for which Pauli was searching. It exists conceptually as the 'Fourfold,' in which masculine and feminine are one, but has yet to be realized in the 'Threefold' as the psychoid archetype's creaturely incarnation.

When Jung declares that he is the glorified Lamb at the centre of the mandala, therefore, he is referring to the Self in himself as this incarnation. The hyperbolic excess of Jung's out-of-body experience, as the divine madness of the Cogito, is an inflation, which protects itself from hubris by returning to the world. 'The parallels I have mentioned [to Pauli's mandala],' Jung writes, 'depict the world-creating or world-ruling deity, or else man in his dependence upon the celestial constellations. Our [Pauli's and Jung's] symbol is a clock, symbolizing time' (*Psychology and Religion* 67). Jung further explores the clock as the feminine Fourth or Space who binds Time to her within a continuum in which the one is known by the other to become the earthly realization of Eternity. As the interceding Virgin Mother, this feminine fourth rounds the masculine Threefold (Trinity) in the earth, which is, of course, what Pauli and Jung, working together to fuse depth psychology and quantum physics, are struggling to achieve. Together they are working to accomplish what the other-worldly medieval church failed to achieve until the 1950 Papal Bull of Pius XII, which affirms as a matter of faith the physical ascent of the Virgin Mother to the marriage chamber of her Son. Jung psychologically interprets this ascent as the extension of the masculine Trinity to include the feminine Fourth as the bodily realization of the Quaternity. But why, Jung asks, has it taken so long dogmatically to recognize her station as the fourth member of the Trinity? 'According to the dogma she is only *beata,* not divine,' he answers. 'Moreover, she represents the earth, which is also the body and its darkness.' Though she clearly has, as intercessor, 'a relationship with the Trinity,' the relationship, as 'the body and its darkness,' is 'rationally not comprehensible, since it is so close and yet so distant' (*Psychology and Religion* 71).

The power of Pauli's mandala, Jung concludes, is that, like the Papal Bull, it 'unites the four and they function together harmoniously.' Without mentioning Pauli by name, and carefully avoiding the anima problem which brought Pauli into analysis (though not with Jung), Jung explains that his patient had been brought up a Catholic and thus, unwittingly, he was confronted with the [...] problem of the Trinity and the exclusion, or the very qualified recognition, of the feminine element, of the earth, the body, and matter in general, which were yet, in the form of Mary's womb, the sacred abode of the Deity and the indispensable instrument for the divine work of redemption. My patient's vision is a symbolic answer to this age-old question. That is probably the deeper reason why the image of the world clock produced the impression of 'most sublime harmony.' It was the first intimation of a possible solution of the devastating conflict between matter and spirit, between the desires of the flesh and the love of God. The miserable and ineffectual compromise of the church dream is completely overcome in this mandala vision, where all opposites are reconciled. (*Psychology and Religion* 72)

For Jung, Pauli's anima problem lay in the 'age-old' Christian conflict between matter and spirit. Jung writes:

Whereas the Mithraic sacrifice was still symbolized by the archaic slaughter of an animal and aimed only at domesticating and disciplining the instinctual man, the Christian idea of sacrifice is symbolized by the death of a human being and demands a surrender of the whole man – not merely a taming of his animal instincts, but a total renunciation of them and a disciplining of his specifically human, spiritual functions for the sake of a spiritual goal beyond this world. This ideal is a hard schooling which cannot help alienating man from his own nature and, to a large degree, from nature in general. (*Symbols* 434–5)

Jung archetypally recognized in Pauli's mathematical genius the danger inherent in such a surrender. Such a surrender, along with the numinosity that accompanies it, can, by virtue of its very impossibility, not only release the animal instincts, but release them as an *enantiodromia* in a manner that no rational discipline like mathematics can control. Indeed, one can relate the moral revulsion that informed Jung's rejection of mathematics to his fear of his own split-off personality, the 'daimon of creativity' that he associated with madness.

# 3

However, time and eternity, which are unconsciously reconciled in the common centre of the two circles – a reconciliation that quantum physics conceptualizes as the human intellect's highest achievement – cannot be reconciled consciously on earth until the anima problem is resolved. Both von Franz and Pauli failed to find this resolution in their mutual relations, a failure that constellates the alchemical hermaphrodite in which the *hieros gamos* assumes the grotesque form of auto-eroticism that constitutes patriarchy. One of the best ways to understand this deformation is in terms of the sexual libido of homoerotic warfare, in which the masculine seeks the phallus he fears he has, in the feminine, lost. In *Totem and Taboo*, his answer to the second part of Jung's *Wandlungen und Symbole der Libido*, Freud writes:

> Sexual desires do not unite men but divide them. Though the brothers had banded together in order to overcome their father, they were all one another's rivals in regard to the women. Each of them would have wished, like his father, to have all the women to himself. The new organization would have collapsed in a struggle of all against all, for none of them was of such over-mastering strength as to be able to take on his father's part with success. Thus the brothers had no alternative, if they were to live to-gether, but – not, perhaps, until they had passed through many dangerous crises – to institute the law against incest, by which they all alike renounced the women whom they desired and who had been their chief motive for despatching their father. In this way they rescued the organization which had made them strong – and which may have been based on homosexual feelings and acts, originating perhaps during the period of their expulsion from the horde. (144)

Freud was inwardly persuaded that Jung wanted to murder him in or-der to usurp his leadership. At the 1912 Psychoanalytic Congress in Mu-nich, Freud fainted while engaged in a tension-ridden conversation with Jung about Ikhnaton's removal of his father's cartouches on the steles. Jung picked him up and carried him in his arms to the next room where he laid him on the couch. 'As I was carrying him, he half came to,' Jung records, 'and I shall never forget the look he cast at me. In his weak-ness he looked at me as if I were his father' (*MDR* 157). Recalling the event, Freud explained to his colleague, Ernest Jones, that 'six and four years ago,' he had, in conversation with Wilhelm Fliess, 'suffered from very similar though not such intense [fainting] symptoms in the same room in the Park Hotel.' 'There is,' Freud wrote to Jones, 'some piece of unruly homosexual feeling at the root of the matter.' Fliess had oper-ated twice on Freud's nose, and believed there was a direct relationship between the mucous membrane of the nose and genital activities. In his first published paper, written in 1897 during Freud's period of intense self-analysis, Fliess announced a new syndrome, 'nasal reflex neurosis,' which could be cured by applying cocaine to the nose. Therefore, as Freud goes on to explain, when Jung 'in his last letter again hinted at my "neurosis" I could find no better expeditive than proposing that every analyst should attend to his own neurosis more than to the other's. After all, I think we have to be kind and patient with Jung and [...] keep our powder dry' (Freud and Jones 182).

Wisely, Freud had no intention of exposing his genital/nasal neurosis to Jung as he had rather disastrously earlier exposed it to Fliess, the two operations leaving him addicted to cocaine. The questionable strength of the movement founded by Freud lay in Jung's own mounting doubts about psychoanalysis. Jung saw in Freud's approach to psychoanalysis in terms of incest the hermaphrodite's sexually distorted strength, whereas for Jung the hermaphrodite's real strength was religious rather than sexual. The source of Fliess and Freud's unruly relations was their recognition of bisexuality, not only of all human beings, but of all living creatures. Both men claimed bisexuality as their own discovery, Fliess insisting that Freud borrowed it from his own elaborate theory without properly acknowledging its source. The origin of this bisexuality was the division of the cell at conception. For Jung, this biological notion was ludicrous. 'I protested that this hypothesis, carried to its logical conclusion,' he explains in his memoirs, 'would lead to an annihilating judgment upon culture. Culture would then appear a mere farce, the morbid consequence of repressed sexuality. "Yes," [Freud] replied, "so it is, and that is just a curse of fate against which we are powerless to contend." I was by no means disposed to agree, or to let it go at that, but still I did not feel competent to argue it out with him' (*MDR* 150). Among the most sinister notions of Jung was the notion that the sole contribution of the Jewish race to an understanding of culture was the fact that religion was merely a facade for repressed sexuality. Such dark notions contributed to Jung's psychotic break.

Yeats describes the danger of a mandala with an empty centre in 'The Second Coming': 'Things fall apart; the centre cannot hold; / Mere anarchy is loosed upon the world' (3–4). For Blake, this anarchy is the free-fall of the four Zoas, Jung's four functions, into endless division, which is the 'Void Outside of Existence' inhabited by Satan. After his break with Freud, Jung fell into this 'Void' and gradually populated it with his own projections. Bound in their early stages to his separation from Freud, these projections assumed various nightmare shapes, most of them related to the hidden Messiah, which lay buried in Freud's psychology waiting for Jung to release Him as a new revelation of Yahweh. Later these mounting horrors – the corpse of Freud's dead God decaying in Freud's arrested libido – became enmeshed in a *Weltanschauung* or world view blindly taking shape in what Jung would later describe as the autonomous operations of the collective unconscious. Unknown to Jung, except in terms of fantasies over which he had no apparent control, this *Weltanschauung* was intimated in his 1916 dream of his mother carried off by the wolfhound to Wotan's sacred grove. This dream's Satanic object was the holocaust Teutonically embraced as the annihilation of the Semitic source of Western culture as its divinely 'chosen seed.' Recognizing this danger from the start, Freud's Jewish disciples viewed Jung as the Trojan horse, which Freud had blindly embraced as his son and heir who would bring psychoanalysis to the promised land. That is to say, Jung instinctively knew that Freud had archetypally recognized him. What now remained was to shape an archetypal psychology rationally able to account for a spiritual recognition of a new revelation of Jahweh Freud's psychology denied.

The 'Void' at the empty centre of a mandala, however, is virtually infinite. Keats describes this infinity in terms of Moneta's 'immortal sickness which kills not; / It works a constant change, which happy death / Can put no end to' (*Fall of Hyperion* 1.258–60). For Keats, the very process of composing the epic, a process over which Moneta presides, is a struggle against this force:

> Prodigious seem'd the toil; the leaves [sacrifice] were yet
> Burning, – when suddenly a palsied chill
> Struck from the paved level up my limbs,
> And was ascending quick to put cold grasp
> Upon those streams that pulse beside the throat:
> I shriek'd; and the sharp anguish of my shriek
> Stung my own ears – I strove hard to escape
> The numbness; strove to gain the lowest step.
> Slow, heavy, deadly was my pace: the cold
> Grew stifling, suffocating, at the heart;
> And when I clasp'd my hands, I felt them not.               (1.121–31)

Jung describes his own struggle against 'immortal sickness':

At the beginning of 1944 I broke my foot, and this misadventure was followed by a heart attack. In a state of unconsciousness I experienced deliriums and visions which must have begun when I hung on the edge of death and was being given oxygen and camphor injections. The images were so tremendous that I myself concluded that I was close to death. (*MDR* 289).

All that Jung wrote after 1944 became his painfully written record of hanging 'on the edge of death.' Tachycardia and arrythmia accompanied the eager motions of his pen as warning signals calling upon him to stop. 'This letter,' he explains to Pauli,

> was already too much of an effort and one that I must avoid repeating for a while. The problem of the *coniunctio* must be kept for the *future*, it is more than I can cope with, and my heart reacts if I exert myself too much along these lines. My essay on 'Der Geist der Psychologie' ('The Spirit of Psychology') of 1946 resulted in a serious attack of tachycardia, and synchronicity brought on the rest. (*Atom* 101)

As Shelley writes, describing the lifting of his pen to write his elegy on the death of Keats,

>        – it can scarce uplift
> The weight of the superincumbent hour.
> It is a dying lamp, a failing shower,
> A breaking billow; – even whilst we speak
> Is it not broken?                          (*A* 282–6)

# 4

The '2,000-year-old' problem of passing from Three to Four is the transformation of the negative feminine, Blake's 'Female Will,' into the positive or creative feminine as the spiritual libido. In terms of Jung's notion of the unconscious as the source of consciousness, this transformation is an extension of Freud's' understanding of the sexual libido, which differs from the spiritual libido in degree rather than kind. The Christian notion of *agape* differs from the sexual libido in kind, descending as grace from the other side of the sexual libido as what Coleridge describes as the 'transcendental' as distinct from the 'transcendent.' In *Symbols of Transformation*, Jung argues that this transformation from the sexual to the spiritual now involves a new understanding of the hero myth 'in which man has always lived.' This new notion also involves a transformation of the animal instincts into a spiritual power. Unlike the '2,000-year-old' Christian notion, this transformation does not require the symbolic form of 'the death of a human being,' a death that renounces the animal instincts 'for the sake of a spiritual goal beyond this world.' While the Christian dogma of radical transcendence consolidated the emergence of one stage of consciousness, it no longer suffices for the new stage of consciousness announced by quantum physics, into which the human mind in its long evolution has now moved. Moreover, the stage of consciousness that is the Christian aeon has now ended. To sustain the dogma of Christianity in the new quantum aeon, Jung argues, is to perpetuate the divine sacrifice of the human, symbolized by the death of God in Christ, in terms of human extinction by weapons of mass destruction. For Jung, then, humanity's survival depends upon its 'adequate understanding and knowledge' of the power the human intellect has now released as its highest achievement.

Jung was critical of Freud's materialist treatment of his new revelation of Yahweh, which Jung saw as the demonic form of revelation, what Blake calls Selfhood or Satan. Jung writes:

> The barrage of materialistic criticism that has been directed against the physical impossibility of dogma ever since the age of enlightenment is completely beside the point. Dogma *must* be a physical impossibility, for it has nothing whatsoever to say about the physical world but is a symbol of 'transcendental' or unconscious processes which, so far as psychology can understand them at all, seem to be bound up with the unavoidable development of consciousness. (*Symbols* 435)

Again, the question that confronted Jung in his struggle with Freud is: '"Why open all gates?"' Why, that is, remove Freud's materialist mask and unveil what lay hidden behind it? Jung's concern with a new revelation of Yahweh, which he believed lay buried alive in Freud's unconscious, began to take shape in Jung's unconscious around 1912 in a series of dreams, some of which he records in his memoirs. In one, a dove descends to the table at which he is seated and speaks to Jung in a human voice: '"Only in the first hours of the night can I transform myself into a human being, while the male dove is busy with the twelve dead"' (*MDR* 172). In another, Jung moved along a long row of tombs where the dead were laid out, apparelled in costumes that located them in various eras starting with the 1830s and moving back to the twelfth century. As Jung stood in front of each of them, they suddenly moved and came to life. When he got to the twelfth century, the corpse was a crusader who seemed to be carved out of wood. 'But suddenly,' writes Jung, 'I saw that a finger of his left hand was beginning to stir gently' (173). Jung explains,

> I had originally held to Freud's view that vestiges of old experiences exist in the unconscious. But dreams like this, and my actual experiences of the unconscious, taught me that such contents are not dead, outmoded forms, but belong to our living being. My work had confirmed this assumption, and in the course of years there developed from it the theory of archetypes. (*MDR* 173)

Like the Romantics, Jung's imagination inhabited a symbolic world in which the actual world became immediately present to him in its eternal or archetypal state. He insists that this state does not emerge from a material source, but rather that the actual emerges from the archetypal as the sensual experience of it, by which the archetypal becomes empirically known. The danger of this 'Corporeal Understanding' is that it solidifies into dogma as the only begotten of the Deistic father. Empiricism, Derrida argues, is the death of philosophy.

Frye rejects this empirical world, what Blake calls the 'Female will,' as the 'object world' of the senses that 'begins in Beulah, the divine garden identified with Eden in Genesis' (*Fearful* 126). Overcome by the beauty and wonder of the divine garden, Albion, as the creative imagination who makes this divine world, falls asleep and 'in a trance sublime and strange' muses on what the active powers of his mind have created. As a result of falling asleep, Albion reduces what his creative, fully awakened power had actively constructed to what Blake in the opening plate of *Jerusalem* calls a 'Phantom of the over heated brain.' Beyond this point Blake requires ninety-two plates to restore to Albion's brain his own creative act of perception. Albion is persuaded that, by 'Holding [what appears to be] an unremitting interchange / With the clear universe of things around,' he is an enlightened materialist who has released himself from the phantoms that wait to possess his mind as the ghosts of all things that formerly inhabited it. Shelley's more secular version of Albion's so-called enlightenment is equally complex: Shelley recognizes that the so-called objective world cannot exist independent of perception. 'Thou art there!' declares Shelley, relieved to discover that Mont Blanc 'yet gleams on high' (127). While the mountain had momentarily fled as Shelley turned inward to contemplate his 'own separate phantasy,' where all that remains are the 'Ghosts of all things that are,' he was relieved to know that 'the breast' from which 'all things that are' fled requires them and therefore 'recalls them' (46–8). Rather than reject the strange phantasmagoric activity that secretly takes place in 'the still cave of the witch Poesy,' Shelley recognizes that the mountain's presence *as consciousness* depends on the unconscious psychic operations informing this consciousness, as Jung will also argue. Without them, the world would be 'vacancy.'

Frye's view of the 'Female Will' as a delusion of 'Ulro beneath Beulah,' which declares itself to be the objective reality of Nature to whose laws all must submit, rejects Jung's alchemical notion of the *hieros gamos*. Frye's reading of Blake, speaking from a left-wing Protestant position, aligns Blake with the Seventh Eye of God as distinct from the 'Starry Eight,' which descends into Blake's garden in 'Felphams Vale' as the return of Jesus. In *Milton*, the 'mild power' (2.9) of Ololon, the New Jerusalem bride of Jesus whose wedding garment is Blake's illuminated text 'Written within & without in woven letters,' releases Jesus from the priestly or hermaphroditic state, which reduces him to the god of natural religion, to become the androgyne, his resurrected form as the 'Starry Eight.' The resurrected Jesus descends into Blake's garden by entering Blake's 'Brain,' in which the 'Eternal Great Humanity Divine. planted his Paradise' so that, through the 'ministry' of the Daughters of Beulah, the fallen 'Vegetable Body' could be released from 'the Spectres of the Dead' and take again 'sweet forms / In likeness of himself' (*M* 2.7–10). For the 'Vegetable Body,' Blake explains, is 'more extensive / Than any other earthly things,' containing as it does 'the secrets of Eternity' (21[23].10–11). Thus, when the hermaphroditic Milton entered the left foot of Blake's 'Vegetable Body, 'the Spirits of the Seven Angels of the Presence' entered with him and 'gave him still perceptions of his Sleeping Body; / Which now arose and walk'd with them in Eden, as an Eighth / Image divine, tho darken'd.' This 'Eighth Image' is, I suggest, the *hieros gamos* of Milton as the masculine and Ololon as the feminine in which Milton casts off his Puritan garments and Ololon casts off her virginity. As the as-yet-unknown operations of the 'Vegetable Body' – the subject of quantum physics – this marriage is the apocalypse itself, distinct from what Frye describes as the *analogia visionis* of it. For this reason, Blake sees the divine marriage 'darkly' or, as he approaches closer before losing consciousness altogether, 'remotely.' At the same time, Blake also explains, this divine marriage of the masculine and feminine takes place 'Within a Moment: a Pulsation of the Artery.' As an illuminated text, *Milton* is the *analogia visionis* of the *hieros gamos*.

My resistance to Frye's reading of the feminine goes back a long way. Frye writes:

> The material world is in a way feminine to the perceiver; it is the body which receives the seed of his imagination, and the works of the imagination which are the artist's children are drawn from that body. We think of Nature as feminine, and so she is. But as the artist develops he becomes more and more interested in the art and more and more impatient of the help he receives from nature. In the world of Eden there is only energy incorporating itself in form, creator and creature, which means that somewhere (on the upper limit of Beulah, as it happens) this permanent objective body which nourishes and incubates the imaginative form drops out. Nature, in simpler language, is Mother Nature, and in the perfectly imaginative state there is no mother. The fall of man began with the appearance of an independent object-world [Eve as Satan], and continued into this state of Generation, where we begin life in helpless dependence on Mother Nature for all our ideas. This independent nourishing force in nature Blake calls the female will.
>
> The worship of a female principle, therefore, specifically a maternal principle, is not imaginative, and is only possible to natural religion. In Eden there is no Mother-God [...] but in the more highly developed ones God is always the supreme Male, the Creator for whom the distinction between the beloved female and created child has disappeared. The reappearance of the Madonna in Christianity is thus a corruption of that religion, and is in direct contradiction to Jesus' own teachings. Mother-worship is womb-worship, a desire to prolong the helplessness of the perceiver and his dependence on the body of nature which surrounds him. (*Fearful* 74–5)

As I stated above, Frye binds Blake to the Seventh Eye of God, which conducts the soul in the direction of Eden beyond Beulah but stops short of Eden, which is the *mise en scène* of Blake's vision as ceaseless 'Mental Fight' (*M* 1). By refusing anagogically to perceive this 'Mental Fight' as the *hieros gamos*, masculine and feminine in one wondrous body, Frye locates its form, while present, beyond the reader's imagination. For Blake, however, this form is the creaturely incarnation of God as the act of perception itself viewed in terms of its 'living Power.'

Plato sees this anagogical or mystical level as divine insanity. 'I certainly have composed no work in regard to it,' he explains in his Seventh Epistle, 'nor shall I ever do so in the future, for there is no way of putting it into words like other studies. Acquaintance with it must come rather after a long period of attendance on instruction in the subject itself and of close acquaintance, when, suddenly, like a blaze kindled by a leaping spark, it is generated in the soul and at once becomes self-sustaining' (1589). As Derrida argues, the divine madness of the Cogito must be tranquillized to become sane, though there is a very fine line between sanity and madness, especially in the case of a genius like Joyce. Jung described Joyce's *Ulysses* as a masterful descent into the collective unconscious, which displays all the evidence of madness yet remains, as the evidence of genius, eminently sane. Frye interprets the 'sanity of genius' as the ability consciously to embrace its madness by creatively shaping madness, which then assures it will be universally recognized. The madness of what Frye calls 'the commonplace mind,' on the other hand, is its failure to recognize 'Eternity' at work in 'the productions of time.' Time is reduced to 'Necessity,' which Shelley in his notes to *Queen Mab* describes as the dialectic of matter that 'governs the moral and material universe' as 'an immense and uninterrupted chain of causes and effects, no one of which could occupy any other place than it does occupy, or act in any other place than it does act' (*Complete Poetical Works* 809).

In his later essay 'On Life,' Shelley describes the real insanity of Necessity as the complete absence of thought. Coleridge, who was also earlier convinced by Necessity, writes that had the immutable law of association 'been really the case,'

> the consequence would have been, that our whole life would be divided between the despotism of outward impressions [Blake's 'Female Will'], and that of senseless and passive memory [Blake's 'rotten rags']. Take his [Hartley's] law in its highest abstraction and most philosophical form [Necessity, which Jung associates with mathematics], viz. that every partial representation recalls the total representation of which it was a part; and the law becomes nugatory, were it only from its universality. In practice it would indeed be mere lawlessness ['the proposition that $a=b$, or that sun=moon, dog=cat [...] might have fooled me endlessly' (*MDR* 28)]. Consider, how immense must be the sphere of a total impression from the top of St. Paul's church; and how rapid and continuous the series of such total impressions. If therefore we suppose the absence of all interference of the will, reason, and judgment, one or other of two consequences must result. Either the

ideas (or relicts of such impression) will exactly imitate the order of the impression itself, which would be absolute *delirium;* or any one part of that impression might recal any other part, and (as from the law of continuity, there must exist in every total impression some one or more parts, which are components of some other following total impression, and so on ad infinitum) *any* part of *any* impression might recal *any* part of any *other,* without a cause present to determine *what* it should be [...] There is in truth but one state to which this theory applies at all, namely, that of complete light-headedness. (*BL* 1:111–12)

Here Coleridge is describing real insanity, which the commonplace mind of his addiction came to recognize, just as the Satan of Blake's Selfhood recognized the 'Void Outside of Existence.' On opium, Coleridge descends into this void's 'sunless sea' ('Kubla Khan' 5) in order to recall himself to the operations of his own genius, like Ololon's descent to recall Milton to his own.

# 5

Perhaps the most powerful encounter in Blake's *Milton*, not unlike Keats's encounter with Moneta, though there tragically unresolved, is Blake's description of Milton's Spectre approaching, confronting, and entering his 'bosom,' where, before it is ejected, it nearly takes possession of him as he lies 'outstretchd upon the path / A moment.' Descending down the path on which Blake has collapsed, Blake in a 'trance sublime and strange' hears the loud thundering of Satan, which recalls him to the familiar world of the 'Vegetable Body,' just as it recalled Shelley to Mont Blanc. Both body and mountain have been transformed to become 'a voice [...] to repeal / Large codes of fraud and woe; not understood / By all' ('Mont Blanc' 80–2). For the sceptical Shelley, the voice personifies a 'Power' that 'dwells apart in its tranquility / Remote, serene and inaccessible.' For the radically heterodox Christian Blake, the voice embodies the prophetic power of the risen Jesus returning to earth in Blake's own body.

'I also stood in Satans bosom & beheld its desolations!' writes Blake, referring at once to the Hell Milton constructs for Satan in the first two books of *Paradise Lost* and to Los at the forge with his Spectre (*M* 38[43].15). Los at his forge is also Blake's 'Printing House in Hell,' Blake's 'furnaces of affliction,' where Los's 'Angels & Emanations / Labour with blackened visages among its stupendous ruins' (38[43].20–1). Addressing his Spectre, Blake's Milton mirrors Blake's troubled relations with his patron Hayley, to whom, in the false heaven of Felpham, Blake, much against his will, must pay homage. One alternative, which would merely reverse their roles, would be for Blake to use his repressed power to annihilate Hayley and claim Hayley's false heaven as his own. 'Satan! my Spectre!' declares Blake's Milton,

> I know my power thee to annihilate
> And be a greater in thy place, & be thy Tabernacle
> A covering for thee to do thy will, till one greater comes
> And smites me as I smote thee & becomes my covering.
> Such are the Laws of thy false Heavens!                    (38[43].30–3)

'Cease!' cries the Chorus in Shelley's *Hellas*, 'drain not to its dregs the urn / Of bitter prophecy' (1098–9). Hermaphroditically bound to his Spectre as it is internalized in Blake's unconscious 'Vegetable Body,' Blake and Milton together become each other's covering Tabernacle in which Satan's will is done. 'I also stood in Satans bosom & beheld its desolations! / A ruind Man: a ruind building of God not made with hands' [*M* 38[43].15–16], declares Blake. Refusing to bow to Milton's epic, Blake in his reading of *Paradise Lost* aloud at Felpham struggles to transform 'the Laws of [Satan's] false Heavens,' as they become in Milton's text what Keats calls 'Language pronounc'd,' into the 'Laws of Eternity.' '[B]ut Laws of Eternity / Are not such,' declares the Milton who in Blake's body has ascended to Blake's brain where his Spectre is cast out:

> know thou: I come to Self Annihilation
> Such are the Laws of Eternity that each shall mutually
> Annihilate himself for others good, as I for thee.          (*M* 38[43].33–6)

'Thy purpose & the purpose of thy Priests & of thy Churches,' Blake's liberated Milton declares, addressing the combined strength of their determination to annihilate the Satan in themselves,

> Is to impress on men the fear of death; to teach
> Trembling & fear, terror, constriction; abject selfishness
> Mine is to teach Men to despise death & go on
> In fearless majesty annihilating Self, laughing to scorn
> Thy Laws & terrors, shaking down thy Synagogues as webs

I come to discover before Heaven & Hell the Self righteousness
In all its Hypocritic turpitude, opening to every eye
These wonders of Satans holiness shewing to the Earth
The Idol Virtues of the Natural Heart, & Satans Seat
Explore in all its Selfish Natural Virtue & put off
In Self annihilation all that is not of God alone:
To put off Self & all I have ever & ever Amen.          (M 38[43].37–49)

This unfolding, highly wrought episode constellates a 'Moment: a Pulsation of the Artery' in which 'the Poets Work is Done' – in essence the entire epic as a single apocalyptic act of perception. During this moment the Spectre whom Blake's Milton addresses is 'Coming in a cloud, with trumpets & flaming fire' along the path where Blake has fallen (38[43].52). 'Fall therefore down & worship me,' he commands Blake, Blake apparently obeying (38[43].54). Stating that 'Seven Angels bear my Name & in those Seven I appear,' Satan declares that the seven Orc cycles culminating in Jesus have turned back to become in their spectral form the Day of Judgment: 'But I alone am God [Urizen] & I alone in Heavn & Earth / Of all that live dare utter this, others tremble and bow' (38[43].55–7). Fearing that Satan has taken possession of him as he took possession of Milton in the dictation of his epic to his 'Sixfold Emanation,' Blake sees Milton coming silently down the path, not as Satan, but 'As the clear Sun' (39[44].5). The 'Starry Seven' spread their 'Starry limbs,' casting off their Spectres to become 'Seven: Forms / Human' (39[44].3, 6–7). In the instant, Judgment is transformed into Resurrection. 'For we must all appear before the judgment seat of Christ; that every one may receive the things done in his body, according to that he hath done,' Paul declares, the 'last trumpet' sounding 'In a moment, in the twinkling of an eye' (2 Corinthians 5.10, 15.52). In a 'mighty Column of Fire,' 'Trumpets innumerable' call upon Albion to awake and 'reclaim [his] Reasoning Spectre,' which had dismissed Blake's vision as the 'Phantom of the over heated brain' (39[44].8, 7, 10). 'Subdue / Him to the Divine Mercy,' the seven Angels declare in the name of the Eighth who dwells in Eden. 'Subdue / Him to the Divine Mercy, Cast him down into the Lake / Of Los, that ever burneth with fire, ever & ever Amen! / Let the Four Zoa's awake from Slumbers of Six Thousand Years' (39[44].10–13).

'Then loud the Furnaces of Los were heard! & seen as Seven Heavens / Stretching from south to north over the mountains of Albion,' Blake explains (39[44].14–15). 'Lest he should fall apart in his Eternal Death,'

Satan 'imitate[s] / The Eternal Great Humanity Divine surrounded by / His Cherubim & Seraphim in every happy Eternity,' his 'Eternal Death' mimicking the apocalypse as the demonic parody of it (39[44].26–8). Here is how Coleridge, speaking of associationism, describes the parody:

> [R]eliques of sensation may exist for an indefinite time in a latent state, in the very same order in which they were originally impressed; and as we cannot rationally suppose the feverish state of the brain to act in any other way than as a stimulus, this fact [...] contributes to make it even probable, that all thoughts are in themselves imperishable; and that if the intelligent faculty should be rendered more comprehensive, it would require only a different and apportioned organization, *the body celestial* instead of *the body terrestrial*, to bring before every human soul the collective experience of its whole past existence. And this, this, perchance, is the dread book of judgement, in whose mysterious hieroglyphics every idle word is recorded! Yea, in the very nature of a living spirit, it may be more possible that heaven and earth should pass away, than that a single act, a single thought, should be loosened or lost from that living chain of causes, to all whose links, conscious or unconscious, the free-will, our only absolute *self*, is co-extensive and co-present. But [...] it is profanation to speak of these mysteries. (*BL* 1:113–14)

Blake's Satan is like the determinism of Coleridge's mechanical philosophy. He contains as eternal damnation the 'reliques' of every sensation recorded on the collective human brain from beginning to end, which Blake, following tradition, describes as six thousand years. He carries these impressions in the fixed and dead arrangement of their original passive reception. Blake associates this passivity with the necessity of Urizen's 'Natural Religion,' the demonic parody of the apocalyptic act of creation that takes place in every 'Pulsation of the Artery.' Coleridge describes the passive brain as 'feverish,' what the fallen Albion calls 'over heated,' rather than 'free.' Freedom lies in the release from natural law or natural religion whose god is what Coleridge calls a 'a *something-nothing-every-thing*, which does all of which we know, and knows nothing of all that itself does.' Those who worship this god are 'merely the causeless and effectless behold[ers] of it when it is done.' 'Yet scarcely can it be called a beholding,' Coleridge continues, 'for it is neither an act nor an effect; but an impossible creation of a *something-nothing* out of its very contrary. It is the mere quick-silver plating behind a looking-glass; and in this alone consists the poor worthless I!' (*BL* 1:119–20). As Jung explains in his Prologue to *Memories, Dreams, Reflections*, 'I cannot employ the language of science to trace this process of growth in myself, for I cannot experience myself as a scientific problem' (3).

Coleridge realized that the confrontation between freedom and Necessity was the ultimate issue confronting the human soul virtually extinguished in a materialistic age to leave natural religion in Satanic charge. Only the poet viewed in '*ideal* perfection' could adequately deal with this issue. For a time, Coleridge projected this ideality onto Wordsworth, who would proclaim

How exquisitely the individual Mind
(And the progressive powers perhaps no less
Of the whole species) to the external World
Is fitted: – and how exquisitely, too –
Theme this but little heard of among men –
The external World is fitted to the Mind;
And the creation (by no lower name
Can it be called) which they with blended might
Accomplish.                                      (Prospectus to *The Recluse* 63–71)

'You shall not bring me down to believe such fitting & fitted I know better & Please your Lordship,' Blake writes in his marginal notes to Wordsworth's Prospectus (*CPP* 667). This 'fitting' is 'not to Mind but to the Vile Body only & to its Laws of Good & Evil & its Enmities against Mind' (667), which constitutes the 'Corporeal Understanding.' For Blake, Wordsworth, like Milton before him, has fitted his mind to Satan. In fact, it was Blake who produced Wordsworth's promised 'great consummation.' *Milton, The Four Zoas,* and *Jerusalem* were conceived together in Blake's 'Pulsation of the Artery' as the 'whole soul of man in activity.' This instant is the awakening Albion arising from his 'Couch of death' (*M* 20[22].44), a 'Couch' which Shelley associates with the 'curse which binds us to be subjected to the accident [necessity] of surrounding impressions' (*DP* 533). Rejecting the curse, Blake writes: 'Then Albion rose up in the Night of Beulah on his Couch / Of dread repose seen by the visionary eye' (*M* 39[44].32–3).

Now distancing himself from the apocalyptic instant, which had taken possession of him as a radical derangement (dissolution) of the senses, Blake describes the agonized building of Jerusalem 'among these dark Satanic Mills' grinding away in the polite society upon which, at Felpham, he found himself becoming increasingly dependent. In *Jeru-*

*salem* Los pleads with Albion to cast off the spectral body of Satan and return to London, where Blake's 'Printing House' awaits him as his own 'vegetating blood in veiny pipes':

> I behold London; a Human awful wonder of God!
> He says: Return, Albion, return! I give myself for thee:
> My Streets are my, Ideas of Imagination.
> Awake Albion, awake! and let us awake up together.
> My Houses are Thoughts: my Inhabitants; Affections,
> The children of my thoughts, walking within my blood-vessels,
> Shut from my nervous form which sleeps upon the verge of Beulah
> In dreams of darkness, while my vegetating blood in veiny pipes,
> Rolls dreadful tho' the Furnaces of Los, and the Mills of Satan.
> For Albions sake, and for Jerusalem thy Emanation
> I give myself, and these my brethren give themselves for Albion.
>
> So spoke London, immortal Guardian! I heard in Lambeths shades:
> In Felpham I heard and saw Visions of Albion
> I write in South Molton Street, what I both see and hear
> In regions of Humanity, in Londons opening streets.     (*J* 34[38].29–43)

Here Blake calls upon Milton, who like Blake knew the streets of London as Blake knew them as if they were his own 'Vegetable Body,' to liberate what had become 'each charter'd street' on which Blake now marks 'in every face' he meets 'Marks of weakness, marks of woe' to rise up from his own 'charter'd' epic and release it from its 'mind-forgd'd manacles' ('London' 1, 3, 4, 8). That is to say, acknowledging England as an empirical/imperial power arising from the Industrial Revolution to envelop the earth, he calls upon Milton, bound to the false Heaven of Newtonian physics, to join him in casting off material empire ('Empire is no more! and now the lion & wolf shall cease' [*MHH* 25]) by transforming it into the New Jerusalem. 'Then they cried out in a chorus,' writes Jung of the spirits who on a Sunday afternoon in 1917 filled his living room from floor to ceiling: 'We have come back from Jerusalem where we found not what we sought.' What they sought was not to be found in the historical city now threatened with destruction by three contending religions. What they were seeking was not the product of religion wrongly understood as allegory addressed to the 'Corporeal Understanding' as opposed to the newly released 'Intellectual powers' that the psychologist Jung embraced as much as the materialist Freud rejected them. Following his break with Freud, Jung, like an exorcist, sought to communicate with the dead 'voices of the unanswered, unresolved, and unredeemed' (*Red Book* 346n78), including his own, in order to alleviate the plight of Jerusalem, especially at a time when, historically, Palestine was already under siege and facing invasion by the British army. Like Blake's 'Seven Eyes [or Seals] of god,' which has to confront how their once spiritual content had turned to the poison of Satan's empire sufficient to destroy the earth, Jung was constructing a new mythology as a spiritual or 'subtle' body understood as the resurrection of a dead one. In his future work with Pauli, Jung shaped this new body to contend with Pauli's mathematical mind, upon whose objectivity Jung increasingly depended. But because of his lifelong and irrational distrust of mathematics, Jung also feared this body as a false heaven produced by the trickster operations of Pauli's mind. Like Blake, Jung had to contend with the 'Opposition' upon which his 'true Friendship' with Pauli depended.

Put another way, Jung feared that he would be unable to distinguish the 'celestial' from the 'terrestrial' body. '[H]is face is toward / The east, toward Jerusalems Gates,' Blake declares of the rising Albion (*M* 39[44].33–4). What follows in *Milton* is an account of the 'groaning' body of Albion 'outstretchd' upon the fragmented body of England, Ireland, and Wales. 'For as the body is one, and hath many members, and all the members of that one body, being many, are one body: so also is Christ,' Paul explains to the Corinthians:

> For the body is not one member, but many. If the foot shall say, Because I am not the hand, I am not of the body; is it therefore not of the body? And if the ear shall say, Because I am not the hand, I am not the body; is it therefore not the body? If the whole body were an eye, where were the hearing? If the whole were hearing, where were the smelling? But now hath God set the members every one of them in the body, as hath pleased him. (2 Corinthians 12.12–18)

Here Paul describes the 'celestial' as distinct from the 'terrestrial' body, which for Paul is Christ's own resurrected body present in the bread digested by the faithful. For Blake, this digestion, as the operations of the imagination, takes place in Bowlahoola, 'the Stomach in every individual man' (*M* 24[26].67), which to the 'visionary eye' is Los's 'Furnaces,' Blake's 'Printing House in Hell.' Here the 'Furnaces rage; / Thundering the Hammers beat & the Bellows blow loud' (24[26].52–3), as they did in Jung's abdomen when Freud dismissed Jung's mental operations as 'a black tide of mud.' John of Patmos enacts this bodily communion, in which Christ's dead body is resurrected in Bowlahoola. John 'went unto the angel, and said unto him, Give me the little book. And he said unto him, Take it, and eat it up; and it shall make thy belly bitter, but it shall be in thy mouth sweet as honey.' 'And I took the little book out of the angel's hand, and ate it up,' declares John; 'and it was in my mouth sweet as honey; and as soon as I had eaten it, my belly was bitter.' 'And he said unto me,' John concludes, 'Thou must prophesy again before many people, and nations, and tongues, and kings' (Revelation 10.9–11). Not surprisingly, Blake, having eaten the entire Bible, *Paradise Lost*, and many other prophetic books, refused medicine to relieve his stomach upsets, which regularly attended the composition, printing, and illuminating of his prophetic works. '[B]ut as none on Earth can give me Mental Distress, & I know that all Distress inflicted by Heaven is a Mercy,' Blake writes to Butts, 'a Fig for all Corporeal Such Distress is My mock & scorn' (*CPP* 716).

Albion's 'left foot near London/ Covers the shades of Tyburn.' His 'instep from Windsor / To Primrose Hill stretch[es] to Highgate & Holloway [...] London is between his knees [...] His right foot stretches to the sea on Dover cliffs [...] [H]is heel is [o]n Canterbury's ruins [...] His right hand covers lofty Wales / His left Scotland [...] [H]is right elbow / Leans on the Rocks of Erins Land, Irelands ancient nation [...] His head bends over London' (*M* 38[44].37–47). What Derrida might call the hyperbolic excess of this instant of the Cogito is the real world of the imagination in which the poet's work is done. This work produces a world that must be patiently reduced to sanity if it is to be rationally perceived, hopefully without being destroyed by the 'Reasoning Negative.' By then Albion is exhausted by this vast outstretching. 'He views Jerusalem & Babylon, his tears flow down,' Blake writes of Albion. 'He strove to rise to walk into the Deep. but strength failing / Forbad & down with dreadful groans he sunk upon his Couch / In moony Beulah' (39[44].48, 50–2).

Albion sinking down again now becomes Milton beholding Ololon standing before him. As one of the 'Daughters of Beulah! Muses who inspire the Poets Song' (*M* 2.1), she has been where Milton's Urania in *Paradise Lost* never went. Urania remains in heaven where she played with her sister, Sophia, before the throne of God, who was pleased with her celestial song. Ololon has been where no other Daughter of Beulah has ever been. She has descended to Ulro to confront there the demonic parody of the throne of God before which she played and sang in *Para-*

*dise Lost.* She has assumed responsibility for the 'Sixfold Emanation' that her celestial song became when the blind Milton dictated it to his wives and daughters. She has sacrificed her innocence and is now ready to assume her destined role as the New Jerusalem whose wedding garment is Blake's illuminated text. As Blake indicates in the invocation of his Muse in the second plate to *Milton,* the entire psychic action of his epic is set in motion as the feminine Muse descends down the nerves of his right arm into his writing hand to tell of the 'False Tongue' before 'the Gates / Of Jerusalem' (2.10, 14–15). Turning eastward, Albion arises to open them. The actual opening becomes the action of the final plates of *Jerusalem* in which, at last, Enitharmon, Los's coy mistress, becomes his true bride, just as Ololon becomes his ravished bride in *Milton.* Blake's epic account of Ololon's astonishing descent into the 'Fires of [Blake's] Intellect,' which the 'Starry Eight' as the return of Jesus sets ablaze as the prophetic power of Blake's imagination, remains unsurpassed in its luminous, though blinding, multidimensionality. In these and subsequent pages I have sought to bring this multidimensionality to bear upon my dream of the Báb as a symbolic rendering in the collective unconscious of the 'living Power and primary Agent' of my advanced 'human Perception.'

# 5 The Hidden Imam

The *Eighth Climate* is the *mundus archetypus,* [...] the world of Images and archetypal Forms. Actually, the only universe that possesses dimensions and extent is the one that is divided into *eight* climates. *Seven* of them are the seven geographical climates with dimensions and extent which are perceptible to the senses. The eighth climate is the one whose dimensions and extent can only be grasped by the imaginative perception.

      – Henry Corbin, *Spiritual Body and Celestial Earth*

With him the Spirits of the Seven Angels of the Presence
Entering; they gave him still perceptions of his Sleeping Body;
Which now arose and walk'd with them in Eden as an Eighth
Image Divine tho darken'd.

      – Blake, *Milton*

## 1

Reading Blake for over sixty years has persuaded me of two things: there are no natural poems and all poems are one. In its fullest sense, a poem is an act of perception. Like all acts of perception, it is a product of what Coleridge calls the primary imagination as the 'living Power and prime Agent of all human Perception.' Poetry is distinguished from this primary act of perception in degree rather than in kind. The secondary imagination brings the primary act to consciousness in which the power and agency become the living experience of perception. That is to say, perception becomes numinous. In the making and reading of a poem, the mind is active rather than passive. In some sense, then, the poem as metaphor is the mind's literal account of its activity rather than a literal account of the external world. This other reality also has a literal presence, but is revealed by other means that seek to undo the work of the imagination, even to declare this work the 'Phantom of the over heated brain.' The distinction between mind and world is essential to the recognition of both, both of which are actual, but in quite different ways. To confuse them is to confront irreality in ways that may conduct to madness, as in schizophrenia, which converts literal reality into a symbolic world without realizing the conversion. The schizophrenic inhabits this world without knowledge, consent, or necessary conscious labour. Coleridge movingly describes the difference between mind and world in his marginal gloss to *The Ancient Mariner*, where the mariner, who without consciousness has shot the albatross, finds himself 'Alone, alone, all, all alone, / Alone on a wide wide sea!' (232–3), isolated from the moon and stars, which in their motions still sojourn since the blue sky everywhere belongs to them. What is more painful, however, is not that the mariner is cut off from the ideal human world symbolized by this analogy to nature, but rather that he is punished for illegitimately existing within this world. Jung devoted his life to explaining that legitimacy resides in locating the act of perception, not in the passive mind's submission to habit and custom as the petrified form of the symbolic, but at its creative or primary source. For Jung, this source is a 'living Power' or what Coleridge calls 'vision nascent' (*BL* 1:286). It is the collective unconscious where the archetypes potentially reside, waiting for the imagination to give them shape and meaning as symbols of the human, which for Blake constitutes the 'Fourfold.'

As the work of the secondary imagination, a poem calls the whole soul of man into *conscious* activity. In this sense a poem is the soul's consciousness of itself. Nature, on the other hand, has no such consciousness. 'Then the man says "I remember,"' writes Nietzsche, 'and envies the animal, who at once forgets and for whom every moment really dies, sinks back into night and fog and is extinguished forever' ('On the Uses' 61). A poem is what may be called conscious nature, that is to say, a revelation of *human* nature. Describing his visit to the Athi Plains in Kenya, Jung watched gigantic herds of animals moving forward like slow rivers.

> This was the stillness of the eternal beginning, the world as it had always been, in the state of non-being; for until then no one had been present to know that it was this world. [...] There I was now, the first human being to

recognize that this was the world, but who did not know that in this moment he had first really created it.

There the cosmic meaning of consciousness became overwhelmingly clear to me. 'What nature leaves imperfect, the art perfects,' say the alchemists. Man, I, in an invisible act of creation put a stamp of perfection on the world by giving it objective existence. This act we usually ascribe to the Creator alone, without considering that in so doing we view life as a machine calculated down to the last detail, which, along with the human psyche, runs on senselessly, obeying foreknown and predetermined rules. In such a cheerless clockwork fantasy there is no drama of man, world, and God; there is no 'new day' leading to 'new shores,' but only the dreariness of calculated processes. (*MDR* 255–6)

However it manifests itself, human nature is one and not many. Therefore, as the revelation of human nature, all poems are what Shelley describes as one 'great poem, which all poets, like the co-operating thoughts [operations] of one great mind, have built up since the beginning of the world.' Coleridge affirms this oneness when, listening to Wordsworth chant his poetry, he felt he had heard 'the ANCIENT of days' proclaiming 'the first creative fiat.'

If any poet in the English language affirms this 'first creative fiat,' it is Blake, so powerfully and comprehensively, in fact, that most readers cannot take in his texts' primary act of creation. Tilottama Rajan argues that Blake's Lambeth prophecies enact their own unreadability as the absence of the meaning Blake's mind is struggling in vain to impose. Significantly, to this point Rajan has resisted Blake's epics, thus rejecting in advance the fact that readers usually impose upon these texts a system in order to deny the fact that there isn't one, absence in Blake becoming the highly wrought form of his presence. To say the least, the struggle Blake imposes upon the reader as Blake's own attempt to unite *Milton*, *Jerusalem*, and *The Four Zoas* is daunting, particularly since he left *The Four Zoas* unengraved, which Frye sees as a major cultural disaster. For me, however, this disaster is crucial to understanding what Blake attempted. I suggest that this attempt points to a reality whose absence reaches beyond human nature to a kind of Archimedean point, Jung's 'real zero point' 'without extension.' It is by this 'point' that human nature may be measured, judged, and forgiven – that is to say, ultimately known beyond this nature's imaginative construction or experience of itself. The challenge confronting the creative imagination is not the mind's inability to know itself as the Cogito, but rather its ability to work creatively with

its madness by rationally absorbing madness without reducing it to a
'*something-nothing-every-thing*, which does all of which we know, and knows
nothing of all that itself does.' Jung calls this mechanical understanding
a 'cheerless clockwork fantasy' where 'there is no drama of man, world,
and God'; there is no 'new day' leading to 'new shores,' but only the
dreariness of calculated processes.

We have seen how Blake explores as parody the demonic pole of the
Cogito's reach beyond the human as 'the Void Outside of Existence,' in
which most of the psychic events described in his early prophecies and
later epics appear to take place. As the work of the 'Reasoning Negative,' however, these events are the negation of action, the non-events
of an 'Eternal Death' from which the soul must ultimately awake. If the
number of plates in Blake's epics is any indication, however, the conscious making of this apocalypse, which occurs 'Within a Moment: a Pulsation of the Artery,' can be the result of a very long sleep over which
Satan presides. When Blake argues that Milton, like all true poets, was 'of
the Devils party without knowing it,' he suggests how the poetic imagination must labour to confront a world that rejects imagination as a 'Phantom of the over heated brain.' That is to say, imagination must labour
mightily to release the 'litteral' reality of the soul buried deep in the delusions of matter. For ninety-six of its ninety-nine plates, Albion, the hero
of *Jerusalem*, opposes Los, the imagination. 'But when he saw blue death
in Albions feet,' Los decides to rejoin his 'Divine Body' (33[37].10, 11),
which he had left behind in order to attend to Albion on his 'Couch of
Death' in the hope of awakening him from the nightmare he is in. Los
decides that he will hereafter remain in his 'Divine Body' – a decision
Blake, like all prophets, struggled in vain to make.

Blake's epic vision ultimately gestures beyond the human revelations
of the imagination toward divine revelation or *kerygma*. As we have seen,
Frye addresses *kerygma* as the mystical dimension in which *Jerusalem* is released from its visible form to become the invisibility of the epic's uncreated form. But the epic does not inhabit this wholeness as perfection, for
the epic's ultimate release, independent of the poet who turns the poem
over to its releaser, is the Archimedean point beyond the poem by which
is it is known to exist at its primal source. Blake indicates this anagogic
recognition by leaving *The Four Zoas* unengraved. As a cultural disaster
in Frye's sense, it is the ground of culture in my sense, which I take to be
Blake's sense. After sixty years of reading Blake, I am thus persuaded of
a third thing: the creative imagination, while repeating the eternal act of
creation, is, as myth, this act's supreme analogy. But it *is* an analogy that

repeats rather than initiates the eternal act. That there is a divine initiator ('Be and It Is') remains in itself the Unknown or 'Uncreated.' 'Veiled in My immemorial being and in the ancient eternity of My essence, I knew My love for thee, therefore I created thee, have engraved on thee Mine image and revealed to thee My Beauty.' At an unconscious level, the descent of the 'Starry Eight' into Blake's garden is the moment that the entire epic is constituted as the ceaseless work of Blake's sometimes mechanical brain. Blake stresses that 'man cannot know / What passes in his members till periods of Space & Time / Reveal the secrets of Eternity' (*M* 21[23].8–10). For this reason, the 'wondrous' acts over which the 'Starry Eight' presides are 'unknown' to Blake 'Except remotely.'

What I find uncanny about Blake's 'unknown' is his mythopoeic access to the archetypal resources of the collective unconscious as Jung would later explore them. That is why, particularly with Blake and Jung in mind, I think of this book as its own figurative engraving and illuminating of my dream of the Báb as a work of the imagination. In the Shia tradition, from which the Báb emerged as its Twelfth or Hidden Imam, the imagination is viewed as an intermediate world joining the literal realm of the senses to the largely unknown world of the spirit. While the imagination participates in both as their shared symbolic form, in itself it is neither world. In this intermediate world analogically binding Blake to the Shia tradition, which I experience as my whole soul in activity, I have over time taken up human residence as one who, however mysteriously, was 'certainly expected.' I moved slowly toward an understanding of the dialectical operations governing the Shia notion of the imagination, particularly as they are mirrored in Blake's vision, and more darkly in Pauli's work with his alchemical dreams – both informed, as we shall see, by a Persian. Through this gradual coming to awareness over sixty years, my climb to the fourth, non-existent floor of the apartment building in which I grew up, after which I cross a parting Persian carpet, rise in the air, and turn a somersault to land at the feet of the figure of the Báb, has assumed a possible meaning that my consciousness now rather awesomely greets with a certain silent joy. The climb to the fourth floor in a dumb waiter pulling on ropes unconsciously enacts the fifth business. This business unites the soul's consciousness of the journey from its undifferentiated beginning to its fully differentiated end to announce the emergence of a new life. As the creative act of perception, this new life is the 'living Power and prime Agent' of Romanticism, which Blake most fully explored in his vision of the 'Starry Eight' as the return of Christ, who in the Shia tradition is the Hidden Imam.

# 2

At the 1932 Easter conference of the Institute of Theoretical Physics, held annually in Copenhagen and founded by Niels Bohr, the father of quantum mechanics, the younger generation of quantum physicists performed for their elders a spoof on Goethe's *Faust* written by Max Delbrück. Bohr, Pauli, and Werner Heisenberg were in the front row. Bohr played God, Pauli played Mephistopheles, and Paul Ehrenfest was Faust. Ehrenfest was unable to abandon Einstein's absolute certainty about the divinely prescribed motions of matter, despite Pauli's dazzling attempts to convert him to the devil's party of Bohr's radical uncertainty, which Einstein dismissed as madness. A year and a half after the performance, Ehrenfest committed suicide. Well before the 1938 discovery of fission, quantum mechanics had already become a matter of life and death.

Michael Frayn takes up this urgency metapsychologically in his 1998 drama, *Copenhagen*. The play explores the indeterminate relations between Bohr and Heisenberg, who came to Copenhagen perhaps to convince Bohr to help the German physicists construct an atom bomb. In 1913 Bohr described atoms as miniature solar systems whose electrons travelled around the nucleus like planets orbiting around the sun. These orbits took discrete values limited by quantum conditions, the release of which energy was destructive but which also constituted a new solar system or order of reality. One image of this new order was Hitler's Third Reich. A counter image was Jung's fourfold mandala, of which Blake's fourfold Jerusalem was an earlier, more elaborate poetic image. Pauli was convinced that this new quantum reality lay in the intuitive grasp of his highly wrought mathematical mind as it took shape in the operations of the collective unconscious, which he called 'unconscious physics.' This conviction became the ground of his relations with Jung.

At the time of the mock performance, Pauli was in analysis with Jung's student, Erna Rosenbaum. Ever since his mother's No. 2 personality had introduced him to the play, *Faust* had lodged in Jung's psyche. For him, Mephistopheles carried forward the mysterious work of progressive revelation fatally arrested in Faust (as in Jung's wounded father) by a *deus ex machina* that arbitrarily casts out Mephistopheles and prematurely redeems Faust. Jung found Mephistopheles still at work in the unconscious laboratory of Pauli's alchemical dreams, which provided Jung with the quantum evidence of a psychic life mathematically manifesting itself in the quantum operations of matter. Even though Jung distrusted mathematics, he believed that Pauli might be able to measure these operations, and so measure the unconscious, which might in turn actualize the psychoid archetype as the inner marriage of psyche and soma – the New Jerusalem 'prepared as a bride adorned for her husband' (Revelation 21.2). 'At bottom it was I myself,' Jung writes of his hallucinogenic experience in 1944: 'I was the marriage. And my beatitude was that of a blissful marriage' (*MDR* 294).

Jung possessed 'no self-consistent mathematics' to view the unconscious like the objective 'Archimedean point' that allowed Pauli to observe the psychic world from a physical point of view. The 'tragic' fact, Jung realized, was that the psyche observes only itself as 'a calculus of subjective prejudices' and 'can only translate the psychic back into the psychic' ('On the Nature' 216). As their relations became more troubled, Jung and Pauli had reason to fear this infinite regress, not unlike the one Shelley explores in *Alastor*. The danger confronting the psyche is its mounting isolation from a larger reality, the 'separate phantasy' in the mysterious operations of Shelley's own human mind in 'the still cave of the witch Poesy.' As Jung knew, this descent into the unconscious psyche conducts to an unknowable source' to become the mind's psychotic revelation, like the anima that can 'utterly destroy a man.' Every human civilization finally becomes the victim of its own demonic shadow, the structures it erects to protect itself becoming in the end mirrors of its own extinction. This demonic shadow cast by divine revelation is the condition for its arising to consciousness, not unlike the archetypal role of the Persian hierophant in Pauli's dreams, who in one dream sets fire to the Eidgenossische Technische Hochschule (ETH) where Pauli held the lifetime chair in theoretical physics.

This shadow is also cast by my dream of thé Báb. Had this shadow possessed my consciousness in the way that many Persian Bábis embraced martyrdom as the Marriage Feast of the Lamb uniting them with their beloved, I would have been, from a Western rather than an Eastern perspective, merely rather than divinely mad. Yet by overtranquillizing divine madness, Blake argues in *The Marriage of Heaven and Hell,* Emanuel Swedenborg reduced his genuine apocalyptic vision to mere analytics. Taking advantage of Swedenborg's announcement of the Last Judgment in 1757, the year of Blake's birth, he dismisses Swedenborg as the angel at the tomb watching over Christ's folded linen clothes. Blake will now unfold this linen – Swedenborg's writings – as the new garment of the risen Jesus never before seen, 'Written within & without in woven letters.' He spent the rest of his life weaving this garment 'intirely new to the Inhabitants of Earth.'

Blake inherited the system of ironies dynamically operative in his imagination from the Enlightenment, a mode of Western cultural communication that assured readers, though barely, of his sanity. My conscious absorption of the garment he was weaving, not unlike the carpet that wraps itself around the Báb in my dream, similarly assured me of my own sanity, although, given the extravagance of Blake's account of the 'Spiritual Acts of [his] three years Slumber on the banks of the Ocean,' this assurance would take the rest of my life. Put another way, my reading of the dream was the *mise en abyme* within my reading of Blake, just as the descent of the androgynous Jesus into the fire of Blake's intellect shaped Blake's life. Following in Blake's footsteps, which at least afforded the distance of his intellectual satire, I thus copied his creations in the book of my own common life. Needless to say, I could not have copied the Báb's life without turning my life into a nightmarish delusion, which Blake recognized as the life of a prophet displayed as revelation. 'An Angel [Swedenborg] came to me and said,' Blake writes, taking the 'perilous path' (*MHH* 2.3) of a Devil as opposed to the Angel's path of ease: 'O pitiable foolish young man! O horrible! O dreadful state! consider the hot burning dungeon thou art preparing for thyself to all eternity, to which thou art going in such career' (17). To which Blake replies: 'perhaps you will be willing to shew me my eternal lot & we will contemplate together upon it and see whether your lot or mine is more desirable' (17). '[T]hy phantasy has imposed upon me & thou oughtest to be ashamed,' the angel finally declares (20). '[W]e impose on each other,' Blake replies, '& it is but lost time to converse with you whose works are only Analytics.'

Jung and Pauli's dilemma was how to observe the unconscious operations of the psyche when their 'supplementary charge' too easily vanished and their 'specific energy' threatened to overwhelm their consciousness. Working by 'only Analytics' wouldn't do the trick. Observing the psyche required moving past science's objective rationality to the subjective psychology of the individual, whose act of observing the world, especially at its quantum level, meant observing the operations of the psyche itself and thus working through the observer's individual psychology, which was itself beyond observation but which intrinsically and fundamentally affected the act of perception. One sees in this circular dilemma – to observe the psyche is to observe the psyche observing itself – the monumental effort confronting Jung and Pauli. This effort is further complicated by the fact of how *two* minds might communicate and keep clear both to oneself and to each other the terms of the exploration.

For Jung and Pauli, as for the Romantics before them, this effort had both an intensely personal and profoundly social, global, and even cosmic dimension. That is to say, the effort has profound implications for the future of the world. In Frayn's play neither Bohr nor Heisenberg knows the other's thoughts, nor indeed does the audience know its own mind. Frayn seems to be postulating what Jung, quoting the late sixteenth-century alchemist Gerald Dorneus, calls the '*unio mentalis*' or '*Unus Mundus*,' the 'one mind' or 'world' that Jung describes to Pauli as 'the one which the unconscious sees and seeks to produce, more or less corresponding to that synthesis which your dreams aspire toward.' In *Copenhagen*, Bohr and Heisenberg do not share their dreams, and so what this silence of the unconscious 'aspires toward' remains unknown, other than the fact that America developed and dropped the bomb ahead of Germany. Had it not, the world might have been far different. Or would it? Bohr explains that 'the whole possibility of science' lies in the fact that science relies on 'measurement,' which as a human act remains immeasurable. He says to Heisenberg that for Einstein measurement is

> a human act, carried out from a specific point of view in time and space, from the one particular viewpoint of a possible observer. Then, here in Copenhagen in those three years in the mid-twenties we discover that there is no precisely determinable objective universe. That the universe exists only as a series of approximations. Only within the limits determined by our relationship within it. Only through the understanding lodged inside the human head. (73–4)

Only, that is, in the dream of this understanding, which Frayn's imagination is mysteriously enacting, drawing his audience into the mystery.

It could be argued that Jung and Pauli set out to dislodge 'the understanding lodged inside the human head' (which included Pauli's dreams) in order to open this understanding to what he calls a new 'series of approximations,' which they explored together as the 'future of the *eternal world*' (*Atom* 129). For Blake, as we have seen, this constitutes the work of the imagination as a perpetual future in which the return of Christ is always already happening since the foundation of the world. The task of the poet is to construct a mythical home for the return in the otherwise uninhabitable foundation, the 'Void Outside of Existence' or the collective unconscious. Agreeing with Pauli that this void is 'bottomless' (128), Jung asserts that the psyche's job is to construct in the 'Abysm' a home wherein the imageless archetypes can assume a symbolic life as 'nascent' or potential forms, unconscious tendencies rather than actualities. For Jung, in a post-religious aeon where the centre of the mandala remains empty, religion constitutes this eternal process as a collective form of madness institutionally still declared sane. Jung would thus agree with Frayn that the numinous, experienced as modes of knowing, is a 'series of approximations.' Having their source in the collective unconscious, these modes are in their sheer potentiality, at least in theory, infinite, what Blake calls 'the bound or outward circumference of Energy' (*MHH* 4). Pauli's self-assigned task as the incumbent of the permanent chair of theoretical physics at the ETH in Zurich, where Jung had been a professor until he resigned following his break with Freud, was to find the mathematical equation that would transform 'approximations' into a demonstrable certainty, a transformation that Jung considered psychologically impossible. Such a certainty, he argues, would sacrifice human wholeness to the tyranny of human perfection.

Jung identified the collective unconscious with what he called 'a Platonic prior or primeval world.' At this archetypal level, like Blake's Eden, there is neither space nor time. Rather, the eternal is *now*. For Blake, this eternal now, 'Every Time less than a pulsation of the artery' (*M* 28[30].63), was, like the Derridean madness of the Cogito, direct revelation. He claimed and thus inhabited this archetypal world as a poetic tale rather than a form of worship by imaginatively exceeding it, opening and founding a mythopoeic world 'intirely new to the Inhabitants of Earth.' This mythopoeia absorbs madness to open and found the sanity within madness, not as an internment, but as the human articulation of the Cogito by which God becomes human as his 'creaturely incarnation,' which Jung treats in *Answer to Job* as poetic rather than religious truth, a *dis*lodging of the mind's psychological truth. Derrida writes:

> The extent to which doubt and the Cartesian Cogito are *punctuated* by this project of a singular and unprecedented excess – an excess in the direction of the nondetermined, Nothingness or Infinity, an excess which overflows the totality of that which can be thought, the totality of beings and determined meanings, the totality of factual history – is also the extent to which any effort to reduce this project, to enclose it within a determined historical structure, however comprehensive, risks missing the essential, risks dulling the *point* itself. Such an effort risks doing violence to the project in turn (for there is also a violence applicable to rationalists and to sense, to *good* sense; and this, perhaps, is what Foucault's book [*Madness & Civilization*] definitely demonstrates, for the victims of whom he speaks are always the bearers

of sense, the *true* bearers of the *true* and *good* sense hidden and oppressed by the *determined* 'good sense' of the 'division' – the 'good sense' that never divides itself enough and is always determined too quickly) – risks doing it violence in turn, and a violence of a totalitarian and historicist style which eludes meaning and the origin of meaning. (57)

Jung and Pauli, like Bohr and Heisenberg in Frayn's play, wrestle with how to release from a 'determined historical structure' – the actual history of the making and dropping of the atom bomb – the 'violence of [its] totalitarian and historicist style,' which is the psychosis of history itself. That is to say, they do not intern or otherwise abandon history, as Shelley was tempted to do in his final fragment, but rather make history a primal source of madness. This source is the tyranny of the psychosis into which the perception of history hardens, which must then be dissolved, diffused, and dissipated to produce the uncertainty or indeterminacy of history itself. Frayn's play settles for 'a series of approximations' as opposed to the delusions threatening to overtake the vulnerable human nature of truth. Like orthodox religious systems governed by fixated fate, these delusions may deny the future by settling well in advance the future's overdetermined 'now' in which time must have a stop. Jung describes such a situation – the hardening of an archetypal image into an infallible system – as a complex, in which the creative life of the collective unconscious lies 'bed-ridden in the dormitory of the soul, side by side, with the most despised and exploded errors' (*BL* 1:82).

For this reason I have sought to absorb my dream of the Báb as a psychological reality by assessing how the historical circumstances of my life in space and time are consciously informed by what Shelley describes as 'the interpenetration of a diviner nature through our own.' This 'interpenetration' transforms these circumstances into a visionary reality resembling a spell. But treated as an act of perception viewed at this act's archetypal source, this reality is, to paraphrase Coleridge, more than magical. Put another way, my dream's archetypal ground as divine revelation is at the same time its literal ground. That the Persian historical figure Siyyid 'Ali-Muhammad Shirazi (1819–50) *did* declare himself as the Báb or return of the Hidden Imam is a historical fact profusely documented in his written revelation and culminating in his martyrdom at high noon on 9 July 1850 in a public square in Tabriz, a martyrdom witnessed by some ten thousand spectators, some of whom described this experience in words and drawings. That said, while I have not rejected these historical facts, I have chosen inwardly to explore their linear record in terms of a vertical or metaphorical understanding of them. This is also to say that I have here chosen largely to ignore these facts because their historical demands upon me as a Baha'i gradually exhausted rather than fed my limited spiritual resources.

In this state of spiritual exhaustion, brought on by an overextended historical participation in the earthly grounding of the Báb's revelation, I was compelled to withdraw from this historical unfolding in order to return to its source. I experienced this source, not as the revelation itself, but as my dream of it, which I embraced as a particular repetition of the source addressed to my finite human mind. In short, I realized that I had been trying to convert the world before I knew what the conversion was in myself. Finding in Romanticism a visionary experience not unlike my dream, I thus chose not to process the dream as my active promotion of the Baha'i faith, which meant, paradoxically and at considerable psychic cost, that I needed to ignore the dream itself. Instead, I withdrew from the extroversion, which in any case increasingly confronted me with a stranger in myself, and attended to the stranger of the Báb of my dream. My vertical or metaphorical understanding of the dream resides in bringing the dream to consciousness, what Jung calls the Self. This Self may now conduct to a further historical understanding of the Baha'i faith as this understanding relates to my inner, still unfolding history. This possibility is as much as I can promise in this book.

Bearing in mind this analysis of my dream projected onto my psychological analysis of Romanticism, most fully embodied in Blake's apocalyptic vision, I now wish to explore further the complex triangulated relations between Jung, Pauli, and Marie-Louise von Franz. What Frayn explores in his play for a larger audience, Jung and Pauli explore rather more privately in their correspondence, each only insofar as the other helped, with the mediating assistance of von Franz, to make conscious what was going on in their highly charged brains, where, as Blake argues, the 'Eternal Great Humanity Divine. planted his Paradise, / And in it caus'd the Spectres of the Dead to take sweet forms / In likeness of himself' (M 1.11–13) In the relationship between Romanticism, quantum physics, psychology, and revelation, I want to confront in the conscious processing of my dream its unconscious source as the shaping of a myth capable of approximating what remains hidden as the collective unconscious. As I have already explored at length, to imagine that one can treat divine revelation as an unveiling of the hidden is delusional, if not entirely mad. Yet I mean to retain Derrida's sense of the Cogito's hyperbolic excess that founds the world in and as the new mythopoeic accounts of it as more than rational 'approximations.' In sane hands, such accounts avoid hubris by returning divine madness to the world as answerable to madness in the name of reason.

# 3

By twenty-one Pauli had published a critique of Einstein's relativity theory that won him a 1945 Nobel Prize, at which point Einstein considered him the heir who would solve problems in physics that had remained too difficult for himself. While still a professor at the ETH, Jung had frequent encounters with Einstein, who was at the University of Zurich. 'He was often in my house,' Jung later explains in one of his Tavistock lectures (1935), 'and I pumped him about his relativity theory. I am not gifted in mathematics and you should have seen all the trouble the poor man had to explain relativity to me' (*The Tavistock Lectures* 68). Jung confessed that the struggle had left him 'fourteen feet deep into the floor.' To illustrate the difficulty for his audience, Jung, when asked about one of his patients, attempted to explain how the patient's dream gave Jung an accurate diagnosis of the patient's mysterious organic disease when it had otherwise stumped Jung's medical colleagues. 'I should have to quote bit after bit from Chinese and Hindu literature, medieval texts and all the things which you do not know,' Jung replied to his somewhat bemused Western audience. 'The Eastern mind, when it looks at an ensemble of facts, accepts that ensemble as it is' (68–9). For Jung, this approach means that from a psychic perspective the dream tells him what is going on psychosomatically in the body at any one of its 'ensembled' moments. To read the dream was to read the patient's diseased body, which the dream diagnoses. Furthermore, for Jung the diagnosis is a synchronistic occurrence, an acausal rather than causal connection between the patient's psyche and his body, there being, so far as we know, no psychic operation that does not include the body as this operation's recipient, or indeed no physical operation that does not include the psyche. Or as the *I Ching* indicates, psyche and matter may yet one day prove to be two aspects of the same thing.

Just as Jung left his audience as Einstein had left him, 'fourteen feet deep into the floor,' he knew when Pauli came to him in 1931 seeking help for an emotional disturbance that to diagnose Pauli's psychophysical situation through his dreams would similarly confound Pauli. 'Special knowledge [whether mathematics or dreams] is a terrible disadvantage,' Jung explains. 'It leads you in a way too far, so that you cannot explain any more.' 'But one day,' Jung concludes, '[Einstein] asked me something about psychology. Then I had my revenge' (*The Tavistock Lectures* 68). Putting down Einstein as much as Einstein put down Jung, Jung was persuaded to turn Pauli over to a woman whose lack of experience would, with the help of Jung's advice, prevent her from interfering with what she was not yet in a position to understand. That is to say, Pauli's understanding of his dreams was likely to be rationally overdetermined, fully demonstrating the severe damage he was inflicting upon his inferior feeling function, which was crucial to this understanding. The paradox was that only through a complete, inevitable collapse could Pauli's feeling function come to its own defence. At this point, Jung would intervene to 'get his revenge' by unlocking in the genius of Pauli's mathematical mind the psychic aptitude or feeling function beyond objective rationality. This answer would essentially prove Pauli's radical point that the psyche's perception of the physical world at a quantum level fundamentally altered – was integrally part of – this world's physical make-up. Put another way, if Pauli could truly confront his own unconscious, he might in fact unlock the secret of how the cosmos functions at a quantum level. He might, that is, confront the 'eternal world' of the *unus mundus*, the point at which psyche and matter, mind and world, touch and do not touch, the still point of perception that was Coleridge's 'living Power and prime Agent of all human Perception.'

To Jung's astonishment and delight, Pauli, who by 1928 held the Chair in theoretical physics at the ETH, proceeded to release in four and a half months of analysis a deluge of dreams. He made some four hundred of these available to Jung. Analysing these dreams supplied the evidence Jung badly needed to support his psycho-physical claims for alchemy, which he eventually published in his 1944 *Psychology and Alchemy* and which Freud had dismissed as 'occultism,' 'sheer bosh,' a 'black tide of mud' (*MDR* 150). In these powerfully archetypal dreams the collective unconscious provided Pauli with a series of mandalas that became crucial to Jung's preparation for a commentary on 'a Taoist-alchemical treatise entitled *The Secret of the Golden Flower*,' which Richard Wilhelm had sent him in 1928. 'I devoured the manuscript at once,' Jung writes, 'for the text gave me undreamed-of confirmation of my ideas about the mandala and the circumambulation of the center. That was the first event which broke through my isolation. I became aware of an affinity; I could establish ties with something and someone' (197). The second event was Jung's work with Pauli. He found in Pauli's dreams 'ties with something and someone' who, more than Wilhelm, had a direct and immediate relationship to the West. To Jung, the 'Oriental point of view and ancient Chinese culture had penetrated [Wilhelm] through and through,' creating a 'clash between his Western and Eastern psyche' that finally brought him down (*MDR* 375–6). Jung persuaded himself that Pauli, being a 'perfectly normal and reasonable person' (*The Tavistock Lectures* 175), would suffer no such collapse.

At first it seemed that Jung was right and that their respective minds and researches were compatible. In his April 1948 address on the occasion of the founding of the C.G. Jung Institute in Zurich, which he described as 'an Institute of Complex Psychology,' Jung argued that a complex, at the core of which is an archetype, 'cannot be adequately explained without the hypothesis of the [collective] unconscious.' Insisting on the importance of 'complex psychology' for a new understanding of various disciplines, physics above all, Jung turned to Pauli, who had already delivered two lectures in February and March on 'The Influence of Archetypal Ideas on the Scientific Theories of Kepler.' In these Pauli related Kepler's scientific theories, affirming a Trinitarian Godhead, to the work of the Oxford alchemist, Robert Fludd, who argued for the Quaternity. In a letter to the physicist Markus Fierz, Pauli declared he was 'not only Kepler, but also Fludd' (cited in Lindorff 90). But his search for the 'longed-for *coniunctio* of the opposites' proved difficult and 'could come to him only if he were able to express himself in a very shocking manner to the representatives of conventional religion as well as of conventional science' (123). 'Thirty years ago [in *Psychological Types*],' Jung explains, 'the problem first presented itself in psychology as a typological phenomenon, i.e., as the relation of three more or less differentiated functions [as in Pauli's differentiation between intuition, sensation, and thought] to one inferior function [as, in Pauli's case, feeling] which was contaminated with the unconscious' ('Address' 473). Like the irritant that makes the pearl or like Blake's Devil serving the imagination, this contamination became the transcendent, though ultimately disruptive, function governing Jung's and Pauli's joint labours. Jung continues:

Since then [my understanding of this problem] has been considerably widened and deepened by the study of Gnostic and alchemical texts. It appears there partly in the form of the social or folkloristic *marriage quaternio*, derived originally from the primitive cross-cousin-marriage, and partly in the form of a differentiation in the sequence of elements, in which one or the other element, usually fire or earth, is distinguished from the other three. The same problem appears in the controversy between the trinitarian and the quaternarian standpoint [Kepler and Fludd] in alchemy. In complex psychology the quaternity symbol has been shown to be an expression of psychic totality, and in the same way it could be established that the *proportio sesquitertia* commonly occurs in symbolism produced by the unconscious. If, as conjectured, the quaternity or above-mentioned proportion is not only fundamental to all concepts of totality but is also inherent in the nature of observed microphysical processes, we are driven to the conclusion that the space-time continuum, including mass, is psychically relative – in other words, that it forms a unity with the unconscious psyche. ('Address' 473)

Between Pauli's two earlier lectures and Jung's statement above we can see the shared energy and idealism at work in their desire to find the 'unity' between matter and 'the unconscious psyche.' In that unity lay for Jung the future of psychology, and for Pauli the future of quantum physics. For both of them the future was the 'future of the eternal world.' Like Blake before them, both men were convinced that 'eternity is in love with the productions of time.'

# 4

But history intervened in less-than-productive ways to curb this enthusiasm. When Jung's mounting heart problems forced him to retire from the C.G. Jung Institute, Pauli became critical of the institute's resistance to science, which by 1956 had ended his work with Jung, though he was careful not to criticize Jung himself. In July he wrote to the president:

In recent years, I have noted with grave concern that the scientific approach *is becoming increasingly neglected* in matters relating to the C.G. Jung Institute and the activities of its members. As the scientific patron of the Institute, I thus regard it as my duty *to draw attention to the standpoint of the sciences* [...] It is clear to me that in addition to the scientific aspect of psychology, there is also a humanistic one, but I do not see it as *my* duty to defend that. [...] I should like to point out that psychology always used to be considered as one of the *humanistic* sciences, but it was precisely C.G. Jung himself who emphasized the scientific nature of his ideas, and it was through his works that the way was paved for an integration of the psychology of the unconscious into the natural sciences. It is my opinion that the progress that has been made in this respect is being seriously jeopardized by the administration of the C.G. Jung Institute. (*Atom* 212)

Becoming characteristically more heated, Pauli continues: 'But it is precisely the scientific investigation of such matters [dreams, fantasies, etc.] that should form the basis for the perception of disturbances in the normal process of these phenomena in neuroses and other patho-logical cases' (213). Instead, he points out, this investigation is becoming increasingly alien to the analyst's egotistical concerns with larger and larger groups. 'I therefore ask the question – with a request for informa-tion – as to *what measures the C.G. Jung Institute is thinking of taking* in order – at least with its members – *to combat the general abuses and deplorable state of affairs of analytical practice at the moment.*' To that question he then adds a further paragraph:

> And this leads me on to another specific question. In his writings, C.G. Jung repeatedly stipulated that *the doctor himself had to undergo analysis.* So I am requesting information as to *what measures the C.G. Jung Institute is thinking of taking to ensure that its members (including the President) comply with this stipula-tion* when Prof. Jung is enjoying a well-earned retirement and *can no longer take over these functions.* (213)

Pauli's insistence on the doctor's own psychoanalysis is rather ironic here in the context of Jung's eventual realization that Pauli was unable truly to confront the necessary 'irritant' of his feeling function as the royal road to his own and thus to the collective unconscious of quan-tum mechanics. For according to the terms of their joint work before their break, the 'scientific' observation of the unconscious psyche and the depth analysis of the scientist were rather intimately linked. Describ-ing Pauli's case in his Tavistock Lectures (though not mentioning him by name), Jung stresses the role of active imagination that Pauli, working on his own, may have invented by writing down his dreams as if they were an assortment of figures in search of an equation. Pauli's later descrip-tion of a dream as 'unconscious physics' would suggest that he related what Jung calls active imagination to mathematics, specifically to his own work as a quantum physicist. If Jung's major contribution to Pauli's search for a hidden equation that defied Newton's law of motion is his discovery that dreams reveal the archetypes of the collective unconscious in the same way that numbers do, then Pauli's work with numbers owed as much to Jung's method of dream interpretation as it did to Pauli's mathematical training.

But the roadblocks weren't all of Pauli's making. For one thing, Jung's invincible ignorance about mathematics, which he rejected as a 'down-right lie or a fraud' to the end of his life, created a chasm between them that could never be completely bridged. Moreover, Pauli became increasingly wearied of his work with Jung, particularly because Jung's health problems increasingly drained him of the energy required to deal with Pauli's superior knowledge in his own field. Pauli, with Jung apparently agreeing, argued that Jung's 'occult' approach to dreams left his psychology without an accepted academic home. That said, Pauli found himself equally homeless when he tried to make a dream answerable to Jung's endlessly regressive method. Arguing in a letter to Pauli that they were drawing closer by virtue of their increasing isolation, Jung concludes: 'for if you feel isolated from your contemporaries when grappling with the unconscious, it is also the same with me, in fact more so, since I am actually standing in the isolated area, striving somehow to bridge the gap that separates me from the others. After all, it is no pleasure for me always to be regarded as esoteric' (*Atom* 129). Jung begins his letter by apologizing for his lengthy silence toward Pauli's substantial one in which Pauli explains in some depth why and how he disagrees with Jung's interpretation of his 'physical-symbolic dreams.' 'Apart from a whole series of external reasons, such as lack of time, fatigue, and poor health,' Jung explains, 'the main reason for my delay in replying was the sheer abundance of problems raised in your letter. I did not feel equal to the task of giving you an adequate response. I doubt whether I can do so even now. Your letter has touched things in me that are vaguely unsettling and which I have in the meantime striven hard to get a grasp of' (125).

One of Jung's fundamental fears was that, by turning toward a more biological notion of the collective unconscious, Pauli appeared to be moving in Freud's direction. Or as Pauli says to von Franz in his active imagination, *The Piano Lesson*, '"This lesson has been going on already for a long time; I must go back to my men's world, among the people"' (133). Here Pauli alludes to the ongoing struggle between the 'symbolic physics' of his dreams and Jung's 'symbolic mythology.' 'Your dreams are physical because this is your natural language,' Jung tries to explain to Pauli, '[...] but in fact the dream means something different.' He continues: 'The unconscious has the tendency to confine you to physics or keep you away from psychology, because psychology, for whatever reason, is not appropriate' (*Atom* 113). Jung then goes on to argue that psychology is equally inappropriate to a fuller understanding of his own dreams:

> It is true that the unconscious produces psychology, but *the more it does so, the more it is against it, which is the case with both you and myself.* Psychological tendencies in the unconscious are found only where psychological insights are urgently necessary. The process of developing consciousness is a very demanding one and is by no means a popular matter in nature. (114; my italics)

It is no popular matter, Jung insists, because nature, left in its native state, remains unconscious, yet in turn is totally alien to a 'developing consciousness' that attempts to bring nature to consciousness. Jung was particularly frustrated in this regard because Pauli's inferior feeling function, especially as it was connected to a confrontation with the feminine in himself, stubbornly resisted the demands of consciousness by repeatedly returning to its natural state, often with the help of alcohol. For this reason Pauli sought the illusion of an easier way out by returning to the 'man's world,' just as in Freud's *Totem and Taboo* the primal horde renounces in common all the women they nevertheless continue to desire. As we shall see, Pauli continues to practice this renunciation in *The Piano Lesson*.

Jung goes on to argue that the most immediate way of avoiding the painful demands 'developing consciousness' makes upon the unconscious psyche, which as nature prefers to remain unconscious, would be in Pauli's case to turn to the unpsychological world of physics, or in Jung's case to the unpsychological world of metaphysics. Jung explains that when he translates the dream figure into the language of consciousness, he reduces its 'meaning to [his] subjective situation.' This experience is painful because the dream figure, belonging to the unconscious world of nature, resists being reduced to a subjective situation to which it is archetypally unrelated. Any reduction of the archetypes to subjective states is, from the perspective of the unconscious, comparable to the tyranny Derrida associates with the internment of the Cogito. How, then, does one absorb the archetype without interning it? 'But as a metaphysician,' Jung continues, 'I could also [like Pauli as a physicist] examine the dream statement for its objective meaning – in other words, not psychologically – which would take me into the sphere of what one might call the spirit or the mind, and from there it might be possible for me to have a sense of archetypal physics' (*Atom* 114). But this 'sense of archetypal physics,' while numinous in the way that numbers as archetypes are clearly numinous for Pauli, bypasses consciousness by transcending it, thereby relieving the ego of the agony of consciousness. Confronted by this agony, as Pauli and Jung confronted each other, 'the *fascinosum*' of the 'constellated archetypes' (114) is infinitely more desirable because in every 'Pulsation of the Artery' it gratifies the natural desire to remain, in obedience to the unconsciousness of nature, felt in the blood. 'These archetypes,' Jung explains to Pauli, quoting Pauli back to himself, 'more or less free us from psychology in the sense that psychology is "relieved of its burden"' (114). 'However important and interesting it may be to deal with the nonpsychic – especially with its archetypal stage,' he warns – and the warning is against madness – 'there is nevertheless the risk that one may lose oneself in the notion itself. But then the creative tension disappears, for it comes into being only when the acknowledgement of the nonpsychic is brought into relation with the observer' (114).

Determined to rescue Pauli from the danger of madness, which Jung associates with a direct mathematical identification with the archetypal realm of numbers rather than the subjective application of mathematics, Jung attempts to bring Pauli back to the role of the observer. However difficult because acausal, this role must be consciously recognized if quantum physics is ever to be mathematically understood:

> What I mean by [the observer] is, for example, that the product is studied critically, not just from the point of view of its objective associations but also its subjective ones. In physics this means the determination of the role played by the observer or the psychological prerequisites of a theory. What does it mean if Einstein establishes a world formula but does not know which reality it corresponds to? [...] With the perception of the archetypal prerequisites in Kepler's astronomy [Trinity] and the comparison with Fludd's philosophy [Quaternity], you have taken two steps, and now you seem to be at the third one – namely, the question of *what Pauli says about it*. (*Atom* 114)

But failing to confront this fact, Pauli returned to the 'men's world' of the natural sciences, of physics and biology, and thus to the intellectual and neutral language of mathematics. Supposedly this return would release him from the emotionally charged realm of narrative or fable into which Jung's understanding of the dream world of the collective unconscious had led him. At the same time, Jung had forced him to recognize the painful role of consciousness that the acausal observer imposed upon him as a quantum physicist. Such a recognition meant that he could not entirely abandon depth psychology without abandoning the new physics, as his colleague Max Delbrück had done. Though he is now going back to his 'men's world,' he assures von Franz he will return:

> *She*: 'What do you want to do among the people?'
> *I*: 'I will try to reconcile the master at all costs.'
> The voice of the master answers immediately, more friendly than before:
> 'That is what I have long waited for.'
> *I* (to the lady): 'Now that he has been reconciled I can give you *your dignity as a woman back.*'
> *She*: (astonished): 'What do you mean? Ah, I see, you allude to what I said earlier about being in bondage to the master.'
> *I*: 'Exactly.'
> *She* only smiles.
> *I*: 'Goodbye for now. Whatever subject I will discuss in the men's world – I shall owe thanks to the lady.'
> Thereupon I made a deep bow and said to myself: 'My consciousness cannot exist without a pair of opposites. That is why, for me as a man, the unity beyond my consciousness will always be with my lady.' (*The Piano Lesson* 133)

But Von Franz knew differently. In a November 1990 interview on Pauli's treatment of the Master (Jung) in his active imagination, von Franz was asked to elaborate on the danger Pauli was in as he describes this danger in *The Piano Lesson*. Von Franz explains:

> The unconscious is a nature spirit in man. It is like the master [Jung], which Pauli describes in his active imagination or Mercurius. He can lead you very easily down the garden path and then you end up in a wilderness or in trouble. It needs great skill to deal with the unconscious properly. So people are afraid of it. ('Wolfgang Pauli' 147)

As we shall see, Pauli believed that von Franz's love of Jung had led her, as his devoted disciple, down a garden path. Though she could not marry, as the piano teacher she had more than necessary prerequisites to facilitate in her work with Pauli a true meeting between the masculine and feminine, matter and psyche, rationality and feeling. But this possibility remained only suspended between them. Pauli's return to the 'men's world' was, they realized, a failure on both their parts. 'So the *Piano Lesson* ends very disappointingly,' von Franz concludes in the interview. 'It makes me sad, like the whole thing makes me sad. If you want me to sum up the relationship: I tried to pull him out and didn't succeed' (143).

# 5

The issue confronting quantum physics that distinguishes it from classical physics is acausality, in which there is a meaningful but unknown connection between the psyche as observer and what is observed outside the psyche, which Jung calls synchronicity. Perhaps the most vivid example of this phenomenon was what became known among Pauli's colleagues as 'the Pauli effect.' For instance, Pauli was sitting alone at the window of a café brooding about his inferior feeling function, which he associated with the colour red. The projected object of his brooding was a large, unoccupied car parked outside the café. Unable to take his eyes off the car, it suddenly burst into flames. By the evidence of such a phenomenon, one can see why Pauli initially sought out Jung in 1931, for by this point his feeling function was wreaking havoc on his emotional life and threatened his work as a leading quantum physicist. This fear reached such an uncanny degree of awareness that Pauli imagined he was struggling with his own extinction, a fantasy enacted by his mother's real suicide, apparently instigated by her husband's extramarital affairs. Pauli's brief marriage to a cabaret entertainer following this suicide was thus likely a futile attempt to reconcile his parents, but in the end his feeling function remained fatally trapped in the construction of a psychological crisis for which he could find no causal or rational solution.

Jung realized the solution lay elsewhere. 'What seems satisfactory to me is that the ordering factor, "consisting of meaning," which contains time (the chronos) as a special case, as the masculine principle, stands in contrast to the feminine-indestructible one (causality in the narrowest sense, energy, collective psyche), as also seems to be the case in microphysics,' Pauli wrote to Jung (*Atom* 39). Pauli is responding to Jung's manuscript on synchronicity, which Pauli persuaded him to write and helped to revise along more scientific lines before publishing it with his own essay on Keppler and Fludd. Unless 'the feminine-indestructible one' is *contained* without being *confined* in the masculine as 'the ordering factor,' the result is fantasy rather than science. As the '*coincidentia opposi-torum*' between them, consciousness is essential if genius is to succeed as the marriage of reason and desire, rather than remain on the verge of collapse, as in Pauli's case. 'It indeed appear'd to Reason as if Desire was cast out,' writes Blake of *Paradise Lost*, 'but the Devils account is, that the Messiah fell. & formed a heaven of what he stole from the Abyss. This is shewn in the Gospel, where he prays to the Father to send the comforter or Desire that Reason may have Ideas to build on, the Jehovah of the Bible being no other than he, who dwells in flaming fire' (*MHH* 5–6).

But this was not how Pauli saw things. Thanking Aniela Jaffé for send-ing him a review of Fred Hoyle's *The Nature of the Universe*, Pauli found it, as a 'mixture of fantasy and science [...] poor taste.' 'I regard it as femi-nine – i.e., more precisely, I see Hoyle as a feeling type,' he explained to Jaffé, whose own feminine he eventually found suffocating, his growing rage abruptly ending their relationship, which was rather ironic given that he had once sought her advice on feminine matters (*Atom* 73). Pauli concludes the letter, 'Do you think that this [difference between the masculine and feminine] is objectively correct, or do you look on such an idea as characteristic of a masculine thinking type and his particular psychology?' (74). Inferior feeling types, Pauli goes on to suggest, deal positively with chaos. '[Hoyle's] "Background Matter" and his continu-ous creation of matter out of nothing strike me as sheer nonsense. I see no reason to doubt the conservation of physical energy. It is clear to me that this type of cosmogony is *not physics but a projection of the unconscious*' (73). Physics, that is, requires consciousness if it is not to be confused with fantasy. If the unconscious is projected, Jung warns, as it can be in any deterministic notion of biology, or in any mathematical immersion in the numinosity of numbers, the result is the sheer pleasure of fan-tasy. In this unconscious state, the feminine assumes control by seducing rather than cooperating with the masculine.

Fantasy is thus chaos masquerading as order, the nightmare of which became for Pauli, as it did for Jung, the making and dropping of the atom bomb as the forbidden fruit of quantum physics, which only a full understanding of the dialectic at work within quantum physics might have prevented. Chosen by Einstein as the son and heir who would solve problems too difficult for the father, Pauli felt that he had, like Einstein, who advised Franklin Roosevelt to make the bomb and even provided the necessary instructions, morally failed. However inflated he might have been, Pauli blamed himself for Hiroshima, the misplaced blame perhaps best revealing how radically inferior his feeling function actually was. What from Blake's point of view his genius never managed to absorb was the archetypal reality of Jehovah, 'who dwells in flaming fire.' The car that exploded in flames outside the café window at which Pauli sat brooding on his dark, inferior feminine is she 'who dwells in flaming fire.' Pauli never psychologically succeeded in bringing her to consciousness, and the failure cost him his life.

Pauli would describe the cause of this failure as 'radioactive.' In physics, radioactivity results from the emission of '(positive) alpha-, (positive or negative) beta-, and (neutral) gamma rays in the spontaneous decay of atomic nuclei' (electrons are negative beta rays, positrons are positive beta rays, photons are high-energy gamma rays) (*Atom* xxiii). Analogously, Pauli describes how the spontaneous decay of the archetypes located at the nucleus of a complex scatter their emissions through the nervous system if the decay is not transformed into consciousness. Reading between radioactive and archetypal decay, Pauli concludes:

> The case where it has not been determined whether the *individual* atom of a radioactive clock [measurable by weight] is in the initial or final stage of radioactive decay corresponds to the connection of the individual with the collective unconscious through an archetypal content *of which he is unconscious.* The ascertaining of the state of consciousness of the individual, which emerges from this collective unconscious and which causes the synchronistic phenomenon to vanish, corresponds to the determination of the energy level of the *individual* atom by means of a special experiment. (41–2)

Here Pauli suggests further that since synchronicity is the acausal (meaningful, though unconscious) connection between an inner, archetypal event and an external, particular one, the synchronistic vanishing of the archetype is measurable by its absorption as the energy level of the synchronistic event resulting from the vanishing form of this event's absorption. The degree to which the archetype's measurable 'radioactive' decay becomes its conscious transformation, the more the archetype's radioactivity is creatively rather than negatively understood. For Pauli, this transformation finds its atomic counterpart in the gamma rays of high-energy photons.

In short, Pauli recognized, to a degree the depth and implications of which we are only now beginning to grasp, how quantum physics and depth psychology are intimately related. In his relations with Jung, this intimacy reached beyond the limits of Pauli's impressive endurance.

Its demands, comparable at times to the perpetual coitus of Shiva and Shakti, drove his inferior feeling function into an *enantiodromia* that produced 'the Pauli Effect.' For Pauli, that this feeling contained within it the alchemical fire in which the analogy itself dissolves into the identity of psyche and matter – Jung's 'point without extension' or 'real zero point' where, as the consciousness of it, psyche and matter 'touch and do not touch' – was an intuitive reality that he both knew and did not know. Blake understood this reality as the new revelation of Jehovah.

In Pauli's dreams this flaming Jehovah took the form of a Persian. Significantly, it was to Emma Jung that he described this figure. Archetypally, Emma Jung represented the mother in her relation to Jung as the father or master. More immediately, she had sent Pauli a 'very instructive' letter about her work with von Franz on the Grail legend, which he had just finished reading, and to which he felt now better equipped to respond. Moreover, he wanted to describe the work he had done on Merlin in relation to his essay on Kepler. Pauli writes: 'I paid special attention to the fair dark form of Merlin. You yourself point out his "dual layer" – namely, his "half-Christian-human": "half-devilish-pagan" [...] and you go on to emphasize his need for redemption' (*Atom* 49). Pauli explores this '"dual layer"' in an earlier letter to Emma Jung, in which he describes his work with Marcus Fierz on the *Romans de la Table Ronde*, particularly the tale of the three wooden spindles found on a revolving mandala island embracing the four elements. The spindles were taken from the island and returned in the Garden of Eden to the Tree of Life, a branch of which Eve was allowed to take with her to Earth. From this branch the spindles were made by Solomon's wife, who added them to David's sword. For centuries sword and spindles travelled by boat until they arrived at the revolving island as the 'chthonic Trinity' (47). On the island (the *primum mobile*) the spindles as the weavers of Fate (Determinism) are restored to the Quaternity, the fourfold releasing consciousness from its triangulated Fate (Freud's family romance) into the freedom of Jung's Fourfold (sensation, intuition, feeling, thought) as 'the whole soul of man in activity.' This fourfold consciousness is the Round Table of the Grail knights from which in its Christian version all that remains pagan has been suppressed. One image of this suppression is Galahad sleeping on a spindle bed until he dies – that is, until he awakens to the 'secret' the bed or boat contains. In short, the tale enacts the psychic journey from Three to Four, which is the recognition of the feminine at work binding Jung and Pauli together for twenty-six years.

In Blake the three spindles belong to the Daughters of Beulah, who in

Blake's lyric are the three virgins who inhabit a Threefold garden where, as a 'Golden Net' that binds the threefold sexual, they weave the pattern of Fate (*CPP* 483). Blake's vision enacts the disentangling of the imagination from this threefold snare by releasing it as a 'golden string' to be wound by the reader 'into a [fourfold] ball,' which will lead 'in at Heavens gate, / Built in Jerusalems wall' (*J* 77.7–10). The infinitely complex weaving of Blake's vision anticipates the psycho-physical issues of quantum physics as they are reflected in the relations between Jung and Pauli. Blake's Los is thus the dark Persian or Stranger of Pauli's dreams. In one of these the Persian uses gasoline to set fire to the ETH and then to drive Pauli to his true destination to do his real teaching, a school where the Persian, the instructor of Pauli's unconscious, also presumably teaches, the ETH having rejected him. Pauli awakens before he arrives. As Pauli struggles with Jung to give to the 'Orient' feminine source an 'Occidental' meaning long considered alien to this source, the Persian merges with a blond figure whom Pauli identifies with Mercurius. Together they form what Pauli calls the 'Stranger' in himself, the same Stranger Jung confronts at the conclusion of his memoirs as an 'unexpected unfamiliarity with [him]self' (*MDR* 359).

Tragically, the 'third step' that Jung urged Pauli to take became the hospital room in which he died after collapsing in the midst of a lecture at the ETH. When Pauli, 'visibly uneasy,' asked Charles Enz, the assistant who took him to the hospital, if he had seen the room number, Enz confessed that he had not noticed. Checking, he told Paul it was 137. As David Lindorff points out,

> The number 137 [...] had been pronounced by Pauli and others to be the most important number in physics. It is a dimensionless quantity composed of three constants that are of central importance to quantum theory: Planck's constant, the charge of an electron, and the speed of light. Pauli believed that future developments in quantum theory depended on an understanding of what lay behind that number. (242)

In *The Piano Lesson* von Franz has a second address, where Pauli 'visited once before' (122). It is 'the Golden Horn,' Istanbul, where Theodore Apt actually did find an Arabic alchemical text by a Shia mystic steeped in the spiritual quest, like all Shia spiritual seekers, for the Hidden Imam whose home is Hurqalya. Hurqalya is the intermediate world between Heaven and Earth, accessible through the dialectical operations of the imagination not as an organ of fiction, but, as throughout Islam, an organ of truth. Working on a commentary on this text, von Franz was herself confronted by a version of Pauli's Persian, who becomes a kind of archetypal figure binding Pauli to von Franz in *The Piano Lesson*, while at the same time separating them. Tragically, von Franz died before completing her commentary. (She once lectured at the University of Toronto on Jung's notion of the Second Coming, and my wife and I spent the day following the lecture with her at Niagara Falls. We stood together behind the falls in yellow rain gear talking about places of power, at which point I was tempted to tell her my dream of the Báb. For some reason I decided not to, though in retrospect at that stage she may well have been the one person to make a real contribution to my understanding of it. At that time, however, such an external source would have been an intrusion upon my very private, not to say sacred, space, which even now I cannot casually enter as if familiar with it.)

'Everything that Prof. Jung says about the "spirit Mercurius" fits him perfectly,' Pauli begins his description of the Stranger in his letter to Emma Jung, whom in one context he associates with 'the mother's lap' on which he is figuratively seated as if on a throne of chthonic power, which he otherwise had reason to fear. He continues:

While reading your work, however, I saw that there is also an important analogy between this figure and *Merlin*. [...] My [Persian] dream figure is also 'dual-layered'; on the one hand, he is a spiritual-light figure with superior knowledge, and on the other hand, he is a chthonic natural spirit. But his knowledge repeatedly takes him back to nature, and his chthonic origins are also the source of his knowledge, so that ultimately both aspects turn out to be facets of the same 'personality.' He is the one who prepares the way for the quaternity, which is always pursuing him. His actions are always effective, his words definitive, albeit often incomprehensible. [...] But now comes the really odd bit, namely the analogy to the 'Antichrist': He is not an Antichrist, but in a certain sense an 'Antiscientist,' 'science' here meaning especially the scientific approach, particularly as it is taught in universities today. This he sees as a sort of *Zwinguri*, as the place and symbol of his oppression, which (in my dreams) he occasionally sets fire to. If he feels he is being disregarded, he does everything in his power to draw attention to himself, for example, by means of synchronistic phenomena (which he calls 'radioactivity') or through moods of depression or incomprehensible affects. [...] When rational methods in science reach a dead end, a new lease of life is given to those contents that were pushed out of time consciousness in the 17th century and sank into the unconscious. [...] And yet, when all comes to all, the relationship of the 'stranger' to science is not a destructive one, which is also true of Merlin's relationship to Christianity. [...] It seems to me that for him the 'bonfire' of liberation will only burn in a form of culture that will be effectively expressed by the quaternity. As far as I can see, it has not yet been determined in detail just when and how this will come about. (*Atom* 50–2)

# 6

The relationships that fully engage the operations of the collective unconscious, by the time they surface, tend to produce a degree of sophistication and complexity likely to challenge the patience of a reader predisposed to reject such things as sheer obfuscation. Like Hamlet's mind subject to infinite delay, 'enterprises of great pith and moment' can all too easily be 'sicklied o'er with the pale cast of thought,' and 'lose the name of action' (3.1.85–8). Hamlet announces the modern rediscovery of the unconscious to which Freud lays claim in his 1900 *Interpretation of Dreams*. As the undertow the mind's interminable operations, the unconscious calls all outward action into doubt and turns the sacred imperative of conscience into a coward. Like most radically introverted events, the mind's unconscious acts are lost upon arrival in consciousness, or if given 'the name of action,' are 'sicklied o'er with the pale cast of thought.'

Jung told Freud that his idea of the unconscious as the amoral operations of the sexual libido was a disaster for civilization. Freud in turn said that culture itself was the catastrophe. Rather than reject Yahweh's curse, Freud boldly renewed it. Eventually Jung decided to release humanity from the 'curse' of Freud's dogma of sexuality, though it took many years for him consciously to absorb the psychic energy inwardly constellated in order to release himself from Freud, an effort that at first literally overpowered his sanity:

I stood helpless before an alien world; everything in it seemed difficult and incomprehensible. I was in a constant state of tension; often I felt as if gigantic blocks of stone were tumbling down upon me. One thunderstorm followed another. My enduring these storms was a question of brute strength. Others have been shattered by them – Nietzsche, and Hölderlin, and many others. But there was a demonic strength in me, and from the beginning there was no doubt in my mind that I must find the meaning of what I was experiencing in these fantasies. (*MDR* 177)

This convulsive state was Jung giving birth to a new creation myth in which the rejected Yahweh was released from Freud's psychotic sexual prison, from which he swore Jung never to release Him. Like Jung, Freud had tapped into a realm of unconscious, archaic images that Freud, having partly explored them, sealed off as taboo. As Freud describes this containment, the taboo created a community of disciples in which men took a vow of chastity. Their repressed incestuous desire for the mother takes the form, in their equally repressed jealousy of the father, of a homoerotic society that Jung, like Blake, personified as a hermaphroditic. Blake describes Tirzah, the 'Mother of [his] Mortal part' ('To Tirzah' 9), embalming Albion 'Within her bosom [...] never to awake' (19[21].57). 'She ties the knot of nervous fibres, into a white brain!' Blake writes: 'She ties the knot of bloody veins, into a red hot heart!' (19[21].55–6). In her bosom as a 'Couch of Death' she then lays the knotted, embalmed hermaphrodite out as a rotting stillborn (the poisoned placenta that killed Mary Shelley's mother memorialized in *Frankenstein*). Blake goes on to enact the entire grisly spectacle of Shelley's *Adonais*, in which Urania feeds on the poet's decaying body, by describing Tirzah feeding the corpse at her breast (the Pieta) as 't[ying] the knot of milky seed into two lovely Heavens / Two yet but one: each in the other sweet reflected!' '[T]hese,' Blake explains, 'Are our Three Heavens beneath the shades of Beulah, land of rest!' (*M* 19[21].61, 20[22].1–2). Beneath Beulah lies Ulro as the nightmare Beulah becomes a land of eternal oblivion.

This condition rather aptly describes Jung's tormented psychological shape under the influence of Freud's sexual dogma until, like Blake, he finally exploded, Blake's apocalyptic trumpets becoming in Jung's erupting diaphragm a red-hot furnace, Blake's 'red-hot blood' in his knotted veins. Nearly bringing down Freud's bookcase on both their heads, Jung realized that, as he also recognized in the second half of his *Symbols of Transformation*, incest had to be affirmed to release him from the homoerotic knot into which Freud's taboo had tied it. As the authentic operations of the spiritual understanding of the libido promulgated by the Papal Bull of Pius XII as the physical assumption of the Virgin Mother to the marriage chamber of her Son, incest at the anagogical level remains the unfinished business bequeathed to us by Jung and Pauli as well as the Romantics before them. (In passages withdrawn by his publisher on the relations between Laon and Cythna or in the relations between Prometheus and his Mother, who is both mother Earth and wife Asia, one could argue that Shelley, like Jung after him, considered the spiritual issue of incest as the release of the human mind from the taboo restricting its divine operations.)

The struggle with the feminine as the Fourth – Sophia as the androgynous Holy Spirit uniting Father and Son – became for Jung and Pauli the bewildering mythical action staged by the collective unconscious as an 'occult' revival of alchemy as well as certain ancient Eastern disciplines engaged with the mandala. Modelling his version of psychoanalysis upon the natural sciences, Freud dismissed Jung's version as mad. Pauli recognized that, however apparently mad this version was when judged by the Newtonian immutability of natural law, it was absolutely essential if the impasse confronting the acausality or synchronicity operative in microphysics was, as quantum mechanics, ever to be resolved. One could not, that is, dismiss the unknown dynamics of the psychic observer as the androgyne. The immense problems they psychologically raised as the *hieros gamos* were problems fully operative in the psychosomatic motions of the atom now fully, if inexplicably, displayed at their subatomic level. In the apparently ever-widening context of a world terrorized by the spectre of weapons of mass destruction, the survival of the human depends upon a conscious understanding of the law governing these psychosomatic motions. As Los declares,

> The Great Vintage & Harvest is now upon Earth
> The whole extent of the Globe is explored: Every scatterd Atom
> Of Human Intellect now is flocking to the sound of the Trumpet
> All of Wisdom which was hidden in caves & dens, from ancient
> Time; is now sought out from Animal & Vegetable & Mineral
> The Awakener is come. outstretchd over Europe! the Vision of God is
>   fulfilled
> The Ancient Man upon the Rock of Albion Awakes.

By Blake's reckoning, approximately one hundred years separate Blake from Milton, a gap bridged by Milton's return in Blake's body. Approximately 150 years separate Jung and Pauli from Blake. The epic tradition binds Blake to Milton in 'an immense number of verses on One Grand Theme Similar to Homers Iliad or Miltons Paradise Lost' (*CPP* 728). This 'One Grand Theme' has its counterpart in what Jung describes as 'the *Aurea Catena* [the Golden Chain] which has existed from the beginnings of philosophical alchemy [Hermes Trismegistos] and Gnosticism down to Nietzsche's *Zarathustra*' (*MDR* 189). Blake my-thopoeically brings the 'One Grand Theme' to its predestined end in his epic enactment of the movement from the 'Threefold' to the 'Fourfold.' In the final plates of *Jerusalem*, Blake's vast bow and arrow slay the false suitors for Albion's Emanation, Jerusalem, much as the bow and arrow of Odysseus shoot the false suitors for Penelope. Though far more ten-tatively (Jung in a dream had shot Siegfried as the false suitor for the New Jerusalem in 1913), Jung brings the *Aurea Catena* to its predestined end in his five-year seminar on Nietzsche's Zarathustra (1934–9) as this goal is more prophetically actualized in Jung's *Answer to Job*, which en-acts Jung's transformation of the madness that claimed the rope dancer, Nietzsche.

Far more mathematically sceptical than Pauli, Jung nonetheless rec-ognized that in the radical shift from classical to quantum physics in-timations of an inner marriage of psyche and matter, which continue now more than ever to haunt and propel the mind as 'the future of the eternal world,' had become urgently immediate. It was as if the dynamic operations of the collective unconscious as the 'living Power and prime Agent of all human Perception' were now within his and Pauli's sight as progressive revelation. It was, indeed, as if the tortoise in its race with the hare was winning, if it had not already won. For Jung, as for Pauli, the inexplicable, though objectively perceived, psycho-physical motions of matter were now an organic, observable part of a vast, newly conceived cosmic order. In this system, its 'Machinery [as Persons] intirely new to the Inhabitants of Earth,' Blake mythopoeically demonstrates that the energy unconsciously released in every 'Pulsation of the Artery' contains, when consciously embraced by the 'Intellectual powers,' a microcosmic enactment of the entire system. To which, thinking of the troubles he was having with his own 'Vegetable Body,' similar to Jung's mounting trouble with his heart, Blake adds:

The Thing I have most at Heart! more than life or all that seems to make life comfortable without. Is the Interest of True Religion & Science & when-ever any thing appears to affect that Interest [...] [i]t gives me the great-est of torments, I am not ashamed afraid or averse to tell You what Ought to be Told. That I am under the direction of Messengers of heaven Daily & Nightly but the nature of such things is not as some suppose. Without trouble or care. (*CPP* 724)

Blake's 'trouble and care' lies in the resistance of his 'Vegetable Body' to the torture inflicted upon its 'Corporeal' nature, even as, for Shelley, the 'unwilling dross' of the 'dull dense world' resists the torture of the 'one Spirit's plastic stress.' Viewing the 'familiar world' as a 'chaos,' Blake's 'Void outside of Existence,' the Romantic imagination, by descending into it, recreates the world 'as if all had then sprang forth at the first creative fiat.' As a prophet in the tradition of Isaiah and Ezekiel, Blake is answerable to the dictates of the imagination as the voice of God heard 'Within the unfathomed caverns of [his] Ear' as Moses heard it 'in mysterious Sinais awful cave.' Jung also claims in his memoirs to have heard the voice of God in the unconscious, out-of-body state described above in which his soul became, not merely the observer of the Marriage Feast of the Lamb, or even a participant in it, but the actual marriage itself understood as the 'litteral expression' of the soul, which is the way Blake describes the illuminated text of *Milton* produced in his 'Printing House in Hell.'

'For thirty years I have studied these psychic processes [conducting to the *hieros gamos*] under all possible conditions,' Jung writes, summing up his alchemical work, 'and have assured myself that the alchemists as well as the great philosophies of the East are referring to just such [quantum] experiences, and that it is chiefly our ignorance of the psyche if these experiences appear "mystic"' (*Mysterium* 535). What 'appear[s] "mystic"' is what Jung, like Blake, actually experienced. Jung describes these experiences in order psychoanalytically to raise them to consciousness and to analyse them, lest, as madness, they take possession of him as they took possession of 'Hölderlin, Nietzsche, and many others.' Embracing madness as a divine revelation, Blake pentecostally enacts the revelation in 'Visionary forms dramatic' bright redounding from 'Tongues in thunderous majesty, in Visions / In new Expanses' (*J* 98.28–30). Their source is the Holy Spirit envisioned as the transfigured Daughter of Beulah (in *Milton*, Ololon) whose woven garment is Blake's illuminated text.

'If the doors of perception were cleansed every thing would appear to man as it is: infinite,' declares Blake (*MHH* 14). Jung writes: 'We should at all events be able to understand that the visualization of the self is a "window" into eternity, which gave the medieval man, like the Oriental, an opportunity to escape from the stifling grip of a one-sided view of the world or to hold out against it' (*Mysterium* 535). This escape, secretly offered to those who did not experience it in the Eucharist, lay in the alchemical vision of the release of '*corpus glorificationis*, the resurrected body' (535) from the inertia of the physical body. Referring to the release of the new physics from Newtonian law, Jung argues that the resurrection depends as much on the rise of the earth to meet the apple as it does upon the fall of the apple. That is to say, the alchemist by 'sublimating [raising] matter [...] concretized [lowered] spirit' (536). For this raising of unconscious matter and lowering of super-conscious spirit, neither of which are the empirical possession of 'man as he is,' a third 'indescribable and super-empirical totality' (*Ubermensch*), 'not encompassed by our knowledge,' must be postulated, though, Jung explains, 'we are not in a position to make any statements about its total nature' (536, 538).

In *Biographia Literaria* Coleridge describes this third as a 'tertium aliquid,' 'a perpetual self-duplication of one and the same power into object and subject, which presuppose each other, and can exist only as antitheses' (1:300, 273). That is, rather than counteracting each other or reducing both to one neutral thing, this 'finite generation' (1:300) produced by two indestructible forces generates a third thing. 'So to one neutral thing both sexes fit,' John Donne writes in 'The Canonization,' describing the sexual act. 'We die and rise the same, and prove / Mysterious by this love' (25–7). The mystery of sex, he suggests, is that it prefigures the ultimate mystery of the *hieros gamos*. From the sexual act, male and female rise the same male and female; in the *hieros gamos*, they merge as the androgyne. Ideally conceived, Pauli and von Franz would arise from Pauli's active imagination, *The Piano Lesson*, not as the same people but as the androgyne, which for Pauli is the mathematical promise held out by the '*ring I*,' which 'the lady slipped [...] from her finger' and 'let [...] float in the air' (133). The androgyne would be the fusion of the dark Persian, westernized as blond (the 'Stranger') in Pauli's dreams and the Chinese lady who is westernized as von Franz, the Chinese lady performing in his dreams the same function as the Stranger. For the alchemists, this third thing is the *lapis* or *caelum*, the philosopher's stone, which is not a stone. 'Microphysics is feeling its way into the unknown side of matter, just as complex psychology is pushing forward into the unknown side of the psyche,' Jung explains. 'Both lines of investigation have yielded findings which can be conceived only by means of antinomies, and both have developed concepts which display remarkable analogies' (*Mysterium* 538).

'If this trend should become more pronounced in the future,' Jung continues,

the hypothesis of the unity of their subject-matters would gain in probability. Of course there is little or no hope that the unitary Being can ever be conceived, since our powers of thought and language permit only of antinomian statements. But this much we do know beyond all doubt, that empirical reality has a transcendental background – a fact which [...] can be expressed by Plato's parable of the cave. The common background of microphysics and depth-psychology is as much physical as psychic and therefore neither, but rather a third thing, a neutral nature which can at most be grasped in hints since in essence it is transcendental.

The background of our empirical world thus appears to be in fact a *unus mundus*. This is at least a probable hypothesis which satisfies the fundamental tenet of scientific theory: 'Explanatory principles are not to be multiplied beyond the necessary.' The transcendental psychophysical background corresponds to a 'potential world' in so far as all those conditions which determine the form of empirical phenomena are inherent in it. This obviously holds good as much for physics as for psychology, or, to be more precise, for macrophysics as much as for the psychology of consciousness. (*Mysterium* 538–9)

For Blake, as prophet, the 'transcendental background' becomes the immediate all-encompassing foreground as what Coleridge describes as 'the IMMEDIATE, which dwells in every man,' and as 'the original intuition, or absolute affirmation of it, (which is likewise in every man, but does not in every man rise into consciousness)' (*BL* 1:243). In Blake, 'Within a Moment: a Pulsation of the Artery' it arises into consciousness. Upon this consciousness, Coleridge argues, 'all the *certainty* of our knowledge depends' (1:243). This '*certainty*,' unconsciously conferred by the dream figure of the Báb, required all the doubt I could muster to bring it to consciousness.

About 1819, when Blake was illuminating *Jerusalem*, he made a visionary drawing of a Persian figure described at the bottom as 'The portrait of a man who instructed Mr. Blake in Painting &c. in his dreams.' The head is haloed in a soft sheath of curls that flow down and round the ears to the shoulders. His eyes are framed by the arched eyebrows that point upward to the forehead, which further extends the arch, as if to connect the forehead to the eyes as an indication of the content of their inward gaze. Below the eyes, directing the viewer's eyes downward, are the nose and nostrils line-linked to faintly curved lips and, further extending the line link to the chin as it becomes, in its arched curvature by a further line-linked extension, connected to the image delineated on the forehead as its pinnacle. Amidst what appears to be the muscularity of the brain the pinnacled forehead is inscribed with what appears to be a Tree of Life as the Burning Bush, the entire visionary head becoming the human face of the Tree or Bush, a dream landscape awakening to the celestial knowledge of what it prophetically contains.

Onto this visionary face I have, on occasion, projected my dream figure of the Persian Báb.

# 6 Mental Fight

I will not cease from Mental Fight

– Blake, *Milton*

## 1

The Greek word *apocalypsis* means the uncovering or unveiling of what has been hidden. Its root is the verb *kalypto*, which means to 'cover' or 'hide.' The prefix is the preposition *apo*, which means 'away' or 'from.' For the Romantic, the organ of this unveiling is the imagination, which the spiritual philosophers of Shia Islam, with reference to the Hidden Imam, treat as truth rather than fiction. The materialism embraced by the Western world since the rise of modern science with Kepler's physics is alien to Islam, in the same way the 'mechanical philosophy' rejected by the Romantics would be for Kepler. Coleridge was partly released from materialism by Kant, for whom the senses are determined *a priori* by the operations of the human mind as they repeat the unknown operations of the divine mind. Shelley rejected Coleridge's notion of an 'eternal act of creation in the infinite I AM' by insisting, as does Kant, that the mind cannot create. The 'Power' or 'secret strength [...] / Which governs thought' ('Mont Blanc' 139–40) remains 'Remote, serene, and inaccessible.' Thought provides the necessary illusion of creation, without which the human mind would be mere 'vacancy,' which it is in metaphysical relation to the unknowable 'Power.' '[T]he existence of distinct individual minds similar to that which is employed in now questioning its own nature,' Shelley writes, 'is likewise found to be a delusion' (*SPP* 508).

Radically disagreeing with Coleridge, though apparently affirming what he rejects as '*something-nothing-every-thing*,' Shelley as poet is forced to embrace the illusions of the imagination, not as merely delusions, but by willingly suspending his disbelief in them. In this fundamental respect, he enacts what the spiritual philosophers of Shia Islam consider the fate of the imagination in the West when it rejects the imagination as an organ of truth as distinct from fiction. Even Kepler in his new physics persuaded himself that measuring the cosmic motions of matter empirically validated the Christian Trinity. His contemporary, the alchemist Robert Fludd, rejected this proof. In the quantifiable motions of matter he saw the death and burial of God. By affirming that he was both Kepler and Fludd, Pauli as a quantum physicist acknowledged in himself the unknown presence of the Fourth as the quarrel between Kepler and Fludd. The alchemical quest for the *lapis* or philosopher's stone *is* the Fourth in something of the same way that the Persian in Pauli's dreams is the Fourth. Ironically, it was Islam's advancing knowledge of the human mind that made the rise of modern science, physics in particular, possible. Muslim philosophers advanced mathematics as a spiritual discipline unveiling, so far as Allah would allow, a deepening knowledge of the mysterious operations of the divine mind as revealed by Muhammad in the Qur'an. In this spiritual sense mathematics was as much a system of meditation and contemplation as was the sublime architecture of the mosque. The secrets of matter remain in the '*body celestial*' of the twelfth or hidden Imam whose return as their unveiling would release what remained hidden in matter as its spiritual nature. As this book argues, the Fourth is, in this sense, the Hidden Imam.

Jung's interest in alchemy, particularly the one enacted in Pauli's archetypal dreams, produced a lifelong effort to unveil the spiritual nature of matter as the *lapis* or philosopher's stone. As he writes in his final book on alchemy, in which he fully announces his indebtedness to quantum physics, though without actually mentioning Pauli:

In general, the alchemists strove for a *total* union of the opposites in symbolic form, and this they regarded as the indispensable condition for the healing of all ills. Hence they sought to find ways and means to produce that substance [equation] in which all opposites were united [in a single unified field]. It had to be material as well as spiritual, living as well as inert, masculine as well as feminine, old as well as young, and – presumably – morally neutral. It had to be created by man, and at the same time, since it was an 'increatum,' by God himself, the *Deus terrestris*. (*Mysterium* 475)

Focusing upon the symbolic nature of the alchemical opus, Jung and Pauli were horrified that the highest achievement of the human intellect, the atom bomb, had become the instrument of its annihilation, in the same way that Shelley's later texts carry the seeds of their own destruction.

In his diatribe to the General Assembly of the United Nations in fall 2007, President Mahmoud Ahmadinejad of Iran identified the return of the Hidden Imam with unveiling the hidden power of the atom, thus literalizing Iran's ability to destroy the earth. Ahmadinejad contrasted America's campaign to dominate the globe with Iran's desire, as the true Shia nation, to bring peace to the world as the celestial Kingdom of Allah (Hurqalya) in its earthly form – *Deus terrestris* – as the return of the Hidden Imam. As he acknowledged in an interview, which he later repudiated, Ahmadinejad spoke to the General Assembly as the messenger of the Hidden Imam announcing on behalf of the Iranian people whom he ruled with an iron hand the imminence of His return. For him, this spiritual mission, in contrast to the 'Satanic' mission of the Jewish and Christian West, which refused to recognize Muhammad, confirmed in Allah's name Iran's divine right to atomic energy. The Shia Islam of Muhammad's divinely appointed imams was the true and faithful custodian of this energy first fully revealed in its spiritual form by Muhammad and then, by divine decree, entrusted to the imans born from the womb of His daughter Fatima.

The Western mind cannot very willingly suspend its disbelief in the sheer madness of such a delusion shaping in a dictator's warped imagination. Later introducing Ahmadinejad, the president of Columbia University denounced him as mad before he had uttered a word. Such denunciation implied that the imminence of the Hidden Imam was beyond the reach of Western sanity, a scandal topped only by Ahmadinejad's actual presence before Columbia faculty and students presumably there to listen. For me, this literalist announcement of the return of the Hidden Imam did not, could not, fall on deaf ears. I can say with some authority that I am one of the few Westerners who could absorb, both implicitly and explicitly, what Ahmadinejad was saying. Hearing it, I found myself listening again to the madness in myself, which, as the spectral form of my dream of the Báb, has never fully ceased to haunt me as Shelley's visionary was haunted in *Alastor*. Certainly I knew upon awakening from the dream that I had confronted my own madness, though whether it was divine or mere madness I was not sure. At the time of the dream, the distinction never occurred to me. It wasn't until *Sanity,*

*Madness, Transformation* that I began the process of absorbing madness by imaginatively – which is to say psychologically – transforming it into a sanity that nonetheless kept madness as its necessary source.

In Ahmadinejad's television appearances I confronted again my original fear of madness in something like its primeval state. Wordsworth idealizes this state at the age of seventeen (the 'eminence' [*P*3.171] to which the two-part *Prelude* ascends) as the 'madness' of 'child-like fruitfulness in passing joy' (*P*3.149-50). With such joy, 'poets in old time, and higher up / By the first men, earth's first inhabitants,' viewed 'things' as they 'matured / To inspiration' (*P*3.153-5). Associating the divine madness of the child ('Mighty Prophet! Seer blest!') with Coleridge's 'first creative fiat,' Wordsworth identifies himself as a poet with its maturing 'Through every change of growth and decay' so that, rather than suffer its suppression or abatement, it remains 'Pre-eminent till death' (2.264-5). I hope that in writing this volume as a process governed by my conscious will informed by my 'Intellectual powers' my dream of the Bàb might mature in a similar fashion. Blake's divine madness is less rationally accessible though at the same time more essential. Still, I have found myself, like Wordsworth, more occupied than Blake with the 'obstinate questionings / Of sense and outward things.' That is to say, my dream has been subject to 'vanishings' in which I have found myself moving about 'in worlds not realized' ('Intimations of Immortality' 142-5). Like Wordsworth, however, the time came when I could no longer accommodate 'questionings' or 'vanishings' to some higher demand to which the mental gymnastics of my somersault in the air had raised me. I had within myself to stand up and be counted. In this sense I slowly realized in turning the first book into a second that I was facing something more apocalyptic than Wordsworth faced when submitting to 'a new control' that had 'humanized [his] soul' as the result of a 'deep distress' ('Elegiac Stanzas' 34-6).

That is to say, I was facing Blake's 'Resurrection & Judgment in the Vegetable Body' as the difference between my 'Corporeal Understanding' and 'Allegory addressd to the Intellectual powers.' As Coleridge understood, the symbol is prior to material fact, for fact as literal perception is the product of the primary imagination as its 'prime Agent.' The symbol is what is perceived as the 'living Power' of the mind by which, in every unconscious 'Pulsation of the Artery,' it is simultaneously perceived as the living 'Vegetable Body.' In this sense the Báb, as the living symbolic form of Siyyíd 'Ali-Muhammad Shirazi, *is* the return of the Hidden Imam as the unveiling of the literal reality of the soul's eternal life, that same 'Eternity' which Blake describes as 'in love with the productions of time.' In *Milton* Blake read *Paradise Lost* in the same allegorical way that his contemporaries in Persia, the followers of Shaykh Ahmad, were reading the Qur'an: as it was 'addressd to the Intellectual powers' as distinct from the 'Corporeal Understanding.' In doing so Blake was confronted by Los, the 'fierce glowing fire' of the prophetic imagination who put on Blake's sandals with which to walk through eternity, unveiling what remained hidden in Milton's epic (*M* 22]24].8). 'I became One Man with him arising in my strength,' Blake declares. 'Twas too late now to recede. Los had enterd into my soul; / His terrors now posses'd me whole! I arose in fury & strength' (22[24].12–14).

At Felpham Blake radically recreated what remained hidden in Milton's epic as a face-to-face encounter with the Second Coming as the 'Starry Eight' descending into the 'Fires of [his] Intellect' wearing the garment of his illuminated text. It is this reading of the Qur'an as the return of the Hidden Imam in which Shaykh Ahmad trained his disciples. From this school came not only Siyyíd 'Ali-Muhammad Shirazi but all His Living Letters. Together they formed the body of His living scripture announcing the coming of Bahá'u'lláh, who described the descent of the Holy Spirit in the guise of the Maid of Heaven in the Tehran prison, much as Blake describes Los's descent wrapped in Ololon's garment. Bahá'u'lláh writes:

> During the days I lay in the prison in Tihrán, though the galling weight of the chains and the stench-filled air allowed Me but little sleep, still in those infrequent moments of slumber I felt as if something flowed from the crown of My head over My breast, even a mighty torrent [Shelley's river Arve in 'Mont Blanc'] that precipitateth itself upon the earth from the summit of a lofty mountain. Every limb of My body would, as a result, be set afire. At such moments My tongue recited what no man could bear to hear. (*Epistle* 101)

What 'no man could bear to hear' is, in another Tablet, proclaimed. 'Pointing with her finger unto my Head,' Bahá'u'lláh writes,

> she addressed all who are in heaven and all who are on earth, saying: 'By God! This is the Best-Beloved of the worlds, and yet ye comprehend not. This is the Beauty of God amongst you, and the power of His sovereignty within You, could ye but understand. This is the Mystery of God and His Treasure, the Cause of God and His glory unto all who are in the kingdoms of Revelation and Creation, if ye be of them that perceive.' (102)

In my reading of the revelation of the Báb as the return of the Hidden Imam, the revelation is essentially the divine process of its making rather than the revelation as complete within itself. In this sense, the revelation of the Báb is the prophetic announcement or Gate of the revelation that was destined to follow nine years later in the sewer in Tehran, where he was imprisoned. He is, again in this sense, what Blake calls the 'poetic' form of religion as the eternal process of its becoming, without which process institutional religion becomes fixed and dead in the same way that for the Romantics Milton's epic hardened into the Puritan religion, whose spectre or shadow became in America the witch hunts that still continue, as Arthur Miller's *The Crucible* dramatically demonstrates. When revelation's progressive unfolding of the otherwise unknown operations of the mind of God in and as the primary imagination ('the power of His sovereignty within you') becomes in any one of its stages final or fixed, the process turns back upon itself to become the 'finite mind' of 'Priesthood,' a demonic parody of itself. In this fixated form, God appears in every revelation of Himself to be conducting His own self-murder, which Blake describes as the Orc-Urizen cycle in which, as an *enantiodromia*, Orc turns into his opposite. This is the spectacle that confronts the three Semitic religions – Judaism, Christianity, Islam – as each in its own barely conscious way conducts a genocidal war upon the others, the family of father Abraham becoming like the family of father Atreus: so dysfunctional that it appears doomed to enact as tragedy or farce its own annihilation.

Confronted by this spectacle, Nietzsche, in the guise of the madman he was on his way to becoming, announced in 1882 the death of God. Nietzsche was born in 1844, the year in which Siyyid 'Ali-Muhammad announced himself as the return of the Hidden Imam. In *Thus Spake Zarathustra,* the first complete edition of which did not appear until 1892, by which point Nietzsche was completely insane, he announced himself as the return, not of the literal Zarathustra, but of his fictional form. In a curiously Western way, Nietzsche treated the return of the Hidden Imam as the fictional work and fictional word of the imagination that as an organ of truth becomes an organ of delusion to which all religions are bound, including National Socialism. Truth, he asserted, is an illusion that has forgotten itself as fiction. By releasing Zarathustra from the delusion in which as the Zoroastrian religion he was left for dead, Nietzsche restored him to the truth of fiction, which is his eternally unfolding life. In this radical undertaking, inspired by a divine madness that descended into mere madness, Nietzsche resurrected Zarathustra in a far more subversive way than even Blake raised Christ as a poetic tale from the dead. In his 1930s Seminars on *Thus Spake Zarathustra*, Jung feared the German Führer as the demonic (psychotic) form of the Nietzsche's Hidden Imam – the return of Zarathustra from which as Zoroastrianism Shia Islam in Persia had emerged. Nietzsche's prophetic madness, Jung argued, had invaded the West as a mass psychosis whose end is nowhere in sight. In his Seminars he struggled psychologically to penetrate the psychosis in order to release the truth it potentially contained as the birth of a new consciousness, especially since this birth had taken the demonic form of the Third Reich as the descent of the New Jerusalem. In something of the same way I now view President Ahmadinejad of Iran, in whose imagination the return of the Hidden Imam continues to haunt the West with a dire spectacle of its imminent collapse, the West's invasive resistance to this collapse increasingly assisting its advent.

# 2

My apparently literalist reading of my dream of the Báb – the Báb of my dream becoming to my immediate understanding upon awakening the same Báb who a few hours earlier had in my reading of Nabil's Narrative declared Himself to his first disciple in the upper room of His house in Shiraz at eight minutes after sunset on 23 May 1844 – was, as literal reality, a dream that my common sense told me to reject as a delusion. Such was the dream's visceral impact that I could no more dismiss it than I could my own physical body. The Báb seemed to be registered there in however stained a condition, demanding some act of purification in order to be properly acknowledged. My step toward this end, though at the time I thought of it as an exorcism, was to join the Royal Canadian Air Force, where my purification rite became the parade square and my training first as a pilot and then as an air-gunner. In this way I bound the truth of the Báb to my senses as if they were the only way my soul could manifest itself. In this respect I carried the Báb rather as Coleridge's mariner carried the albatross about his neck. I was as yet unaware of the difference between blessing and cursing and thus of the true friendship their opposition contained. What was required was what Jung describes as the surrender of the ego to the Self, which writing this book has helped me to recognize. Jung has in mind the difference between the imagination in the service of the ego, which usurps the eternal act of creation, and in the service of the Self, which repeats the eternal act in the human mind. In my earlier life, struggling to enlist the imagination in an act of 'usurpation' rather than 'repetition,' I chose, despite all strenuous psychological efforts, to remain unaware.

Of course, there is a further twist to this process. My wife Marion would argue that unawareness can be a blessing that reaches beyond human understanding to the realm of grace. For her, the instant the albatross falls off the mariner's neck and sinks like lead into the sea is a moment of divine awareness of which the human may remain unaware. In this 'Pulsation of the Artery,' the mariner is allowed spontaneously to pray, which is for her anything but an act of usurpation. For more than thirty years in her psychoanalytic work, she has, of course, understood this state in terms of a distinction between the inner feminine (Sophia) and the patriarchal masculine. Fortunately or unfortunately, in my earlier life she never brought this distinction to bear on my understanding of the dream of the Báb because I was not, in truth, prepared to let her. When Wordsworth describes the imagination's 'strength / Of usurpation,' as we have seen, he goes on to compare it to 'the mighty flood of Nile / Poured from his fount of Abyssinian clouds / To fertilise the whole Egyptian plain' (P 6.614–16). Far from enlisting this 'strength' under 'banners militant, the soul seeking 'trophies,' struggling for 'spoils / That may attest her prowess' (6.609-11), remains in the 'beatitude / That hides her' as the 'Abyssinian clouds' hide the 'mighty flood of Nile.' Wordsworth remained persuaded that this 'strength' remained hidden in Coleridge's 'Abyssinian maid' ('Kubla Khan' 39) which Coleridge had brutally abused by forcing her to submit to doses of opium that usurped her real power. At most, the 'mighty flood of Nile' thus became in dream 'the silly buckets on the deck / That had so long remained' filled up with nothing more than 'dew' (*The Ancient Mariner* 297–9). Coleridge continues, describing the mariner awakening from his dream:

> My lips were wet, my throat was cold,
> My garments all were dank;
> Surely I had drunken in my dreams
> And still my body drank.
>
> I moved, and could not feel my limbs:
> I was so light – almost
> I thought that I had died in sleep,
> And was a blessed Ghost.                          (301–8)

Coleridge himself returned from Malta as one who 'had died in sleep, / And was a blessed ghost,' and in chanting *The Prelude* to him, Wordsworth gave him a decent burial.

Blake, of course, was horrified by the egotistical sublime of Wordsworth's 'strength / Of usurpation' in his Prospectus to *The Recluse*, which asserts that he will pass beyond the throne of Jehovah 'alarmed' to unveil behind it the 'mind of man.' In his annotations to Wordsworth's Preface to *The Excursion*, Blake writes:

> Solomon when he Married Pharohs daughter & became a Convert to the Heathen Mythology Talked exactly in this way of Jehovah as a Very inferior object of Mans Contemplations he also passed him by unalarmd & was permitted. Jehovah dropped a tear & followd him by his Spirit into the Abstract Void it is called the Divine Mercy Satan dwells in it but Mercy does not dwell in him he knows not to Forgive. (*CPP* 666)

For Blake, imagination is perpetual forgiveness of sin, which restores the fallen creation to its unfallen state, not by usurping the strength of Jehovah, but by repeating this strength as the true act of perception, Coleridge's primary imagination. Humanity only remains in the 'Abstract Void' of Ulro because, as Satan, humanity 'knows not to forgive.'

# 3

Satan personifies what Blake calls the 'Reasoning Negative.' Coleridge speaks of this state as the 'fearful resolve to find in [the Will] alone the one absolute motive of action, under which all other motives from within and from without must be either subordinated or crushed.' He distinguishes this perverted isolation of the will from the free will, which is 'our only absolute *self*.' As the will's freedom, this 'self' repeats the spirit's relation to itself on a 'finite level.' Because he does not wish to profane the mystery of this process, Coleridge names it 'the infinite I AM' rather than the 'I AM that I AM,' lest it be confused with 'any form of "I" or "ego," even if modified by "pure" or "absolute"' (1:114 n.4). Coleridge insists that the will is free because it recognizes itself as 'co-extensive and co-present' with spirit, whether affirming itself as 'wisdom' in relation to the 'indwelling' spirit's intuitive mode of operations or as 'love' in its relation to the 'indwelling' spirit of the Christian God. Of these two modes, Coleridge finds wisdom 'more frequent' in the Old Testament and love 'more frequent' in the New. They become one in Milton's sacred Muse Urania, who as love sings nightly before the throne of God with her sister Sophia, or wisdom. Blake believed that in dictating their celestial song to his 'Sixfold Emanation,' Milton compromised his own freedom, which Blake's *Milton* attempts apocalyptically to restore through his twelve-year-old Muse, Ololon, who finds Milton's freedom too 'unbounded.'

For Blake, Milton's worship of Urizen, however 'unaware,' allied him with Satan, which is why as an act of 'Divine Mercy' Blake takes Milton into his own sense-bound 'Vegetable Body.' Working together as 'conscious, or unconscious,' 'co-extensive and co-present,' they shape the spiritual body lying dormant within the 'Vegetable Body' as a living corpse or spectral form within a grave. As I have already suggested, I took Blake as my unconscious model in Frye's graduate class and gradually brought it to consciousness as a result of the nameless trauma into which I settled as a 'Void Outside of Existence.' In ways not dissimilar to the role Blake played in Frye's own life, over sixty years I have come unsteadily closer to an understanding of Blake and, by extension, myself. That is to say, my release from the trauma constellated in Frye's class came in the form of my commitment to Romanticism, though in 1948–9 I still completely repressed the possibility that the release should finally resolve itself into the return of the Hidden Imam, already announced in my dream of the Báb. This repression was *my* 'Reasoning Negative,' what Frye calls 'the absolutizing of circumstances' (*Fearful* 189) that permits no dialectic between 'Contraries,' which would release the mind from the prison of its denial. The absence of dialectic, he goes on to say, constitutes death: 'The deader a thing is, the more obedient it is to circumstances, and the more alive it is the less predictable it becomes' (189).

Over time I have considered various reasons why I became in Frye's class 'obedient' to the 'circumstances' in which I found myself after the delivery of my paper, which Frye dismissed. The paper argued that in Blake's epic Milton enacted in Satan's fall his own despair over the failure of the Puritan Revolution, which, during the period of the Restoration, released everything Milton despised. Frye concluded that, as the 'Female Will,' I had bound Milton's imagination to the tyranny of circumstance. The judgment was likely accurate enough, but it left me no room to manoeuvre, for it told me that by absolutizing circumstance, I was essentially dead. The restoration to life lay ahead of me as a long and circuitous journey unmarked by any sudden awakening. And even if some 'Divine Mercy' had shown its luminous face, I was ill prepared to recognize it. To put Frye's dismissal another way, by submitting the soul to historical circumstance in my 'Corporeal' account of Blake's *Milton*, I had constructed a demonic parody of the will's freedom. Coleridge describes this as the ego's exploitation of circumstance for its own glory, which he finds in the 'COMMANDING GENIUS' of Milton's Satan, 'a *systematic* criminal, self-consistent and entire in wickedness, who [...] has removed a world of obstacles by the mere decision, that he will have no obstacles, but those of force and brute matter' (*Lay Sermons* 66). Coleridge suggests that such power, dedicated to perverse ends, issues darkly from the sublimity of the Semitic vision when this power remains politically focused upon its apocalyptic object: the descent of the New Jerusalem as the Kingdom of God on earth. Both he and Wordsworth saw this dark end in the Reign of Terror, which perversely constellated the French Revolution as the ego's absorption of the sublime into itself as the visionary source of the ego's own willful power. It was for this reason that many of the Romantics feared the imagination's subjection to the immediate historical demands of the ego's insatiable desire. This is why, by arguing that 'Power dwells apart in its tranquillity / Remote, serene, and inaccessible,' Shelley, against his desire as a social being, is sure, by reflection, to distance himself from the 'Dizzy Ravine' as an image of the 'mind in creation' mirroring the 'one mind.'

Every strong Romantic instinctively knows that this egotistical sublime has the satanic power to slay the gods who obstruct the ego unless the power arising from 'the mind's abyss' is transformed into a 'beatitude' capable of turning a 'flood of ruin' into a 'mighty flood' of soul-fertilizing grace, which blesses 'unaware.' To confront and transform this dark instinct, which Freud located at its archetypal source in Sophocles' Oedipus, into a lyrical vision, is an *opus contra naturam* that brings the whole soul of man into harmonious activity. The composition of an epic, however, is a much more dangerous undertaking because, as the enactment of the struggle itself, this composition engages as a ceaseless 'Mental Fight' the forces that oppose creation. In Milton's case, at least for Blake, it may end in an impasse, or worse. Having prepared himself to begin his Father's work of salvation by rejecting Satan's offer of the kingdoms of the world now in Satan's hands, Christ returns at the end of *Paradise Regain'd*, privately and unobserved, to his 'Mother's house' (4.639). Milton counters Satan, still heaping damnation upon himself, with Michael, whose humanistic attempt to educate Adam in a moral scheme of salvation bypasses the Crucifixion without dismissing its vicarious atonement as a *deus ex machina*. The Romantics hoped to complete the work they felt

Milton had begun: the transfer of God's self-sacrifice through His Son to the human imagination, although for them the ego's crucifixion, Keats's negative capability, remained a problematic issue that placed severe demands on the Romantic imagination equal to those faced by Milton. 'Did he smile his work to see? / Did he who made the Lamb make thee?' Blake asks his tiger.

Toward the end of his life Shelley saw in *Don Juan* Byron's recognition that humanity could not usurp the role of the Christian God by crucifying the ego for man's redemption. For Byron, the satanic hero who attempts this becomes instead the want of a hero who is never defeated: knowing he cannot win, he never sets out to triumph. This facet of Byron's genius virtually silenced Shelley because it reduced his unbound Prometheus to a mock-heroic figure and his Promethean vision to ruined fragments, or worse, demonic parody. In turn, Shelley wanted to 'eradicate from [Byron's] great mind the delusions of Christianity, which, in spite of his reason, seem perpetually to recur and to lay ambush for the hours of sickness and distress' (*Letters* 2:959). For Shelley, that is, Don Juan's lack of heroism did not solve the problem. Shelley wanted to accomplish what Milton's Samson accomplished in relation to the Philistines. '"I mean to show you of my strength, yet greater,"' declares Samson:

'As with amaze shall strike all who behold.'
This utter'd, straining all his nerves he bow'd,
As with the force of winds and waters pent
When Mountains tremble, those two massy Pillars
With horrible convulsion to and fro
He tugg'd, he shook, till down they came, and drew
The whole roof after them with burst of thunder
Upon the heads of all who sate beneath,
...
*Samson* with these inmixt, inevitably
Pull'd down the same destruction on himself.   (*Samson Agonistes* 1644–58)

But Samson's *agon*, destroying himself by destroying his enemies, is in fact the fatal triumph of the egotistical sublime. Like Satan, Samson identifies himself with his 'COMMANDING GENIUS,' though unconsciously as the Spectre or Shadow of his own creative power. His show of greater strength is a 'vain attempt' (*PL* 1.44) to usurp 'the Tyranny of Heav'n' (1.124), an act of the will turned in upon itself that becomes 'yet more miserable!' (*Samson Agonistes* 101):

Myself my Sepulcher, a moving Grave,
Buried, yet not exempt
By privilege of death and burial
From worst of other evils, pains and wrong.                    (102–5)


# 4

In the 1960s I confronted, along with the rest of my generation, the innocence of an emerging popular culture whose outward signs of joyous liberation belied the wholesale destruction being enacted within it as a kind of new reign of terror that was its spectral form. In this culture's various Bacchic festivals I saw what appeared to be Shelley's 'winged seeds' driven 'like ghosts from an enchanter fleeing' or like 'pestilence-stricken multitudes' (AIDS had not yet been diagnosed) 'charioted to their dark, wintry bed' under the 'pale, and hectic' intoxication that, like the 'dreaming earth,' they would arise from within it as newborns ('Ode to a West Wind' 3–10). During this period many of these 'winged seeds' appeared in my university courses on Romanticism wearing the ritual costumes in which they assumed identities as fragile as those of *A Midsummer Night's Dream* so enchanted that, as Titania, Queen of the Fairies, explains, spring, summer, autumn, and winter so changed their wonted liveries that one cannot tell which is which. Tempted to play Oberon, I was initially too fearful to encourage the masque laid out before me waiting for permission to play its wonted way out. I suspected it would be nothing more than a demonic parody of the Romantic apocalypse I was waiting to explore. At the same time, I was aware – who could not be? – of an energy springing from a primeval source, which, Wordsworth warns, some called 'madness,' particularly by those for whom 'in these tutored days,' it can 'no more be seen / With undisordered sight' (*P* 3.156–7). My task, I had to remind myself, should be closer to Shakespeare's than to Oberon's: to raise to consciousness what was waiting to happen in front of me by transforming rather than repressing it. In this sense, the 1960s were in many ways the ideal time to explore the transforming power of the imagination in the work of many of the English Romantics.

But where to begin? I could feel that the students in front of me, or at least some of them, whom I thought of as the 'Reprobate,' had an instinctive awareness of what Romanticism was about, even though their contact with it, if contact they had, might not have advanced far beyond – or perhaps even arrived at – Blake's *Songs of Innocence*. I trusted this instinct and was persuaded that there were others in the class, whom I thought of as the 'Redeemed,' who were at least willing to learn. For the 'Reprobate,' a laughing child on a cloud asking a piper mindlessly piping a song of pleasant glee to pipe a song about a lamb was for them nothing more than asking them to open their *Norton Anthology* to page 31. Asking them later to sit down and write an essay about this expression that, if not 'all' would read, at least I would read was a different matter. But they knew that to write the essay was a different matter in which the spontaneity in the classroom would vanish, just as Blake's child vanished. Some of them, by no means all, would recover this vanished child as their own inner vanished child in the writing of the essay. And these few, I soon realized, were the ones with whom I was eager to work as an incentive to continue my own. In my own way, then, the classroom – 'Mark well my words! they are of your eternal salvation' (*M* 2.25) – was divided into Blake's three classes. The 'Fourfold,' which is the 'Human,' became myself to the degree that in 'true Friendship,' I could imaginatively hold the class together. The problem was the third group: the Elect, whom I could safely ignore so long as I was prepared to give them exact instructions on how to write an essay and pass a final examination. But could I give them hope enough to pass the final exam by explaining why it was necessary to use the exact words of the question in their effort to answer it, knowing that if they repeated them often enough they probably would find their way to the answer, which the question, however hidden, contained. (An examiner seldom asked a question without having an answer in mind.)

Having known the war in a way my students did not, and having used it to discipline the chaos within me arising from my dream of the Báb, my classes in Romanticism, particularly in the 1960s, continued for me the process I had already been through and was still going through. I became increasingly aware of the essential role of the liberal arts in civilizing the soul. I knew what was waiting to devour students in the name of liberation at a time when few of them knew what liberty was: Coleridge's 'free will' as 'our only absolute *self*.' I had to move slowly toward this, as I had to move even more slowly in myself. The 'eternal act of creation' that was never far from the surface in any of my post-graduate courses at Toronto was always there treated as civilization perpetually on trial. To put it on trial in my classes before my students barely understood what civilization was, many of them eager to overthrow it, was an incremental process in which taking the pulse of the artery became a necessary psychic measure if the fever of the students was to subside.

For my students, however few or many, to experience their own 'sensual pleasure' with 'new feelings' was, as Coleridge describes it, a 'mental convalescence' that the 1960s rarely managed to distinguish from 'sensual pleasure' understood as a 'bodily convalescence' from the social and moral pressures that repressed this pleasure. What needed to be learned, for it is not innately known as instinct, is that in any poem of any worth a 'dark inscrutable workmanship' is taking place, in which the 'whole soul' is brought into 'activity' both in the poet and in the reader. This 'activity' – and here my students had to absorb it slowly, if they were to absorb it at all – involves 'the subordination of [the soul's] faculties to each other, according to their relative worth and dignity.' The power by which the subordination of the faculties to each other *are* subordinated, Coleridge explains, is 'the magical power' of the 'imagination.' It is, he further explains,

> first put in action by the will and understanding, and retained under their irremissive, though gentle and unnoticed, controul (*laxis effertur habenis*) that reveals itself in the balance or reconciliation of opposite or discordant qualities: of sameness, with difference; of the general, with the concrete; the idea, with the image; the individual, with the representative; the sense of novelty and freshness, with old and familiar objects; a more than usual state of emotion, with more than usual order, judgement ever awake and steady self-possession, with enthusiasm and feeling profound or vehement; and while it blends and harmonizes the natural and the artificial, still subordinates art to nature; the manner to the matter; and our admiration of the poet to our sympathy with the poetry. (*BL* 2:16–17)

Needless to say, I never, at least with my undergraduates, managed to work my way through this long passage, which I consider about the length of a lifetime. But I have worked it through for myself. It has brought me, by a most circuitous path, to where I am. Coleridge compares it to

> the motions of a serpent, which the Egyptians made the emblem of intellectual power; or like the path of sound through the air; at every step he pauses and half recedes, and from the retrogressive movement collects the force which again carries him onward. Precipitandus est *liber* spiritus, says Petronius Arbiter most happily [The *free* spirit must be hurried onward.]. The epithet, *liber,* here balances the preceding verb; and it is not easy to conceive more meaning condensed in few words. (*BL* 2:14)

Coleridge's 'more meaning condensed' is the free will carrying along the spirit as the only 'absolute *self*.' That 'free will,' however much I questioned it – 'half recedes,' 'collects the force,' 'carries' on – has, by 'indirection,' long experienced as a maze, brought me, as my own collective process, to the Hidden Imam as the centre of the 'labyrinthine soul' (*PU* 1.805).

# 5

But who or what is the Hidden Imam? Is he the martyred Siyyíd 'Ali-Muhammad Shirazi? Or is he not a flesh-and-blood person at all in the same sense that the 'Persons & Machinery intirely new to the Inhabitants of Earth' unveiled to Blake in what he calls his 'Spiritual Acts' are not flesh and blood? They cannot be seen as flesh and blood, Blake explains, 'unless [some unknown reader] has seen them in the Spirit or unless he should read My long Poem descriptive of those Acts.' Here Blake refers to *The Four Zoas*, which he left un-illuminated because he could find no customer for it. (It needs to be noted that many of the manuscripts of both the Báb and Bahá'u'lláh, the central sacred texts of the Baha'i faith, have yet to be published.) In its barely discernible manuscript form, which Blake first described as 'A Dream of Nine Nights,' he managed in his final night to bring his scattered epic to a triumphant end, at which point he writes, 'End of the Dream.'

Blake was perhaps persuaded that a reader, sufficiently spiritually advanced, might be able to read his poem without actually seeing the manuscript in the flesh. But he was equally persuaded that no person *could* read it until he got back to London and subjected it to his 'Printing House in Hell.' He was equally convinced, that is, that once printed the reader, including Blake, would behold the poem in the flesh as one awakening from a dream. As Keats states when describing his 'sensations' as opposed to his 'consequitive reasoning,' 'The imagination may be compared to Adam's dream, – he awoke and found it truth' (*KL* 37). In the transformative act of reading, Blake's reader would hopefully in 'the Litteral expression' undergo 'Resurrection & Judgment in the Vegetable Body,' an awakening that, as revisions of it, became *Milton* and *Jerusalem*. As we have seen, Blake's central metaphor of this transformation is Milton's *Paradise Lost* entering Blake's 'Vegetable Body' where in Bowlahoola, his 'Stomach for digestion,' the poem is both excreted and transformed as the death and resurrection of Milton's epic.

Over sixty-five years I have submitted my dream of the Báb to a similar flesh-and-blood process in my 'Vegetable Body,' which has also undergone a slow and painful transformation into a spiritual body, which is the Hidden Imam. To worship the Hidden Imam as the eternal form of oneself would constitute the madness of primary narcissism, which is frequently the shape taken by religious faith in the guise of the egotistical sublime of Coleridge's Satan, too often identified with the Devil of Blake's *Marriage of Heaven and Hell*. In Frye's graduate class, I clearly had not yet sufficiently progressed to sort out the complex issue of 'the Devil's party.'

Blake's writings are driven by his ceaseless reading and rereading of *Paradise Lost* in which he gradually found a way fully to embrace as true friendship his opposition to Milton's epic account of his fallen self. The Hidden Imam is constellated in this embrace, what Jung calls the Self, not in opposition to the ego but as the 'Divine Mercy' by which the Self requires the ego for its unveiling. Jung's idea of the Self in relation to the ego casts a rather different light upon Milton's account of Urizen casting out Satan, not knowing that he is Satan. In *Paradise Lost* Milton's God leaves Satan at large darkly to enact what God, withdrawing his goodness from Messiah's act of creation, leaves open to Satan:

> nor ever thence
> Had ris'n or heav'd his head, but that the will
> And high permission of all-ruling Heaven
> Left him at large to his own dark designs,
> That with reiterated crime he might
> Heap on himself damnation, while he sought
> Evil to others, and enrag'd might see
> How all his malice serv'd but to bring forth
> Infinite goodness, grace and mercy shewn
> On Man by him seduc't, but on himself
> Treble confusion, wrath and vengeance pour'd.          (1.210–19)

To which Adam replies:

> O goodness infinite, goodness immense!
> That all this good of evil shall produce.
> And evil turn to good; more wonderful
> Than that which by creation first brought forth
> Light out of darkness! full of doubt I stand,

Whether I should repent me now of sin
By mee done and occasiond, or rejoice
Much more, that much more good thereof spring,
To God more glory, more good will to Men.                    (12.469–77)

Willingly suspended between repentance and rejoicing, I find in Adam's situation, in which Milton will not allow him to remain despite Milton's unorthodox misgivings, my own existential position. I cannot repent the process I have been through, nor can I unambiguously rejoice in it.

The Hidden Imam, to whatever degree unveiled, then, remains in his essence hidden, as indeed essence itself remains forever hidden. 'Exalted, immeasurably exalted, art Thou above the strivings of mortal man to unravel Thy mystery, to describe Thy glory, or even to hint at the nature of Thine Essence' (*Gleanings* 3–4), declares Bahá'u'lláh. To unveil the Glory of God ('to God more glory') is not finally to embrace the naked truth. Rather it is to embrace the Glory (Baha) as Blake embraced it: in a new apparel as its 'Litteral expression,' its old apparel or 'rotten rags of Memory' having exploded under the pressure of the new, as in Revelation. This breaking of the vessels is like Christ's parable of the new wine in old bottles: 'And the heavens departed as a scroll when it is rolled together' to release a poisonous content no longer fit to drink (6.13). I associate this revelation partly with Byron's 'vitality of poison,' a perception of the human mystery largely set aside in this book. This much: for the apocalyptic imagination of the Romantics, especially Blake, the vitality of Satan's poison calls the 'whole soul' of Milton's 'uncircumscribed' God 'into activity' by rejecting the limitations imposed upon Milton's Messiah by his restricted use of Newton's compasses, 'prepar'd / In God's eternal store to circumscribe / The Universe, and all created things' (*PL* 7.225–7).

Modelling his Lucifer on Milton's Satan, Byron argues that Messiah's creation leaves Jehovah alone in the 'Uncreated.' Withdrawing his goodness into himself, this becomes his 'unparticipated solitude' (*Cain* 1.1.151). In *Cain* Lucifer takes Cain into a 'Void Outside of Existence' which, unlike Blake's impregnated 'Void,' remains void. Reading Byron's drama, Blake identifies Cain's journey into the uncreated with 'the Sleep of Ulro.' 'Can a Poet doubt the Visions of Jehovah?' Blake asks Byron ('The Ghost of Abel' 1.1). 'Nature has no Outline; / But Imagination has. Nature has no tune: but Imagination has! / Nature has no Supernatural & dissolves: Imagination is Eternity' (1.2–4). Since Abel's ghost swears vengeance on Cain for murdering him, Jehovah declares that Abel must 'go to Eternal Death / In Self Annihilation even till Satan Self-subdud Put off Satan / Into the Bottomless Abyss whose torment arises for ever & ever' (2.19–21). When Shelley hurls Jupiter into the 'Bottomless Abyss,' his 'vast and solitary throne' (*Cain* 1.148) 'Stand[s], not o'erthrown, but unregarded now' (*PU* 1.1.148, 3.4.179). It is merely vacant or 'no more remembered' (3.4.169) until the mind in creation confronts its own dissolution as what Shelley calls 'Invulnerable nothings' that 'decay / Like corpses in a charnel' (*A* 348–9). Before *Cain*, Shelley was anxious to release Byron from self-destruction. Now seeing Byron's genius nourished by the 'vitality of poison,' he seems prepared to embrace it as an 'apocalyptic [...] revelation not before communicated to man' (*Letters* 2:388). Shelley explores this silence in *The Triumph of Life* as 'thoughts which must remain untold,' as if discovering for the first time the spectre his imagination was never fully able to absorb or transform. That is to say, Shelley saw Byron's Shadow, which, properly embraced, lifts the soul from Three to Four.

For Jung, this Shadow resides in the dark feminine, which in Romanticism continues to haunt a masculine vision bound to its own patriarchal remnants. For example, though Newton's physics announced the 'Trump of the last doom,' which 'awake[s] the dead to Judgment [in the "Vegetable Body" (*Europe* 13.2–3)],' it does not in Blake's *Europe* succeed. Enitharmon, Los's Emanation, the weaver of Blake's text, 'Written within & without in woven letters,' does not awake the dead. As Rajan argues, she is 'put to sleep,' 'curiously absented from the history of which she is said to be the cause.' 'It would seem,' Rajan suggests, 'that prophecy is possible only through the bounding off of the female within a crisis pushed back into prehistory' ('Gender' 202). The androgyne as *hieros gamos*, however devoutly to be wished for, remains more psychologically feared than desired by male Romantics, which often leaves its female authors to lament their exile from a male Eden. 'I would give / All that I am to be as thou now art!' declares Shelley's Urania, 'but I am chained to Time, and cannot thence depart!' (*A* 241–3). Rajan rejects the patriarchal foreclosure of vision that leaves the feminine in the exile situation of the Threefold Sexual, which Blake calls Beulah.

In an essentially psychoanalytical framework, Rajan has argued Byron's metaphysical position, which often sets him apart from the other Romantics, though in his final fragment Shelley becomes Byron's sole convert. Arguing that the creative imagination is answerable to a 'primal scene of trauma' that resists enlightenment, Rajan explores the operations of the imagination in the context of this 'primal scene' ('*ig-*

*notum per ignotius*') as what Schelling calls, in *Ages of the World* (1815), 'the self-lacerating madness [that] is still now what is innermost in all things' (103). Fully embracing Blake's madness, while critiquing the determination of humanist critics (including myself) to view it in spiritual terms, she explains how, unlike myself, she resisted Frye's and other like-minded idealistic readings of Blake by insisting that his visionary poetry, like that of the other Romantics, remains bound to the trauma that it unconsciously enacts as the '(im)possible' creative struggle to resolve it. Focusing upon the '(im)possible' as the 'still born and still to be born' ('Dis-figuring' 231), Rajan provides the most deeply disturbing, critically discerning feminist reading of Romanticism, to which as a *failed apocalypse* I assent. Unlike Rajan, however, I locate my assent in a larger apocalyptic context in which the sublation (*Aufhebung*) of poetic truth into the androgyne (marriage of the opposites) becomes the *a priori* reality of the soul, which Coleridge boldly equates with the act of perception. Rajan, on the other hand, would equate the apocalyptic act of perception with the megalomania that for her patriarchally inhabits epic vision.

As this book explores it, Romanticism is apocalyptically announced less by *Lyrical Ballads* with its 1800 Preface than it is by Blake's removal from London to Felpham in 1800. Here, as Palamabron, he calls down 'a Great Solemn Assembly' with the purpose of announcing the radical recreation of the English prophetic tradition in which the poet 'who will not defend Truth, may be compelled to / Defend a Lie, that he may be snared & caught & taken.' 'And all Eden descended into Palamabron's tent,' Blake declares. There they listen to the 'Bards prophetic Song,' which serves, not only as a Preludium to *Milton*, but in a larger sense as the Preludium to this book. At the anagogical or 'Fourfold' level, which announces itself in every 'Pulsation of the Artery,' this book, like Blake's *Milton*, serves as a Preludium to a larger vision, which on a personal level I identify with my dream of the Báb. Getting from Three to Four lies, for Blake, in entering the 'Pulsation' itself, where it becomes, as the body's consciousness of its own operations, the risen or resurrected body. Unless it is entered, Blake further explains, the 'Pulsation' remains in 'the Void Outside of Existence,' where it is frozen into a corpse-like state described by Blake as 'Eternal Death.' (Urizen's 'cold hand' scoops up 'water from the river Jordan,' pouring its 'icy fluid' on to 'Miltons brain' [*M* 19[21].7–9].) In *Jerusalem* this corpse-like state is 'Albion's Couch' where Albion lies asleep. Albion awakening is Blake awakening every morning 'at sun-rise' to 'see the Saviour over [him] / Spreading his beams of love, & dictating the words of [his] mild song' (4.4–5). The awakened Blake is calling the sleeping Albion in himself as his 'Vegetable Body' to awake.

With the English pastoral tradition in mind, including his own contribution to it, Blake recognizes the way in which the pastoral, the 'Threefold' Beulah as the sexual or married land, becomes the 'marriage hearse' unless the Daughters of Beulah 'who inspire the Poets Song' can receive the Sons of Eden, whom Blake has called down into his tent at Felpham, not as the equals of the Sons, but as the limited containers of their unlimited energy, which they know to be 'too exceeding unbounded.' Blake knows that the 'Fourfold' Eden is the only possible 'Human' state. He knew it in 1800 when Los announced his return to him after six thousand years to accomplish what he could not accomplish, as surely and as clearly as Jung and Pauli knew that, with the dropping of the atomic bomb in 1945, quantum physics as the resurrected form of Newton's 'Vegetable Body' was now the only possible global, human habitation.

Deeply aware of the ghostly presence of the patriarchy informing this vision, Rajan cries out in defence of Enitharmon trapped by Blake in 'the demonisation of the female' ('Gender' 202). Drawing upon Jean-François Lyotard's notion of three levels of the figure, Rajan equates Blake's female figures with 'the matrix figure,' which 'does not belong "to plastic" or "textual space" at all, and is "no more visible than readable," being instead the general conditions of possibility for a kind of figuration' (227–8). This 'matrix figure' mirrors Jung's understanding of the archetype as the 'general conditions' for which the image or figuration provides the 'possibility.' Rajan goes on to say that 'Blake's actual images of women are a point of access to a more archaeological [archetypal?] level at which the very nature of form and imaginative work is constituted and put into question.' This statement describes the function of the anima. That is to say, Blake's 'actual images of women' suggest Jung's understanding of the anima, the dangerously problematic 'nature of form and imaginative work,' which 'can utterly destroy a man.' Rajan continues:

It is *both* constituted and questioned because Blake's female figures [like Jung's], at least in the 1790's, are at once symbolically encoded and released, by being given their own voice, from the 'solid form' with which they have been 'stamp[ed].' Thus one cannot speak of images of women in the sense of stereotypes; rather Blake's images of women are already deeply conflicted, whether they are symbolically deformed like Enitharmon, or allowed to cry out against the identities thrust on them like Oothoon and the nameless shadowy female of *Europe*. As such, Blake's females at the level of the image-figure are correlated with a profound crisis at a more archaeological level where gender forms part of a matrix from which the very space of literature is generated. This space has conventionally been configured in Blake criticism as systematic, which is to say fully organized, or as illuminated: the space of the illuminated book where seeing and saying coincide. And these ways of configuring mastery, needless to say, are invisibly masculine, since they involve a certain mastery: illuminated space, as Levinas says, 'collects about a mind which possesses it' and 'is already like the product of a synthesis.' ('Gender' 203–4)

Lest it be assumed, however, that Rajan's position supports the position of Jung, it perhaps needs to be made clear that Jung himself, at 'a more archaeological level,' is subject to a patriarchal fear of the feminine, which tends systematically to subordinate the feminine to what he considers the stronger logocentric demands of the masculine.

The generation of literature from a 'Void Outside of Existence' is the unnamed 'Female Space' that becomes a womb in which the poem takes shape only to be discarded as the poem's embryonic container when it finally assumes completed form. I suggest that this radically limited role constitutes the patriarchal limits imposed by the secondary imagination on the *hieros gamos*. My dream of a somersault in the air that lands me at the feet of the Báb could not assume its awakened or illuminated form as the logocentric system that governs the Baha'i Administrative Order without being anything more than a 'Poor earthly casket.' I slowly realized that integrating the dream lay in the androgyne as the inner, equal marriage of masculine and feminine. Rajan's analysis of Blake's Lambeth texts has confronted me with the limitations of the patriarchal apocalypse in terms of the role it assigns to the bride at the wedding feast. Frye argues that Beulah is a 'moony habitation' where 'no dispute can come, where everything is an equal element of a liberal education, where Bunyan and Rochester are met together and Jane Austen and the Marquis de Sade have kissed each other' ('Reflections' 143). I can now see that Beulah is less the 'liberal education' I thought I received at the University of Toronto than its patriarchal parody. Here, literature students are nursed by the great Alma Mater as a return to the soul's source from which the soul could retrace its steps up to a patriarchal eminence. Such a place, pastoral rather than epic, remains for the genuinely androgynous apocalyptic imagination a tempting 'spell' in which the barrel of a loaded gun becomes a fanciful receptacle for a daffodil or daisy, a lunatic paradise of wanton isolation, which some fondly see as the only solution to an otherwise suicidal engagement with a chaos now beyond human reckoning. Viewed in terms of the androgyne not yet constellated by the epic imagination, the retreat of Prometheus and Asia, presumably accompanied by her two sisters, into an enchanted cave as the recovered Atlantis of the oceanic imagination ('a Sea profound, of ever-spreading sound') is a parody of the psychic action that conducts to this cave. Comparable to what Rajan describes as Urizen's act of self-construction in *Urizen*, the enchanted cave lyrically mirrors the dramatic action, now 'claustrophobically' contained 'inside its own womb' ('Gender' 205). Again, as Rajan argues in her reading of the abortive creative process in *Urizen*, Shelley in *Prometheus Unbound* creates 'an ectopic pregnancy,' a '"human heart struggling & beating" inside its own womb.'

In Romanticism the new human life shaping within the womb of Beulah is, as the process of its making, not yet released from this process into a fully independent life, which classically understood constitutes a work of art. At the end of his life, Blake was still at work on his copious designs for Dante's *Divine Comedy*. He was continuing the 'Mental Fight,' which for Blake Dante's Threefold Christian vision had abandoned by failing to see the Inferno as the essential condition of ascent to the Fourfold in which, Shelley argues, Dante 'feigns himself to have ascended to the throne of the Supreme Cause' (*DP* 526). Commissioned by Linnell and paid two to three pounds a week while engaged, Blake began the drawings in 1824 while in bed with a sprained foot and learning Italian the better to execute them. Few of the drawings were completely finished and only seven were engraved. These seven engravings, done by himself, were published in 1827. On 25 April 1827 (he died on 12 August), he wrote to Linnell: 'I am too much attachd to Dante to think much of anything else – I have Proved the Six Plates & reduced the Fighting Devils ready for the Copper I count myself sufficiently Paid If I live as I now do & only fear that I may be unlucky to my friends & especially that I may not be so to you' (*CPP* 784). All 120 drawings were sold, along with the manuscript of *The Four Zoas*, as the Linnell Collection at Christie's on 15 March 1918. They fetched £7,665. For Blake, making the drawings and engravings was pay enough, so long as he could live to finish them. The process itself belonged to Blake, as my process belongs to me as the Hidden Imam in myself struggling to reveal Himself. The danger of the dream lies in its tendency to roll back its impulse on the vacant brain. But the danger also lies in the dream's ability to assume the autonomous

life of an active imagination that seduces the dreamer to take up phantasmagoric residence in an enchanted cave. Such a vitality can cost the
dreamer his actual as distinct from virtual life, as Keats well knew in *The
Fall of Hyperion*. The struggle between the virtual and actual is focused in
the Shadow, the conscious integration of which constitutes the dialectic
of the Self. As the will's free rather than possessed expression, this dialectic becomes what Coleridge calls the only absolute self, the Uncreated,
understood as 'groundless; but only because it is itself the ground of all
our certainty.'

The Báb of my levitating dream in which I float like a feather to his
feet – 'A molded feather, an eagle feather,' writes Browning, describing
his response to a stranger who had talked to Shelley – is what Derrida
calls the Cogito, the 'proper and inaugural moment' (56) of its madness
that 'opens and founds the world as such by exceeding it.' By momentarily exceeding the world – Blake's 'Pulsation of the Artery,' which for Derrida 'is possible only in the direction of infinity or nothingness'–madness
releases the mind's inaccessible desire *for* the world, which 'acknowledges madness as its liberty and very possibility' (56). It is virtual rather than
actual. As such, madness 'keeps itself within the world' – that is, within
its necessary tranquillization as what Derrida calls economy. Revelation
as Plato's divine insanity does not tranquillize its madness, does not betray the 'fading coal' of inspiration. I understand knowledge to be this
betrayal as economy. I understand revelation to be its unknown or unconscious source, whose symbol in my particular dream is the figure of
the Báb.

# 7 Revelation and Madness

The God seems purposely to have deprived all poets, prophets, and sooth-sayers of every particle of reason and understanding, the better to adapt them to their employment as his ministers and interpreters; and that we, their auditors, may acknowledge that those who write so beautifully are possessed, and address us, inspired by the God.

– Shelley's translation of Plato, *Ion*

## 1

Wordsworth's *The Prelude* is a mythopoeic account of the ascent of consciousness from its mortal or 'inland' ('Intimations of Immorality' 166) source, which Wordsworth describes as the soul's 'first outset' (*P* 9.7), to its pinnacle as the 'philosophic mind' in which, in faith, the soul 'looks through death' ('Intimations of Immortality' 190). As such, *The Prelude* presents three interlocking perspectives: ascent, descent, and reconciling murmur. Together these enact a 'dark / Inscrutable workmanship' by which otherwise 'Discordant elements [...] cling together / In one society' (*P* 1.341–4). Understood in terms of the Logos or Word, *The Prelude* thus looks 'Towards the Uncreated with a countenance / Of adoration' that ecstatically binds Wordsworth's imagination to its biblical source as what Frye calls *kerygma*. By the 'sweet breath of heaven,' Wordsworth has been 'singled out' as a 'renovated spirit' for 'holy services' (1.53–4). Apparently opposing this priestly calling, Wordsworth describes his experience of the French Revolution as a demonic descent, 'juvenile errors' that left him, like 'Adam, yet in Paradise / Though fallen from bliss' (11.54, 8.659–60). Extending the two-part *Prelude* beyond his seventeenth year, Wordsworth at twenty-eight found himself in a very different world. His 'voice / Labouring, a brain confounded,' in nightly dreams he pleaded before 'unjust tribunals,' where he felt a 'Death-like' sense 'of treacherous desertion' in his 'last place of refuge – [his] own soul' (P 10.412–15). These unresolved feelings, however repressed, initiated *The Prelude* as the therapeutic composition of his thoughts 'to more than infant softness,' which Coleridge describes as 'the constant accompaniment of mental, no less than bodily, convalescence.'

This 'softness' is the sound of the river Derwent blending with Wordsworth's nurse's song as the created voice of the 'Uncreated.' Not surprisingly, the *kerygma* of the Uncreated is 'most audible' when his 'fleshly ear / O'ercome by humblest prelude of that strain, / Forgot her functions, and slept undisturbed.' *The Prelude* as *kerygma* is Wordsworth's prelude to the 'Uncreated.' Raised to consciousness in his 'finite mind,' the 'ceaseless music' of the Derwent gave him 'a dim earnest' of the 'infinite I AM.' What flowed along his dreams was 'the first creative fiat,' even as the Báb, as the prelude to this book, flowed along mine at its primal source. In Wordsworth's 'Intimations of Immortality' ode, the Derwent is inwardly linked to 'that immortal sea / Which brought us hither.' The composed soul can in the instant of *kerygma* 'hear the mighty waters rolling evermore' (169–71). Discomposed, however, the soul is devoured by a 'ravenous sea' (P 9.4). The expanded *Prelude* confronts this devouring context as a process of 'intricate delay' in which, 'swayed / In part by fear to shape a way direct,' Wordsworth turns 'back his course, far back, / Seeking the very regions which he crossed / In his first outset' (9.2–8). This shift between vertical ascent and descent and horizontal progress and regress, particularly as they later join existentially in Wordsworth to form a cross, enact *The Prelude*'s dialectical struggle, which resolves itself in a faith fed by hope.

'Oh! yet for a few short years of useful life, / And all will be complete' (14.432–3), Wordsworth concludes *The Prelude*, referring to his projected completion of *The Recluse*, which in Coleridge's absence he had barely begun. But he still consoles himself that the mind that *might* produce 'the FIRST GENUINE PHILOSOPHIC POEM' is 'A thousand times more beautiful' (P 14.451) than the sheer duress that produced *The Prelude* and *The Excursion*. Frye argues that *kerygma*, being itself 'Of quality and fabric more divine' (P 14.456), comes from the other side of poetry's myth and metaphor, which is at best an inspired prelude to *kerygma*. Poetry prepares the mind for revelation, much as Romantic poetry prepared my mind to receive and absorb the revelation of the Báb.

In *Words with Power*, Frye describes the body of his work as a mandala whose centre and circumference is the *kerygma* of the Bible perceived as the archetypal form of Western culture. Extending Frye's vision to embrace the Báb as the return of Christ, I have in this book affirmed a vision of a world culture embracing East and West.

In Book Nine of *The Prelude*, Wordsworth turns from the metaphor of the river in order to argue that the 'intricate delay' of his ceaseless recourse to the fading 'eagerness of infantine desire' has in fact prepared him for a final confrontation. He thus reduces the bold perspective of Mount Snowdon to an 'aerial Down' where he halts 'For breathing-time' (9.10–11). There he is 'tempted to review / The region left behind him,' not as a devouring sea but 'from that height,' to decide 'if aught / Deserving notice have escaped regard' (9.11–13, 15). With mounting detachment approximating dismissal, Wordsworth, 'with one and yet one more / Last look,' makes 'the best amends he may' (9.15–16). Having thus 'lingered,' he is now ready to 'start afresh / With courage, and new hope risen on our toil,' though suggesting a kind of nervous exhaustion that accompanies what 'now / Awaits us! Oh, how much unlike the past' (9.17, 18–22). Published posthumously, *The Prelude* had both outlived and replaced its author's reason for writing it. The reason became as an apparent outward defeat the point within his soul where, beyond words, he stood single before the uncreated Godhead. His 'breathing-time' diminished, Wordsworth has instead written 'Breathings for incommunicable powers' (3.190). Drawing this book to an end rather than a conclusion, I find myself standing single, making similar breathings. A correspondent breeze vexing its own creation.

# 2

In *Gate of the Heart: Understanding the Writings of the Báb*, Nader Saiedi provides an English commentary on some of the major works of the Báb. Many of these have yet to be translated into English or commented upon in a way that adequately explores the various symbolic rather than literal levels upon which they were clearly intended to be read. As a result, the few English-speaking scholars who have attempted to read them have been able to make of them about as much sense as a 'Corporeal' reading of Blake. One of these readers was Edward G. Browne, author of the still-standard *Literary History of Persia* (first edition 1902–6) and one of the first Westerners to treat the Bábi and Bahá'i religions in any serious way, though his colleagues at Cambridge saw his devotion to this study a waste of his impressive scholarly skill. In his introduction to *The Tarikh-i-Jadid* or *New History of Mirza 'Ali Muhammad the Báb*, Browne, whose scholarship reflects Britain's imperial mission, describes the books of the Báb as 'for the most part, voluminous, hard to comprehend, uncouth in style, unsystematic in arrangement, filled with iterations and solecisms, and not unfrequently quite incoherent and unintelligible to any ordinary reader' (cited in Saiedi 49). In *From Shaykhism to Bábism*, Denis MacEoin speaks even more severely of 'the innumerable obscurities and vagueness of even the most reliable texts.' He singles out the Báb's commentary on the Súrih of Abundance as 'for the most part, almost unreadable, consisting of highly abstract and insubstantial speculations on the verses, words, and even letters of the Súra on which it is supposed to be a "commentary"' (cited in Saiedi 49).

At the same time, however, Browne follows in the footsteps of Count Gobineau's *Religions et Philosophies dans L'Asie Centrale* (1865), which recounts the origins of the Bábi religion up to 1852, by extending its narrative to the 1880s, including Browne's year among the Persian followers of the Báb. Gobineau's text, which he read while preparing an essay on Sufi philosophy, was Browne's first encounter with the Bábi religion, and in it he found the 'most perfect presentation of accurate and critical research in the form of a narrative of thrilling and sustained interest, such as one may, indeed hope to find in the drama or in romance, but can scarcely expect from the historian' (x). The book produced in Browne 'in a certain sense a complete revolution in my ideas and projects,' including, above all, his dawning notion of history as a divine drama. He thus decided to go to Persia, particularly Shíráz, 'not because it was the home of [the Sufi poets] Háfiz and Sa'dí,' but 'because it was the birthplace of Mírzá 'Ali Muhammd the Báb' (xi). He was further anxious to document the Bábi religion because its first eyewitnesses and participants formed a persecuted spiritual community dwindling in number. He thus went 'amongst those who professed it, winning their confidence, and eventually [...] obtaining copies of their sacred books and a clue to their contents' (xi). He devoted the rest of his life to a 'systematic examination' of all the basic texts involved in the revelations of the Báb and Bahá'u'lláh, as well as 'a host of more or less important letters, memoranda, poems, and abstracts,' first presenting this material in two July and October 1889 articles in the *Journal of the Royal Asiatic Society* (xiv).

Browne's *Literary History of Persia* culminates in his four interviews with Bahá'u'lláh, the only Westerner to be so honoured. Browne's tone of awe and reverence indicates the meeting's profound impact upon him, particularly because of his intimate relations to that point with the Bábis, most of whom (though not all) had, in accordance with the Báb's instruction, turned to Bahá'u'lláh as the One to whom the Báb addressed everything he had written as 'Him Whom God will make manifest.' Browne writes:

> So here at *Behjé* [the home of Bahá'u'lláh in the final years of his exile to Acre] was I installed as a guest, in the very midst of all that Bábism accounts most noble and most holy; and here did I spend the five most memorable days, during which I enjoyed unparalleled and unhoped-for opportunities of holding intercourse with those who are the very fountain-heads of that mighty and wondrous spirit which works with invisible but ever-increasing force for the transformation and quickening of a people who slumber in a sleep like unto death. It was in truth a strange and moving experience, but one whereof I despair of conveying any save the feeblest impression. [...] Persian Muslims will tell you often that the Bábis bewitch or drug their guests so that these, impelled by fascination which they cannot resist, become similarly affected with what the aforesaid Muslims regard as a strange and incomprehensible madness. Idle and absurd as this belief is, it yet rests on a basis of fact stronger than that which supports the greater part of what they allege concerning this people. The spirit which pervades the Bábís is such that it can hardly fail to affect most powerfully all subjected to its influence. It may appal or attract: it cannot be ignored or disregarded. Let those who have not seen disbelieve me if they will; but, should that spirit once reveal itself to them, they will experience an emotion which they are not likely to forget. (*Traveller's Narrative* xxxviii–xxxix)

Finally admitted to Bahá'u'lláh's presence,

> a mild dignified voice bade [him] be seated, and then continued: – 'Praise be to God that thou has attained! [...] Thou hast come to see a prisoner and an exile. [...] We desire the good of the world and the happiness of the nations; yet they deem us a stirrer up of strife and sedition worthy of bondage and banishment. [...] That all nations should become one faith and all men as brothers; that the bonds of affection and unity between the sons of men should be strengthened; that diversity of religion should cease, and differences of race be annulled – what harm is there in this? [...] Yet so it shall be; these fruitless strifes, these ruinous wars shall pass away, and the 'Most Great Peace' shall come. [...] Do not you in Europe need this also? Is not

this what Christ foretold? [...] Yet do we see your Kings and rulers lavishing their treasures more freely on means for the destruction of the human race than on that which would conduce to the happiness of mankind. [...] These strifes and this bloodshed and discord must cease, and all men be as one kindred and one family. [...] Let not a man glory in this, that he loves his country; let him rather glory in this, that he loves his kind.' (xl)

It seems clear from Browne's description of his encounter with Bahá'u'lláh and his followers that Browne's interest in Persian poetry, particularly its embrace of Persian history, had found its 'primal Point' in the figure of the Báb. This is the mystic centre around which the entire creation revolves as a ceaseless revolution in which every 'Pulsation of the Artery' repeats 'the eternal act of creation in the infinite I AM.' In Sufi tradition, this movement assumes a ritual form in the mystical dance of the dervish, which enacts ceaseless motion as a perfect stillness or equilibrium in which matter and spirit, Yin and Yang, masculine and feminine, become reconciled. Jung hypothesizes this mystical transcendence in his notion of the psychoid archetype, in which 'psyche and matter are two different aspects of one and the same thing, [...] two cones, whose apices, meeting in a point without extension – a real zero point – touch and do not touch.' In the Bayán, 'the most important of the Báb's works' (Saiedi 1), the Báb describes this as the 'primal Point' around which all the prophets revolve to become one, each new revelation becoming a return to the 'primal Point' as the judgment and resurrection of the previous revelation. Thus the revelation of Jesus during his lifetime as prophet becomes the judgment and resurrection of Judaism, and the revelation of Muhammad during his lifetime as a prophet becomes the judgment and resurrection of Christianity. And thus, as the Báb goes on to explain, his revelation during his lifetime as a prophet (23 May 1844–9 July 1850) becomes the judgment and resurrection of Islam. Together each of these forms a single revelation, what Nietzsche calls the '*amor fati*' or psychic recognition 'that one wants nothing to be different, not forward, nor backward, not in all eternity' (*Ecce Homo* 258). For Nietzsche, the return of Zarathustra is this renewal of the primal Point of creation, symbolized by Shelley in his lyrical drama by Asia as the Orient or primal source.

'Since their essential being is unconscious to us,' Jung writes of the archetypes,

and still they are experienced as spontaneous agencies, there is probably no alternative now but to describe their nature, in accordance with their chiefest effect, as 'spirit.' [...] If so, the position of the archetype would be located beyond the psychic sphere, analogous to the position of physiological instinct, which is immediately rooted in the stuff of the organism and, with its psychoid nature, forms the bridge to matter in general. In archetypal conceptions and instinctual perceptions, spirit and matter confront one another on the psychic plane. Matter and spirit both appear in the psychic realm as distinctive qualities of conscious contents. The ultimate nature of both is transcendental, that is, irrepresentable, since the psyche and its contents are the only reality which is given to us *without a medium*. ('On the Nature' 215–16)

For Jung and Pauli, the recognition of the archetypal ground in which matter metaphorically enacts the unconscious life of the psyche to become its symbolic form is the intersection of eternity and time in which the horizontal plane of history and the vertical axis of the psyche spiral together around their primal point.

Like the Romantics before him, Jung devoted his life to understanding this transformation. As progressive revelation, this act is a ceaselessly unfolding process alarmingly presented to me in my dream of the Báb. I have attempted to explore this dream *as* a dream, which is to say, as psychically given '*without a medium*' as it issues directly from the unconscious. As an archetype in the Jungian sense shared by Pauli with reference to numbers, however, this immediacy transcends as spirit the reality of the psyche. My dream experience of the Báb is what Jung would call an 'instinctual' perception in which 'spirit and matter,' without in my case a history to support it, 'confront one another on the psychic plane.' Elsewhere Jung suggests that this confrontation is the human experience of animals as the guardians or totems of instinct. My experience of the dream had this force of animal instinct, which Jung describes as the primordial presence of the archetype.

In 'Instinct and the Unconscious,' Jung makes the following distinction: 'whereas instinct is a purposive impulse to carry out some highly complicated action, intuition is the unconscious, purposive apprehension of a highly complicated situation' (132). Intuition, like imagination, focuses upon a 'highly complicated situation,' which as poetic truth it seeks to raise to consciousness in order to display the whole soul in activity. Instinct, on the other hand, is less concerned with the inner display of the soul brought into harmony with its complex operations than with carrying out those operations as an extroverted rather than an introverted action. As outer rather than inner behaviour, instinct demands active belief rather than a willing suspension of disbelief. Therefore, when in apparent opposition to poetic truth I bind my dream to instinct rather than intuition, I have in mind Jung's description of instincts as 'impulses to carry out actions from necessity, without conscious motivation,' in the same way that an animal is compelled to carry out actions 'without conscious motivation' (133). At the same time, Jung argues, animal 'necessity' is distinct from human 'necessity.' In the human state, 'instincts compel man to a specifically human mode of existence, so the archetypes force his ways of perception and apprehension into specifically human patterns.' Together the instincts and archetypes form what he calls the 'collective unconscious,' which, 'unlike the personal unconscious,' is 'not made up of individual and more or less unique contents but of those that are universal and of regular occurrence' (133–4). 'Instinct,' he insists, 'is an essentially collective, i.e., universal and regularly occurring phenomenon which has nothing to do with individuality. Archetypes have this quality in common with the instincts and are likewise collective phenomena' (134). It is this collective, impersonal, and universal quality to which I was necessarily drawn in the absence of anything historical or personal to which to attach my experience of the dream. The danger of this absence as a splitting should be obvious.

Jung describes this danger as the psyche's descent into the unconscious realm of Nature, which Blake describes as a 'Void Outside of Existence' into which Ololon descends, the 'Void' in her descent becoming a 'Womb.' Describing at the human level a highly complex operation in which instinct becomes intuition – 'the irruption into consciousness of an unconscious content, a sudden idea or "hunch"' – Jung insists that for Nature what appears to us as complicated or wonderful is for Nature 'quite ordinary' ('Instinct' 132). 'We always,' he argues, 'tend to project onto things our own difficulties of understanding and to call them complicated, when in reality they are very simple and know nothing of our intellectual problems' (132). To reduce human behaviour to natural law (deism or natural religion) is to reduce it to the level of the 'Corporeal Understanding,' thereby rejecting poetic vision 'addressd to the Intellectual powers' as the 'Phantom of the over heated brain.' It is this rejection of poetic power that Romanticism, confronted by the scientific triumph of the 'Corporeal Understanding,' opposed.

Jung provides what amounts to a psychological account of what Coleridge explored metaphysically as the primary imagination:

Just as we have been compelled to postulate the concept of an instinct determining or regulating our conscious actions, so, in order to account for the uniformity and regularity of our perceptions, we must have recourse to the correlated concept of a factor determining the mode of apprehension. It is this factor which I call the archetype or primordial image. The primordial image might suitably be described as the *instinct's perception of itself,* or as the self-portrait of the instinct, in exactly the same way as consciousness is an inward perception of the objective life-process. Just as conscious apprehension gives our actions form and direction, so unconscious apprehension through the archetype determines the form and direction of instinct. If we call instinct 'refined,' then the 'intuition' which brings the instinct into play, in other words the apprehension by means of the archetype, must be something incredibly precise. Thus the yucca moth must carry within it an image, as it were, of the situation that 'triggers off' its instinct. This image enables it to 'recognize' the yucca flower and its structure. ('Instinct' 136–7)

So powerfully and immediately is this primordial presence archetypally operative in revelation that the Báb declares precisely what Coleridge declares with reference to the primary imagination:

God hath created in the truth-sign of any thing that is called a thing, the signs of *all* beings, that it should not be difficult for anyone to recognize the manifestations of the tokens of His grace, and the effulgences of His modes of justice, so that all beings may witness the revelation of His sovereignty in the creation of all things [the eternal act of creation], manifestly and truly, in such wise that none may see anything but that he would behold Him before seeing that object. (Cited in Saiedi 60)

Jung's identification of 'instinctual perceptions' with 'archetypal conceptions,' which reflects how spirit is the perception of matter as the beholding of God, finds perhaps its boldest affirmation in the Báb's assertion that 'Every created entity in itself reflecteth the Greater World.' 'Verily,' He declares, 'God hath fashioned all things in the form of His Divine Unity in such wise that when a servant is purified from all protestation and doubt and instead reflecteth the splendours of the divine revelation unto him and through him, in utmost equity, he will be naught but the sign of the Divine Self, that "verily there is none other God but Him, the Beloved, the Compassionate."' 'Therefore, in this day,' the Báb continues, 'should a tiny ant desire to unravel all [the Qur'an's] verses, and its abstruse meanings, and its stations, through the black of its own eye, it shall be capable of achieving that, inasmuch as the mystery of

Lordship and the effulgence of the Eternal vibrate within the very atoms of all created things' (cited in Saiedi 58–9). The 'yucca moth,' that is, '"recognize[s]" the yucca flower and its structure.'

On the human level, instincts understood as recognition unconsciously carry at the collective level an archetypal identity, which Bahá'u'lláh describes as 'the attributes and names of God.' 'How resplendent the luminaries of knowledge that shine in an atom, and how vast the oceans of wisdom that surge within a drop!' He declares, and continues:

> To a supreme degree is this true of man, who, among all created things, hath been invested with the robe of such gifts, and hath been singled out for the glory of such distinction. For in him are potentially revealed all the attributes and names of God to a degree that no other created being hath excelled or surpassed. All these names and attributes are applicable to him. Even as He [Muhammad] hath said: 'Man is My mystery and I am his mystery.' (*Gleanings* 177)

Again and again the instinctual reality of this archetypal identity has surfaced in my life. It surfaced in my levitating dream of the Báb, earlier intimated at the end of a Bahá'í meeting when I unexpectedly rose and declared everything the speaker said to be true. It surfaced in a converted army hut at the University of Manitoba when I stood up with Euripides' *Electra* in my hand and said to forty veterans that 'what we are about to do is more real than anything we have yet done.'

# 3

The Báb's revelation moves from its seed to its fruition in the revelation of Bahá'u'lláh. Together they proclaim a 'new creation' awakened in the soul as the consciousness of it. 'Lo, the entire creation hath passed away!' declares Bahá'u'lláh. 'Nothing remaineth except My Face.' 'Verily, We have caused every soul to expire by virtue of Our irresistible and all-subduing sovereignty. We have, then, called into being a new creation, as a token of Our grace unto men' (*Gleanings* 29–30). 'Could ye apprehend with what wonders of My munificence and bounty I have willed to entrust your souls,' Bahá'u'lláh further declares of His 'new creation,' 'ye would, of a truth, rid yourselves of attachment to all created things, and would gain a true knowledge of your own selves – a knowledge which is the same as the comprehension of Mine own Being' (326–7). The revelations of the Báb and Bahá'u'lláh introduce a notion of progressive revelation in which, as the renewal of 'the eternal act of creation in the infinite I AM,' the act of perception enacts a new revelation of its 'living Power and prime Agent' in which what is perceived as object *is* 'the Face of God.' In this radical sense, the twin revelations of the Báb and Bahá'u'lláh are a single revelation announcing the end of the cycle from Adam to Muhammad and the opening of a new one. This return to the 'primal Point' is a renewal issuing from an unprecedented outpouring of energy in which every atom contains within it the *unus mundus* or one world.

Describing Nietzsche's descent into madness, Jung turns to quantum physics to find a physiological explanation that, as if for the first time, understands animal instinct archetypally. In the same sense, the Báb cites the 'black' of a tiny ant's eye to account for 'the mystery of Lordship and the effulgence of the Eternal' that vibrates 'within every atom.' Nietzsche's fall into matter as the *enantiodromia* resulting from his out-of-body ascent into spirit lies in his failure to recognize instinct as spirit, the two as opposing 'Contraries' constituting one 'eternal body,' Blake's Human Fourfold. As Coleridge argues, subject and object exist 'as a perpetual self-duplication of one and the same power into object and subject, which presuppose each other, and can exist only as antitheses.' Making the same point, Jung argues that an 'opposition either exists in its binary form or it does not exist at all, and a being without opposites is completely unthinkable, as it would be impossible to establish its existence.' He continues:

> Absorption into the instinctual sphere, therefore, does not and cannot lead to conscious realization and assimilation of instinct, because consciousness struggles in a regular panic against being swallowed up in the primitivity and unconsciousness of sheer instinctuality. This fear is the eternal burden of the hero-myth [of which Nietzsche's Zarathustra is the prime modern example] and the theme of countless taboos. The closer one comes to the instinct-world, the more violent is the urge to shy away from it and to rescue the light of consciousness from the murks of the sultry abyss [Freud's 'black tide of mud']. Psychologically, however, the archetype as an image of instinct is a spiritual goal toward which the whole of nature strives; it is the sea to which all rivers wend their way, the prize which the hero wrests from the fight with the dragon. ('On the Nature' 212)

What perhaps I most feared upon waking from my dream was a fall into

the instinctual level of my life. To that point I had at least managed to
ignore the darkness, if not escape it entirely. But now awake I was suspended between instinct as 'the spiritual goal' and instinct as 'the murk
of the sultry abyss.' Unknown to me at the time, the dream had constellated 'the prize which the hero wrests from the fight with the dragon,'
which mythically informs the *agon* of this book.

This *agon* lay in my waking fear of the Báb as the dangerous, somersaulting release of instinct as a dissolution into air accompanied by lightning and a distant thunder. Describing the process of transformation,
Jung argues that the god

> appears at first in a hostile form, as an assailant with whom the hero has to
> wrestle. This is in keeping with the violence of all unconscious dynamism.
> In this manner the god manifests himself and in this form he must be over-
> come. The struggle has its parallel in Jacob's wrestling with the angel at
> the ford Jabbok. The onslaught of instinct then becomes an experience
> of divinity, provided that man does not succumb to it and follow it blindly,
> but defends his humanity against the animal nature of the divine power.
> (*Symbols* 338)

Ironically, the danger of my dream lay in the appearance of the Báb,
not 'in a hostile form,' but as an eagerly awaited figure whose psychic
presence I greet with abandoned joy, which I would increasingly blindly
confront in myself as 'the animal nature of the divine power.' In this
murky respect my passion for the Báb became, like the passion of Shelley's Visionary for the veiled maid, a nightmare that conducts to death.
In *Alastor* the 'interpenetration' of eternity and time becomes a catastrophic collision best described as psychosis. Treated in a religious rather than poetic sense, revelation essentially protects against this collision
of spirit and matter. In this sense it obeys the moral imperative to absorb
revelation rather than experience it imaginally as the whole soul creatively displayed in aesthetic activity for a reader's progressively unfolding
pleasure. Such a protection is present in the Administrative Order of
Bahá'u'lláh.

Absent in Nietzsche's Zarathustra is 'the fight with the dragon' in
which the absence of consciousness becomes a delusional transcendence
that brings about Nietzsche's fall from divine into mere madness, his
soul dead before his body. Jung analyses this fall from spirit into matter, as opposed to their reconciliation, in terms of the Chinese perception of Yin and Yang enacted in the sixty-four hexagrams of the *I Ching*,

which laid the foundation for his work in synchronicity as it shaped his
psychological understanding of quantum physics. For Jung, Chinese philosophy 'always foretold' the explosion of matter in quantum physics:
'Yin increases till it overcomes Yang. Yang disappears into utter darkness.
[...] But then Yang is seeking the heart of darkness and overcomes the
darkness from within, and suddenly out of the power of Yin appears the
Yang again' (*Nietzsche's Zarathustra* 244). Illustrating this process in the
various hexagrams as they bring the whole soul of man into activity, Jung
declares:

> now physics has done the trick. The Yin condition is exploded and the
> first Yang line is appearing. There is no return to material matter now, no
> chance. It is completely gone. For the last thing you really can observe is
> the mind. You disturb whatever there is by means of your mind, and what
> you are able to disturb, you can observe: you can perceive your disturbance.
> (244–5)

What has replaced matter is mind, which disturbs 'whatever there is.'
'Whatever there is' is 'your disturbance.' 'As when you look into a black
hole where you see nothing, after a while you see yourself. That is the
cognitional principle of the Yoga: you create the void and out of the void
comes the beginning of all knowledge, all real understanding' (245).

The 'void' into which Nietzsche fell became madness rather than 'the
beginning of all knowledge, all real understanding.' Jung confronted
this void after his break with Freud. Gratefully, he was not sufficiently a
poet to 'utterly destroy' himself. His fear of the anima as the poet's muse
who opens the flood gates of the collective unconscious was matched by
an even greater fear of divine revelation on the edge of whose 'abysm'
his 'daimon of creativity has ruthlessly had its way with [him].' 'A creative person,' he writes, 'has little power over his own life. He is not free.
He is captive and driven by his daimon' (*MDR* 357). What emerged from
Nietzsche's madness was the recognition of the energy it released as a
revelation of the mind's unlimited 'Intellectual powers,' which could no
longer be subjected to the materialism of a 'Corporeal Understanding.'
In the interior life of the mind, like that of an atom, lay 'the mystery of
Lordship, and the effulgence of the Eternal,' which 'vibrate[s] within
the very atoms of all created things.' For Jung, this was the Gate that had
now been opened.

As a patriot Wordsworth suffered the *enantiodromia* of the French Revolution as the reduction of his mind to a void or 'conflict of sensation

without name,' a madness that, like the imagination's strength of usurpation, produced a 'stride at once / Into another region' (10.275–6). For
Blake and Shelley, Wordsworth radically betrayed his own apocalyptic encounter with this void to produce a false memorial to its god-like power,
which Coleridge 'no sooner felt, than [he] sought to understand' (*BL*
1:82). In this current study, Coleridge's understanding of Wordsworth's
creative imagination finds an earlier analogue in the Shi'ite notion of
the imagination as the unveiling of the Hidden Imam in the human soul,
which in Persia becomes attached, with alarming consequences, to the
revelation of the Báb. This exploration of my dream of the Báb as it embraces the full range of my 'Intellectual powers' finds in Wordsworth's
withdrawal from the heroic a less satisfactory resolution of madness than
the 'fable' constructed by Jung. Jung argues that in 'a moment of unu-
sual clarity' he realized that in *Symbols of Transformation* he had found a
key to the mythology of the hero, but had still not answered the more
radical question, 'But in what myth does man live nowadays?' or, more
importantly, 'But then what is your myth – the myth in which you do
live?' To go on with his life Jung would have to 'unlock all the gates of the
unconscious psyche.' Opening them was painful. Like Keats in his 'Ode
to Psyche,' Jung knew he had entered a previously untrodden region of
his mind, that he had released a torrent like Wordsworth's Nile flooding
the Abyssinian plain, for which he was initially unprepared. He thus continued to revise *Symbols* as a way of finding in himself the myth ceaselessly
shaping itself in the collective unconscious as the myth in which 'we,' not
simply himself, continue to flow.

In 1950 Jung recalled that he was thirty-six when he wrote *Symbols of
Transformation*, 'the beginning of the second half of life, when a meta-
noia, a mental transformation, not infrequently occurs' (*Symbols* xxvi). In
1937 he had written: 'History teaches us over and over again that, contrary to rational expectation, irrational factors play the largest, indeed
the decisive, role in all processes of psychic transformation.' To which
he adds: 'It seems as if this insight were slowly making headway with the
somewhat drastic assistance of contemporary events' (xxvii). At the time
Jung was exploring these events in his seminars on *Thus Spake Zarathustra*, which explored Nietzsche's descent into madness in the context of
Hitler's rise to power. My dream of the Báb released in me a process of
psychic transformation governed by what appeared to be 'irrational factors,' upon which I sought to impose a 'rational expectation.' With the
exception of Blake, who remained until the end committed to ceaseless
'Mental Fight,' this imposition led to what, in the name of sanity, Derrida describes as a necessary betrayal of the apocalyptic imagination of

madness, a tranquillization of its hyperbolic powers, which are at the same time the mind's 'limit and profound resource.' Describing the act of revelation in which the prophets speak with the 'Voice of Divinity,' Bahá'u'lláh declares: 'Were the eye of discernment to be opened, it would recognize that in this very state, they have considered themselves utterly effaced and non-existent in the face of Him Who is the All-Pervading, the Incorruptible. Methinks, they have regarded themselves as utter nothingness, and deemed their mention in that Court an act of blasphemy' (*Gleanings* 55).

By arguing that the total absence of the Cogito as the Logos or Word would reduce 'the eternal act of creation' to a nothingness 'that neutralizes everything,' Derrida essentially agrees with Bahá'u'lláh (55). At 'the very moment proceeding His Revelation,' Bahá'u'lláh declares, God is alone 'without a creation.' At that moment, 'each and every created thing shall be made to yield up its soul to God' (*Gleanings* 151). Haunted by this madness ('Lo, the entire creation hath passed away!'), Derrida suggests, writing partakes of a madness, which, the more diaphanous it becomes, the more it unveils its betrayal of sanity by making the Cogito as madness numinously present. 'Crisis of reason, finally, access to reason and attack on reason,' Derrida concludes his essay, which he insisted be printed precisely as it was orally delivered, forcing readers, if they hoped to comprehend, to listen to the silence of his absent speaking voice. 'For what Michel Foucault teaches us to think is that there are crises of reason in strange complicity with what the world calls crises of madness' (63). This 'strange complicity,' as Derrida describes it, is the role of *logos* in the life of reason as it relates to the Logos or Word. Beginning with the rise of modern science in the seventeenth century, reason incrementally (progressively) dismissed this 'complicity' as madness, while yet remaining as madness what Derrida describes as reason's 'liberty and its very possibility.' Confronted by some such crisis and having explored it at some length, I return in the end to find in the precise figuration of my dream the form and direction of instinct in which fate as the cyclic Wheel of Fortune becomes, as the radical transformation of it – 'its liberty and its very possibility' – what Jung calls destiny.

# 4

Madness, which Foucault calls 'the absence of a work,' becomes for Derrida the unknown and unknowable essence of the Godhead unveiled in a metaphysics of presence. As the ground of thought, this metaphysics

must, as the operations of the human brain, be deconstructed in order
to become conscious of itself as mind or thought. This deconstruction
does not reject metaphysics, but rather establishes a relationship to it,
which avoids the solipsistic madness of the 'I Am that I Am,' when and
if this identity is embraced as the deification of the self-created human.
Describing in *Timaeus* the Demiurge's creation of the world soul, Plato
writes:

'And in the centre [of the world] he set a soul and caused it to extend
throughout the whole and further wrapped its body round with soul on
the outside; and so he established one world alone, round and revolving
in a circle, solitary but by reason of its excellence able to bear itself company, needing no other acquaintance or friend but sufficient to itself. On all
these accounts the world which he brought into being was a blessed god.'
(Cited in *Symbols* 266)

Recognizing in Plato's account the presence of the mandala, which became for Jung a symbol of the Self, Jung comments: 'This utter inactivity
and desirelessness, symbolized by the idea of self-containment, amounts
to divine bliss. Man in this state is contained as if in his own vessel, like
an Indian god in the lotus or in the embrace of his Shakti' (*Symbols* 266).
'"There is in us too much of the casual and random, which shows itself
in our speech," Plato continues; "but the god made soul prior to body
and more venerable in birth and excellence, to be the body's mistress
and governor"' (cited in *Symbols* 266). Further describing the body contained in the soul as the Demiurge's splitting of the body-soul fabric into
two halves, Plato explains that he made the two halves cross each other
at their centres in the form of the letter X. He then bent each of the
two halves round into a semicircle and joined them up. This separation
of feminine and masculine, Yin and Yang, becomes in their joining the
mandala that, following the alchemists, Jung calls the *hieros gamos* or inner marriage.

As 'utter inactivity and desirelessness,' this 'alone with the alone' constitutes for Bahá'u'lláh a state that none save God Himself can enter,
before which the entire creation, including the human creation, is nothingness. The desire to enter this non-existence propels the mind toward
a 'divine madness' in which the possessed poet 'draws honey and milk
from the rivers' only to discover that it is 'nothing but simple water.' But
the propulsion itself as the life of metaphor understood as the transformation of the actual is the very foundation of language itself. As the sign

of the actual, language is in its own inherent reality the symbol of the divine. That is to say, words partake of the Logos or Word understood as the revelation of God. Thus in *The Hidden Words* Bahá'u'lláh declares: 'Veiled in My immemorial being and in the ancient eternity of My essence, I knew My love for thee; therefore I created thee, have engraved on thee Mine image and revealed to thee My beauty.' The mystery of creation is that, though no metaphysics of presence, however refined, can penetrate God's eternal hiddenness, within which the Godhead, as His knowledge of Himself, knows 'His love for thee,' He, in His hiddenness, 'created thee.' This creation is not His unknown 'essence' but His 'image,' not as 'fixed and dead,' but as a living, eternally evolving, single unfolding Will. For the Báb this 'primal Point' is progressive revelation in which, for Blake, all religions are one. For me this was the 'Primal Point' around which the works of the Romantics revolved and to which I inwardly referred these works as the operations of the creative imagination that, with the possible exception of Blake, nevertheless remained anagogically hidden. What remained hidden in Romantic poems became for me in the dream figure of the Báb the unveiling of the object of their progressive revelation, described by Blake as the 'Starry Eight,' by Wordsworth as the 'Uncreated,' by Coleridge as the 'infinite I AM,' by Keats as a 'fellowship with essence' (*Endymion* 1.779), by Shelley as the 'One,' and by Byron as 'Forgetfulness' (*Manfred* 1.1.136).

The conscious unveiling of this hidden object as the Báb, the Hidden Imam of Shia Islam unconsciously presenting itself to me in my dream, has been the subject of this book. Its *agon* resides in the psychological process of bringing this veiled presence to consciousness, a process explored in part in terms of Jung's painful absorption of his break with the sexual theory of Freud as the burial ground in which a new revelation of Yahweh remained, as the death of God, still hidden. (I went to my first Baha'i meeting – a first date – with sex rather than Yahweh in mind.) Freud's sexual theory struck Jung with an 'eruption of unconscious religious factors': 'I had the feeling that I had caught a glimpse of a new, unknown country, from which swarms of new ideas flew to meet me.' He continues:

> Sexuality evidently meant more to Freud than to other people. For him it was something to be religiously observed. [...] Just as the psychically stronger agency is given 'divine' or 'daemonic' attributes, so the 'sexual libido' took over the role of a *deus absconditus*, a hidden or concealed god. [...] At bottom, however, the numinosity, that is, the psychological qualities

of the two rationally incommensurable opposites – Yahweh and sexuality – remained the same. The name alone had changed, and with it, of course, the point of view: the lost god had now to be sought below, not above. But what difference does it make, ultimately, to the stronger agency if it is called now by one name and now by another? If psychology did not exist, but only concrete objects, the one would actually have been destroyed and replaced by the other. But in reality, that is to say, in psychological experience, there is not one whit the less of urgency, anxiety, compulsiveness, etc. The problem still remains: how to overcome or escape our anxiety, bad conscience, guilt, compulsion, unconsciousness, and instinctuality. If we cannot do this from the bright, idealistic side, then perhaps we shall have better luck by approaching the problem from the dark, biological side. (*MDR* 151–2)

While my dream of the Báb presented me with 'the bright, idealistic side' of spirituality, I had still at the age of twenty-one to deal with it 'from the dark, biological side' in order existentially to absorb it into my thoroughly Western, rather than Eastern, consciousness. The meeting and joining of East and West became for me, as for many of my contemporaries, the meeting and joining of a new vision of Yahweh with Freud's mythical or Oedipal understanding of sexuality.

In Shelley's *Prometheus Unbound*, readers, should they manage to penetrate the text or be penetrated by it 'To the Deep, to the Deep / Down, Down!' 'Even to the steps of the remotest Throne,' will encounter what Jung describes as the 'primitive idea of reproducing oneself by entering into the mother's body.' He argues that this notion 'has become so remote that the hero, instead of committing incest, is now sufficiently far advanced in the domestic virtues to seek immortality through the sacrifice of the incest tendency' (*Symbols* 262). Disregarding the advancement of 'domestic virtues,' which in visionary poetry he found abhorrent, Shelley's lyrical drama enacts the unbinding of Prometheus as his penetration of his mother Earth. Long wasted and infertile, she feels in her son's embrace the touch of his lips running down 'Even to the adamantine central gloom / Along these marble nerves.' '[T]is life, tis joy,' she cries, 'And through my withered, old and icy frame / The warmth of an immortal youth shoots down / Circling.' The result is that all living things shall 'Drain[ ] the poison of despair' and 'interchange sweet nutriment' (3.3.86–96). Mother Earth as the bride of her son, which indicates a spiritual understanding of incest that Jung shares with Shelley, becomes as her 'wedding garment' the transformed Asia, who after long separation from Prometheus has produced 'Some good change / [...] working in the elements which suffer / [Her] presence thus unveiled' (2.5.18–20). Panthea compares this unveiling to the birth of Venus from the 'veined shell, which floated on / Over the calm floor of the chrystal sea' (2.5.23–4).

In *Symbols of Transformation*, Jung goes on to describe the painful awakening to consciousness from the dream of the unconscious, an awakening he identifies with Adam's fall, as what he calls 'the sacrifice of the incest tendency.' 'This significant change,' he argues, 'finds its true fulfilment only in the symbol of the crucified God. In atonement for Adam's sin a bloody human sacrifice is hung upon the tree of life. Although the tree of life has a mother significance, it is no longer the mother, but a symbolical equivalent to which the hero offers up his life.' 'One can hardly imagine a symbol which expresses more drastically the subjugation of instinct,' Jung continues, with his experience of Freud's 'bitterness' in mind, a 'bitterness' which at their first encounter had remained 'inexplicable':

> Even the manner of death reveals the symbolic content of this act: the hero suspends himself in the branches of the maternal tree by allowing his arms to be nailed to the cross. We can say that he unites himself with the mother in death and at the same time negates the act of union, paying for his guilt with deadly torment. This act of supreme courage and supreme renunciation is a crushing defeat for man's animal nature, and it is also an earnest of supreme salvation, because such a deed alone seems adequate to expiate Adam's sin of unbridled instinctuality. The sacrifice is the very reverse of regression – it is a successful canalization of libido into the symbolic equivalent of the mother, and hence a spiritualization of it. (262–3)

Jung then goes on to quote Saint Augustine by way of describing the Christian scheme of vicarious salvation (God performing the act that must, for Jung, now be performed by man as the sign of his coming of age) as it assumed its medieval shape essentially untouched by the revelation of Muhammad: the death and resurrection of God nailed to the cross as the mother tree:

> 'Like a bridegroom Christ went forth from his chamber, he went out with a presage of his nuptials into the field of the world ... He came to the marriage-bed of the cross, and there, in mounting it, he consummated his marriage. And when he perceived the sighs of the creature, he lovingly gave

himself up in place of his bride, and [as the *hieros gamos*] he joined himself
to the woman for ever.' (Cited in *Symbols* 269)

Jung interprets the passage as Christ's marriage with the Church as the
Virgin Mother who is the Mother of God, a marriage which he will later
identify with the move 'from Three to Four.' The neurotic, he explains,
is in this Catholic context the son who, as the guilt-ridden product of the
'incest prohibition,' cannot leave the mother because 'it is the fear of
death that holds him there,' the mother in holding him becoming what,
for Freud, she essentially is: the death mother of the Pieta. Jung explains:

> It seems as if no idea and no word were powerful enough to express the
> meaning of this [Reformation] conflict. Certainly the struggle for expres-
> sion which has continued through the centuries cannot be motivated by
> what is narrowly and crudely conceived as 'incest.' We ought rather to con-
> ceive the law that expresses itself first and last in the 'incest prohibition' as
> the impulse to domestication, and regard the religious systems as institu-
> tions which take up the institutional forces of man's animal nature, organ-
> ize them, and gradually make them available for higher cultural purposes.
> (*Symbols* 271)

In Jung's understanding, the Protestant revolution robbed Christianity
of its symbolism, an absence that for the human soul constituted the
death of God. As a result, the cultural domestication of the animal instinct, once the province of religion, has now become the work of depth
psychology, particularly as it seeks to release the human being from what
Freud conceives still 'narrowly and crudely' as 'incest.' The higher spiritual goal of incest is the *hieros gamos*, the inner marriage of the masculine
and feminine as the true androgyne emerging from the *agon* of differentiation as the psychological meaning of the crucifixion.

This marriage constitutes for Jung the goal of individuation as the
emergence of the Self. My own conscious recognition of the Báb emerges from this process of differentiation of the masculine and feminine in
myself. It constitutes my recognition of him as my 'primal Point.' This
point of the Self remains within what is now for Jung at the end of the
Christian dispensation a mandala with an empty centre waiting to be
filled in and as the process of individuation, the *ignotum per ignotius*, the
unknown endlessly becoming the more unknown. While recognizing
the unknowable nature of human or divine essence, I embrace as progressive revelation this radical existential process of the unknown mov-

ing deeper into the more unknown, in which, declares Bahá'u'lláh, 'a true knowledge of your own selves is the same as the comprehension of Mine own Being.' With this essential proviso:

> So perfect and comprehensive is His creation that no mind or heart, however keen or pure, can ever grasp the nature of the most insignificant of His creatures; much less fathom the mystery of Him Who is the Day Star of Truth, Who is the invisible and unknowable Essence. [...] Ten thousand Prophets, each a Moses, are thunderstruck upon the Sinai of their search at His forbidding voice, 'Thou shalt never behold Me!'; whilst a myriad Messengers, each as great as Jesus, stand dismayed upon their heavenly thrones by the interdiction, 'Mine Essence thou shalt never apprehend.' (*Gleanings* 62)

Following Jung, I have submitted my dream of the Báb to depth analysis in order to understand how it issued from the collective unconscious. This unknown and unknowable source is not, as Freud suggests, the site of all that consciousness rejects, but rather the creative source of what it progressively embraces as the unfolding image and likeness of God. Jung posits the unconscious as the site of the unknowable God to which the soul has metaphorical access in dreams. The arts enact their limited understanding of them, what the Romantics call a waking dream. Jung suggests that the imagination remains suspended between dreaming and waking, the danger of waking lying in the loss of the dream. As abundant recompense, his depth psychology struggles to overcome this loss, not by recovering the dream as it exists in the unconscious, but as it emerges from its unconscious state into the symbolic life of its conscious absorption, which Jung calls its authentic human form. I interpret God in His 'immemorial being' in Jung's rather than Freud's sense: as creating the human as the image and likeness of Himself. But I am equally aware that the human likeness and image of God can become 'the bliss of solitude,' which is the intended subject of Wordsworth's *Recluse*. In his dream of the crazed Bedouin, Wordsworth confronts his unwritten epic as a madness from which he retreats in fear. The imagination's 'strength / Of usurpation' becomes a divine insanity, a dream encounter with the Cogito that, in dream, Descartes experienced and that, along with Wordsworth's reading of *Don Quixote*, produced Wordsworth's own dream.

The God present in divine revelation is not the 'I Am that I Am.' It is the God Who is what He will become. As progressive revelation His becoming is the process in which the entire creation participates as it assumes the form in which, as the operations of Coleridge's primary imagination, it is humanly perceived. Persuaded that the 'prime Agent and living Power of all human Perception' resides in progressive revelation as an eternal process of human becoming, I bind religion to the evolution of human consciousness in which, as relative rather than absolute, it remains the evolving human form of the divine as the otherwise unknowable absolute. Its present responsibility to which the ethos of previous dispensations stretching from Adam to Muhammad is inadequate, lies in the present task as the offspring of a new revelation of shaping a global consciousness grounded in the oneness of humankind. Shaping this consciousness is now a categorical moral imperative. Unless fully awakened, the overwhelming demands of this shaping may cause the soul neurotically to retreat in terror into a delusional solitude. Worse, the cause may descend into a militant vision of empire understood as global conquest with genocidal designs upon all those who resist. As a process of becoming, genuine religion requires an active moral engagement in the continuing life of the planet as the shaping of a consciousness capable of perceiving it as our human home.

Coleridge reminds us that perception is an action of the mind calling the whole soul of man into activity. Its 'primal Point' is 'the IMMEDIATE which dwells in every man.' Upon the 'original intuition or absolute affirmation of it (which is likewise in every man, but does not in every man rise into consciousness), all the *certainty* of our knowledge depends.' This certainty as 'self-intuition,' he explains, 'becomes intelligible to no man by the ministry of mere words from without.' Rather, it becomes 'intelligible' by what he calls 'the consciousness of freedom' in which 'words from without' unveil, as what, with reference to Demogorgon, Shelley describes as 'a universal sound like words.' Coleridge describes this sound as 'tremulous reciprocations,' which 'propagate themselves even to the inmost of the soul' (*BL* 1:244). Language as sound issuing from *pneuma* or breath is, as the Logos or Word, the voice of divinity itself, Shelley's 'sea profound of ever-spreading sound.' It is Shelley's 'divinity in man' upon which, named or unnamed, human freedom depends – unnamed because, for Shelley at least, 'there is no portal of expression from the caverns of the spirit which [as the vanishing apparitions that haunt the interlunations of life] they inhabit into the universe of things' (*DP* 532). I suggest that the *becoming* rather than the *being* of divine revelation provides the 'portal of expression from the caverns of the spirit,' which gate Shelley's poetry lacks. Addressing the 'Spirit of BEAUTY,' he laments that 'No voice from some sublimer world hath ever / To sage or poet' given a satisfactory response to mutability. 'Therefore,' he writes, 'the name of God and ghosts and Heaven / Remain the records of their vain endeavor,' which he describes as 'Frail spells' ('Hymn to Intellectual Beauty' 14, 25–9).

The 'universal sound' heard in the undulations of the luminous carpet, which in my dream causes me to rise up into the air and turn a somersault before floating downward to the feet of the Báb, is the sound of freedom described by Jung and Coleridge before him, a transformation of animal instinct into 'self-intuition.' Because, as 'IMMEDIATE,' this sound is first potentially present in the unconscious, it must, as freedom, be subjected to the intelligibility inherent in human consciousness. Only then can it, as self-evident, become the existential '*certainty*' upon which knowledge, as knowledge, finally depends.

# Bibliography

Bahá'í *World Faith: Selected Writings of Bahá'u'lláh and 'Abdu'l-Bahá*. Wilmette, IL: Bahá'í Publishing Committee, 1943.

Bahá'u'lláh. *Epistle to the Son of the Wolf*. 1943. Trans. Shoghi Effendi. Wilmette, IL: Bahá'í Publishing Trust, 1988.

– *Gleanings from the Writings of Bahá'u'lláh*. 1935. Trans. Shoghi Effendi. Wilmette, IL: Bahá'í Publishing Trust, 1983.

– *The Hidden Words of Bahá'u'lláh*. 1858. Trans. Shoghi Effendi. Wilmette, IL: Bahá'í Publishing Trust, 1985.

– *Kitáb-i-Íqán: The Book of Certitude*. 1862. Trans. Shoghi Effendi. Wilmette, IL: Bahá'í Publishing Trust, 1950.

– *The Seven Valleys and the Four Valleys*. 1856–63. Trans. Ali-Kuli Khan, with Marzieh Gail. Wilmette, IL: Bahá'í Publishing Trust, 1952.

Blake, William. *The Complete Poetry and Prose of William Blake*. Rev. ed. Ed. David V. Erdman. New York: Doubleday, 1988.

Blondel, Eric. 'Nietzsche: Life as Metaphor.' *The New Nietzsche*. Ed. David B. Allison. Cambridge, MA: MIT P, 1985. 150–75.

Bloom, Harold. *Shelley's Mythmaking*. New Haven, CT: Yale UP, 1959.

Brewster, David. *Letters on Natural Magic, Addressed to Sir Walter Scott*. London: John Murray, 1832.

Brown, Norman O. 'The Prophetic Tradition.' *Studies in Romanticism* 21 (Fall 1982): 367–86.

Browne, Edward G., trans. *The Tarikh-i-Jahid or New History of Mirza Àli Muhammad the Báb*. Cambridge: Cambridge UP, 1893.

Byron, George Gordon. *Byron's Letters and Journals*. 9 vols. Ed. Leslie A. Marchand. London: John Murray, 1973–94.

– *Lord Byron: Major Works*. Ed. Jerome J. McGann. New York: Oxford UP, 2000.

Caruth, Cathy. *Empirical Truths and Critical Fictions: Locke, Wordsworth, Kant, Freud.* Baltimore: Johns Hopkins UP, 1991.
– 'Introduction.' *Trauma: Explorations in Memory.* Ed. Cathy Caruth. Baltimore: Johns Hopkins UP, 1995. 1–10.
Coleridge, Samuel Taylor. *Biographia Literaria.* Ed. James Engell and W. Jackson Bate. Princeton, NJ: Princeton UP, 1983.
– *Coleridge's Poetry and Prose.* Ed. Nicholas Halmi, Paul Magnuson, and Raimondo Modiano. New York: Norton, 2004.
– *Collected Letters of Samuel Taylor Coleridge.* 6 Vols. Ed. Earl L. Griggs. Oxford: Clarendon P, 1956–71.
– *The Collected Notebooks of Samuel Taylor Coleridge.* Ed. Kathleen Coburn. 4 Vols. New York: Bollingen Series: Pantheon Books, 1957–90.
– *The Collected Works of Samuel Taylor Coleridge.* Gen. ed. Kathleen Coburn. 16 vols. Princeton, NJ: Princeton UP, 1969–2003.
– *Lay Sermons.* Vol. 6. Ed. R.J. White. 1972. *The Collected Works of Samuel Taylor Coleridge.*
– *Lectures 1808–1819 on Literature.* Vol. 5.1. Ed. R.A. Foakes. 1987. *The Collected Works of Samuel Taylor Coleridge.*
– *On the Constitution of Church and State.* Vol. 10. Ed. John Colmer. 1976. *The Collected Works of Samuel Taylor Coleridge.*
– *Table Talk.* Vol. 14. 2 parts. Ed. Carl Woodring. *The Collected Works of Samuel Taylor Coleridge.*
Corbin, Henri. *Spiritual Body and Celestial Earth: From Mazdean Iran to Shi'ite.* 2nd ed. Trans. Nancy Pearson. Princeton, NJ: Princeton UP, 1989.
*The Dawn-Breakers: Nabíl's Narrative of the Early Days of the Bahá'í Revelation.* 1932. Trans. and ed. Shoghi Effendi. Wilmette, IL: Bahá'í Publishing Trust, 1970.
De Man, Paul. 'Shelley Disfigured.' *Deconstruction and Criticism.* New York: Continuum, 1979. 39–74.
De Quincey, Thomas. *Works of Thomas De Quincey.* 21 vols. Ed. Grevel Lindop et al. London: Pickering and Chatto, 2000–3.
Derrida, Jacques. 'Cogito and the History of Madness.' *Writing and Difference.* Trans. and intro. Alan Bass. Chicago: U of Chicago P, 1978. 31–63.
Donne, John. 'The Canonization.' *The Norton Anthology of English Literature.* Vol. 1. 6th ed. Gen. ed. M.H. Abrams. New York: Norton, 1993. 1086–8.
Effendi, Shoghi. *God Passes By.* 1944. Intro. George Townshend. Willmette, IL: Bahá'í Publishing Trust, 1974.
– *The Promised Day Is Come.* 1943. Rev. ed. Willmette, IL: Bahá'í Publishing Trust, 1980.
Eliot, Thomas Stearns. *The Wasteland. The Norton Anthology of English Literature.* Vol. 2. 6th ed. Gen. ed. M.H. Abrams. New York: Norton, 1993. 2146–60.

Frayn, Michael. *Copenhagen: A Play in Two Acts*. New York: Samuel French, 2000.

Freud, Sigmund. *On the History of the Psycho-analytical Movement*. 1914. Vol. 14. *The Standard Edition of the Complete Psychological Works of Sigmund Freud*. 3–66.

– 'The Question of a Weltanschauung.' 1932. Vol. 22. *The Standard Edition of the Complete Psychological Works of Sigmund Freud*. Trans. and ed. James Strachey. 24 vols. New York: Vintage, 2001. 158–82.

– *Totem and Taboo*. 1913. Vol. 13. *The Standard Edition of the Complete Psychological Works of Sigmund Freud*. 1–162.

Freud, Sigmund, and Ernest Jones. *The Complete Correspondence of Sigmund Freud and Ernest Jones 1908–1939*. Ed. R. Andrew Paskauskas. Intro. Riccardo Steiner. Cambridge, MA: Belknap P of Harvard UP, 1993.

Frye, Northrop. *The Collected Works of Northrop Frye*. Gen. ed. Alvin Lee. Toronto: U of Toronto P, 1997–.

– *The Diaries of Northrop Frye 1942–1955*. Ed. Robert D. Denham. *The Collected Works of Northrop Frye*. Vol. 8. Toronto: U of Toronto P, 2001.

– *Fearful Symmetry: A Study of William Blake*. Princeton, NJ: Princeton UP, 1947.

– *The Great Code: The Bible and Literature*. New York: Harcourt, Brace, Jovanovich, 1983.

– *Northrop Frye's Late Notebooks, 1982–1900: Architecture of the Spiritual World*. 2 Vols. *The Collected Works of Northrop Frye*. Vol. 5. Ed. Robert D. Denham. Toronto: U of Toronto P, 2000.

– *Northrop Frye's Notebooks and Lectures on the Bible and Other Religious Texts*. Vol. 13. Ed. Robert D. Denham. *The Collected Works of Northrop Frye*. Gen. ed. Alvin A. Lee. Toronto: U of Toronto P, 2003.

– 'Reflections in a Mirror: Letter to the English Institute, 1965.' *Northrop Frye in Modern Criticism*. Ed. Murray Krieger. New York: Columbia UP, 1966. 133–46.

– *The 'Third Book' Notebooks of Northrop Frye, 1964–1972: The Critical Comedy*. Vol. 9. Ed. Michael Dolzani. *The Collected Works of Northrop Frye*. Toronto: U of Toronto P, 2002.

Giegerich, Wolfgang. *The Soul's Logical Life: Towards a Rigorous Notion of Psychology*. 2nd rev. ed. Frankfurt: Peter Lang, 1999.

Harding, Anthony John. 'Imagination, Patriarchy, and Evil in Coleridge and Heidegger.' *Studies in Romanticism* 35 (1996): 3–26.

Hogg, James. *The Private Memoirs and Confessions of a Justified Sinner*. Ed. John Carey. London: Oxford UP, 1970.

Hume, David. *An Enquiry Concerning Human Understanding*. Ed. Eric Steinberg. 2nd ed. Indianapolis: Hackett, 1993.

– *A Treatise of Human Nature*. Ed. L.A. Selby-Bigge. 2nd ed. Oxford: Clarendon P, 1978.

Jung, Carl Gustav. *The Collected Works of C.G. Jung.* 20 vols. Ed. Herbert Read,
Michael Fordham, Gerhard Adler, and William McGuire. Trans. R.F.C. Hull.
Princeton, NJ: Princeton UP, 1954–79.
– 'Address on the Occasion of the Founding of the C.G. Jung Institute, Zurich,
24 April 1948.' Vol. 18. *The Collected Works of C.G. Jung.* 471–6.
– *The Archetypes of the Collective Unconscious.* 1934/54. 2nd ed. Vol. 9.1. 1969. *The
Collected Works of C.G. Jung.*
– 'Foreward to Werblowsky's *Lucifer and Prometheus.*' 1952. Vol. 11. 1958. *The
Collected Works of C.G. Jung.* 311–15.
– 'Instinct and the Unconscious.' 1948. Vol. 8. *The Collected Works of C.G. Jung.*
129–38.
– *Memories, Dreams, Reflections.* Ed. Aniela Jaffé. Trans. Richard and Clara Win-
ston. New York: Vintage Books, 1965.
– *Mysterium Coniunctionis.* 1955/6. 2nd ed. Vol. 14. 1970. *The Collected Works of
C.G. Jung.*
– *Nietzsche's Zarathustra: Notes of the Seminar Given 1934–1939.* 2 vols. Ed. James
L. Jarrett. Princeton, NJ: Princeton UP, 1988.
– 'On the Nature of the Psyche.' 1947/54. Vol. 8. 1954. *The Collected Works of
C.G. Jung.* 159–236.
– *The Practice of Psychotherapy.* 1954. 2nd ed. Vol. 16. 1966. *The Collected Works of
C.G. Jung.*
– *Psychology and Alchemy.* 1944. 2nd ed. Vol. 12. 1968. *The Collected Works of C.G.
Jung.*
– *Psychology and Religion: East and West.* 1958. 2nd ed. Vol. 11. 1969. *The Collected
Works of C.G. Jung.*
– *The Red Book.* Ed. Sonu Shamdasani. Trans. Sonu Shamdasani, Mark Kyburz,
and John Peck. New York: Norton, 2009.
– *Symbols of Transformation.* 1911–12/1952. 2nd ed. Vol. 5. 1967. *The Collected
Works of C.G. Jung.*
– *The Tavistock Lectures.* 1935. Vol. 18. 1976. *The Collected Works of C.G. Jung.*
5–184.
– 'Théodore Flournoy.' Trans. Sonu Shamdasani. http://www.survivalafterdeath
.org.uk/articles/jung/flournoy.htm. Accessed 2 February 2009.
– 'Why I Am Not a Catholic.' 1944. Vol. 18. 1976. *The Collected Works of C.G.
Jung.* 645–7.
Jung, Carl Gustav, and Wolfgang Pauli. *Atom and Archetype: The Pauli/Jung Letters
1932–1958.* Ed. C.A. Meier. Intro. Beverley Zabriskie. Princeton NJ: Prince-
ton UP, 2001.
Lindorff, David. *Pauli and Jung: The Meeting of Two Great Minds.* New York: Quest
Books, 2004.

Keats, John. *Letters of John Keats.* Ed. Robert Gittings. Oxford: Oxford UP, 1977.
– *Poems of John Keats.* Ed. Jack Stillinger. Cambridge, MA: Belknap P of Harvard UP, 1978.
Kierkegaard, Søren. *Fear and Trembling.* Ed. C. Stephen Evans and Sylvia Walsh. Trans. Sylvia Walsh. Cambridge: Cambridge UP, 2006.
Kushner, Tony. *Angels in America: A Gay Fantasia on National Themes.* New York: Theatre Communications Group, 1993–4.
Milton, John. *Complete Poems and Major Prose.* Ed. Merritt Y. Hughes. New York: Macmillan, 1957.
Moore, Thomas. *Life of Lord Byron: With His Letters and Journals.* 6 vols. London: John Murray, 1854.
Nancy, Jean-Luc. 'Church, State, Resistance.' *Political Theologies: Public Religions in a Post-Secular World.* Ed. Hent de Vries and Lawrence E. Sullivan. New York: Fordham UP, 2006. 102–12.
Nietzsche, Friedrich. *Ecce Homo.* On the Genealogy of Morals *and* Ecce Homo. Trans. and ed. Walter Kaufmann. New York: Vintage, 1966. 215–335.
– 'On the Uses and Disadvantages of History for Life.' *Untimely Meditations.* Ed. Daniel Breazeale. Trans. R.J. Hollingdale. Cambridge: Cambridge UP, 1997.
– 'On Truth and Lies in a Nonmoral Sense.' *Philosophy and Truth: Selections from Nietzsche's Notebooks of the Early 1870's.* Ed., trans., and intro. Daniel Breazeale. Atlantic Highlands, NJ: Humanities P International, 1979. 79–100.
Pauli, Wolfgang. '*The Piano Lesson*: An Active Fantasy About the Unconscious.' *Harvest* 48, no. 2 (2002): 122–34.
Plato. 'Letter VII.' *The Collected Dialogues of Plato, Including the Letters.* Ed. Edith Hamilton and Huntington Cairns. Princeton, NJ: Princeton UP, 1961. 1574–98.
Rajan, Tilottama. 'Dis-figuring Reproduction: Natural History, Community, and the 1790s Novel.' *The New Centennial Review* 2, no. 3 (Fall 2002): 211–52.
– 'En-Gendering the System: *The Book of Thel* and *Visions of the Daughters of Albion.*' *The Mind in Creation: Essays on English Romantic Literature in Honour of Ross G. Woodman.* Ed. J. Douglas Kneale. Montreal: McGill-Queen's UP, 1992. 74–90.
– 'The Gender of Los(s): Blake's Work in the 1790s.' *Women Reading William Blake.* Ed. Helen P. Bruder. New York: Palgrave MacMillan, 2007. 200–8.
Saiedi, Nader. *Gate of the Heart: Understanding the Writings of the Báb.* Waterloo, ON: Wilfrid Laurier UP, 2008.
Schelling, F.W.J. *The Ages of the World.* 1815. Trans. Jason M. Wirth. Albany: State U of New P, 2000.
Schopenhauer, Arthur. *The World as Will and Representation.* 2 vols. Trans. E.F.J. Payne. New York: Dover, 1958.

Shaffer, Elinor. 'Religion and Literature.' *Romanticism*. Ed. Marshall Brown.
   Vol. 5. *The Cambridge History of Literary Criticism*. Cambridge: Cambridge UP,
   2000. 138–61.
Shakespeare, William. *Antony and Cleopatra*. Ed. Burton Raffel. New Haven, CT,
   and London: Yale UP, 2007.
– *The Complete Sonnets and Poems*. Ed. Colin Burrow. Oxford: Oxford UP, 2008.
– *Hamlet*. Ed. G.R. Hibbard. Oxford: Oxford UP, 2008.
– *The Tempest*. Ed. Virginia Mason Vaughan and Alden T. Vaughan. London:
   Thomson Learning, 2007.
Shelley, Percy Bysshe. *The Complete Poetical Works of Percy Bysshe Shelley*. Ed.
   Thomas Hutchinson. London: Oxford UP, 1960.
– *The Complete Works of Percy Bysshe Shelley*. Ed. Roger Ingpen and Walter E. Peck.
   Julian Editions. 10 vols. New York: Charles Scribner's Sons, 1926–30.
– *The Letters of Percy Bysshe Shelley*. Ed. Frederick L. Jones. 2 vols. Oxford: Claren-
   don P, 1964.
– *Shelley's Poetry and Prose*. 2nd ed. Ed. Donald H. Reiman and Neil Fraistat New
   York: Norton, 2002.
Siskin, Clifford. *The Historicity of Romantic Discourse*. New York: Oxford UP,
   1988.
Von Franz, Marie-Louise. *Number and Time: Reflections Leading Towards a Unifica-
   tion of Psychology and Physics*. Trans. Andrea Dykes. London: Rider, 1974.
– 'Wolfgang Pauli, the Feminine and the Perils of the Modern World.' Inter-
   view with Hein Stufkens. *Harvest* 48, no. 2 (2002): 142–8.
Winnicott, Donald. Rev. of *Memories, Dreams, Reflections*, by Carl Gustav Jung. *D.
   W. Winnicott: Psycho-Analytic Explorations*. Ed. Clare Winnicott, Ray Shepherd,
   and Madeleine Davis. Cambridge, MA: Harvard UP, 1989. 482–92.
Wordsworth, William. *The Fenwick Notes of William Wordsworth*. Ed. Jared Curtis.
   London: Bristol Classical P, 1993.
– *The Letters of William and Dorothy Wordsworth*. Ed. Ernest de Selincourt. 2nd ed.
   Vol 1. *The Early Years, 1787–1805*. Rev. Chester L. Shaver. Oxford: Clarendon
   P, 1967. Vol 2: *The Middle Years, Part 1, 1806–1811*. Rev. Mary Moorman. Ox-
   ford: Clarendon P, 1969.
– *William Wordsworth: The Oxford Authors*. Ed. Stephen Gill. Oxford: Oxford UP,
   1984.
– *The Prelude: 1799, 1805, 1850*. Ed. Jonathan Wordsworth, M.H. Abrams, and
   Stephen Gill. New York: Norton, 1979.
Yeats, William Butler. 'The Second Coming.' *The Norton Anthology of English Liter-
   ature*. Vol. 2. 4th ed. Gen. ed. M.H. Abrams. New York: Norton, 1979. 1973–4.
Žižek, Slavoj. *How to Read Lacan*. New York: Norton, 2007.
– *On Belief*. New York: Routledge, 2001.

# Index

48–9, 54, 55, 60, 64, 78, 80, 82–4,
93, 110, 116, 120–4, 134–6, 156,
162, 165–7, 183, 209, 213–14, 216,
217. *See also,* Jung, Carl Gustav
Frye, Northrop, xxii–xxiii, 27–31,
34–5, 39–40, 74, 125–8, 140–1,
182–3, 189, 192, 197–9; *Anatomy of
Criticism,* 28; *Fearful Symmetry,* 28

German Idealism, 54, 78
Giegerich, Wolfgang, 15–17, 83
Gobineau, Arthur de: *Religions et
Philosophies dans L'Aise Central,*
200
God, xix, xxv–xxvii, xxviii, xxx, xxxv–
xxxvi, xli, xlv, xlvi, xlix, 5, 8, 10, 11,
12, 21, 23–5, 26, 28, 29, 33, 34, 38,
40, 47, 49, 50, 52–3, 62, 63, 66–9,
72, 74, 80, 81, 89, 90, 95, 97, 100,
102, 108, 109, 119, 122, 124, 126,
127, 130, 131, 134–6, 140, 141, 143,
147, 167, 169, 174, 177–8, 181–4,
189–90, 197, 201, 205–6, 207, 211–
13, 215–17, 219
Goethe, Johann Wolfgang von, 143
*gnosis. See* knowledge

Harding, Anthony John, xxxii
Hartley, David, 22, 52, 59, 84
Hayley, William, 107, 130
Hegel, G.W.F., xxv, 28, 78
Heidegger, Martin, xxvi
Heisenberg, Werner, 143, 146, 148
hermaphroditism, 100, 106, 115–16,
120, 121, 166
*hieros gamos,* 38, 55–6, 70, 80, 88, 91,
100, 106, 120, 126–7, 167, 169–70,
194, 212, 216
Hitler, Adolf, 79, 143, 179, 210
Hogg, James, xxxiii–xxxiv

Hölderlin, Friedrich, 87, 92, 115, 165,
169
Holzer, Jenny, xiii
Hoyle, Fred, 160
Hume, David, xxx; and belief, xxi; *An
Enquiry Concerning Human Under-
standing,* xxx; 'On Miracles,' xxi; *A
Treatise of Human Nature,* xxx
Hurqalya, 163, 175

*I Ching,* 150, 208–9
*ignotum per ignotius,* xxii, 9, 63, 216
imagination, xxiv, xxxii, 11, 23, 44,
54, 57, 141–2, 146, 154, 169, 180–4,
187, 188, 190, 194, 196, 198, 203,
210–11, 213, 217; and fancy, 23,
57; as myth, 141; primary, xxix,
19–21, 23, 25, 34, 41, 53, 66, 68, 86,
138, 176, 181, 204–5, 218; of the
Romantic poet, 38, 101; secondary,
xxix, 19–20, 23, 27, 79, 138–9, 194.
*See also* Coleridge, Samuel Taylor
incest, 55, 83, 109–10, 113, 120–1,
166–7, 214–16
intuition vs. instinct. *See* Jung, Carl
Gustav
Islam, xxii, xxiv, xxx, 21, 23–6, 28,
30, 37–8, 41, 43–4, 52, 107, 142,
163, 173–9, 202, 213; the Eighth
Climate, 24, 107, 138; the Hidden
Imam, 25, 26, 107, 138–72, 173–9,
182, 188–90, 195, 210, 213; Shia,
21, 23–4, 25, 26, 37–8, 41, 107,
173–5, 179, 213; Sunni, 25, 37–8

Jaffé, Aniela, 160
Jones, Ernest, 120
Joyce, James, 62, 128
Judaism, 24–5, 44, 121–2, 175, 178
Jung, Emma, 162, 164